Open Road's
Italy with Kids

by Barbara Pape & Michael Calabrese

Open Road Family Travel Guides
The only travel guide your family needs!

Open Road Publishing

Open Road's new travel guides cut to the chase.
You don't need a huge travel encyclopedia – you need a
selective guide to steer you right. If you're going on vacation for
a few weeks or less, get a guide that brings you the *best* of any
destination for the amount of time you *really* have for your trip!

Open Road – the guide you need for the trip you want.

The New Open Road *Best Of* Travel Guides.
Right to the point.
Uncluttered.
Easy.

4th Revised Edition

For Beatrice Ricci Pape, who taught me all she knew about being an Italian mother.

OPEN ROAD PUBLISHING
P.O. Box 284, Cold Spring Harbor, NY 11724
www.openroadguides.com

Text Copyright©2011 by Barbara Pape & Michael Calabrese.
Maps by Douglas Morris
- All Rights Reserved -
ISBN 13: 978-1-59360-124-9
ISBN 10: 1-59360-124-7
Library of Congress Control No. 2009924898

About the Authors
Barbara Pape and Michael Calabrese are a husband-wife writing team who have published in and worked on political, education and economic issues. They have two children, Anthony and Caravita, whose many tips and suggestions find their way into each revised edition of this book! They live in Chevy Chase, Maryland.

For important Italian phrases turn to page 7.
For photo credits turn to page 8.

CONTENTS

What's The Word I Want?

I do not speak Italian.	*Non parlo italiano.*
Do you speak English?	*Parlate inglese?*
Illness	*Mallattia*
I need a doctor.	*Ho bisogno d'un medico.*
Where is the hospital?	*Dove è l'ospedale?*
Take me to the hospital.	*Prenderlo all' ospedale.*
My child is allergic to penicillin.	*Il mio bambino è allergico a penicillina.*
Where is the pharmacy?	*Dove è la farmacia?*
I need medication.	*Ho bisogno del farmaco.*
I need penicillin.	*Ho bisogno della penicillina.*
I need insulin.	*Ho bisogno dell' insulina.*
Please call the police.	*Chiamare prego la polizia.*
Take me to the police station.	*Prenderlo alla stazione di polizia.*
Where's the American Embassy?	*Dove è l' Ambasciata Americana?*
I would like to make a reservation at your restaurant.	*Vorrei fare una prenotazione al vostro restauranti.*
I would like to make a reservation at your hotel.	*Vorrei fare una prenotazione al vostro hotel.*
I need a hotel room please.	*Ho bisogno d'una stanza dell'hotel prego.*
Does your hotel have babysitting?	*Il vostro hotel ha "babysitting?"*
We need a babysitter.	*Abbiamo bisogno d'una "babysitter."*
Do you offer a discount for kids?	*Offrite uno sconto per i bambini?*
Where can I exchange money?	*Dove posso scambiare i soldi?*
Where can I exchange currency?	*Dove posso scambiare la valuta?*
Where can I buy diapers?	*Dove posso comprare i "diapers?"*
Where can I buy baby food?	*Dove posso comprare gli alimenti per bambini?*
Do you sell diapers?	*Vendete i "diapers?"*
Where can I buy milk?	*Dove posso comprare il latte?*
Where is the grocery store?	*Dove è il deposito della drogheria?*
Where is the supermarket?	*Dove è il supermercato?*
How much does this cost?	*Quanto questo costo?*
What is the price?	*Che cosa è il prezzo?*
Can you find me a taxi?	*Potete trovarli un tassì?*

Maps

PHOTO CREDITS

1. INTRODUCTION

Italy is for lovers. Lovers of art. Lovers of music. Lovers of fine food and wine. And, lovers of children. Parents who trekked through Italy as students, or parents who have only dreamt of visiting *Italia* and its ancient and modern splendors, may envision a sensual Italy, resplendent in art, opera, haute couture and take-your-breath-away landscapes. But, visit the country again with a child and a new magic embraces you. From the cat who has made his home in the castle at Sirmione and the musical Venetian gondoliers, to the cavernous catacombs of Rome and Collodi's fanciful Pinocchio Park, Italy plays with children, tempting them and you to linger just a little longer.

Tiny hill towns speckled throughout the region of Tuscany are now world-famous. The lure of lush Capri and the bedazzling Amalfi Coast have been tourist havens for millennia. The increase in travel to Italy today includes a high percentage of families, with many pondering how they can possibly entertain their children for two or more weeks. Rest assure: Italy and the Italians make travel with children *molto facile* (very easy).

This book features points of interest for children of all ages. It features those special sites that particularly grab the attention of the younger traveler. And, we offer tips on how to keep your children and young teens engaged, at least for some time, while you enjoy the art museums, fine dining and more of what Italy has to offer.

To help you and your children prepare for a trip to Italy, we have selected a list of books that tell tales of Italian cities, famous Italians and the rich history of this Mediterranean country. Peppered throughout this book are comments

by our two children (five and seven on their first trip to Italy, now 16 and 18) for you to better see from a youngster's perspective what is delightful in Italy. So, *buono viaggio*! And, welcome to Italia, where family living is *la dolce vita.*

2. OVERVIEW

Where to go with children in Italy? To Venice? Tuscany? How about Rome? Or Capri? Just about anywhere you travel with children in Italy, there are special places to enchant every child – and the child in you.

Part of the excitement of Italy is its diversity. In the north, framed by the snowy Alps, the country is more rugged and alpine – no surprise here. Skiing and hiking are national pastimes. The Lake region, north of Milan, provides plenty of beauty, history and water sport activities. The eastern part of the northern area extends to the Adriatic Sea, while the west stretches to the Ligurian Sea. Most of Italy's population resides in the north, engaged in farming and industry.

Central Italy, north of Rome, is primarily lowlands and also boasts strong farming, including world-famous vineyards and olive groves. The Apennines, a mountain range that forms a backbone to Italy's boot, run through central Italy, with the stunning Abruzzo National Park beckoning hikers. Etruscan ruins, Tuscan farmhouses and ancient Rome makes central Italy a hot spot for tourism.

Southern Italy for most travelers means Naples, Pompeii and the Amalfi Coast – Italy's and the world's playground and beach resort. The south also lays claim to Italy's spectacular islands – Sicily, Sardinia and a group of smaller islands, including the lush isle of Capri.

Sample one or two, or try them all. Italy is bound to delight and surprise every member of the family.

TRAVELING WITH KIDS

Our first long-distance flight with kids was when our oldest was only seven months old. Seasoned travelers – both from business and pleasure – we didn't think twice about traveling with an infant when we boarded the plane in Washington, DC, for fun and work in California. Perhaps we should have. On the way over, we had, shall we say, a bit of a diaper emergency. How could this happen? And, in business class, no less. Neighboring passengers were left gasping for breath, and so were we. Flight attendants fluttered over to help the oh-so-obviously inexperienced parents. Where are the diapers? Did we bring any onto the plane?

No, we did not. After a few minutes of finger pointing – "It was your job to pack the diapers." "No, yours!" – we cleaned up the baby with an airplane napkin and swaddled him in Mom's sweater. Thank goodness we were only a few minutes from LAX.

Traveling with children requires more planning than solo trips, we discovered, but it can be equally as enjoyable. And Italy is a splendid place to test the waters of traveling with kids. All of Italy is family-friendly. Children are national shrines. Even the maitre d' in the most posh of restaurants has a special smile for the youngest of diners.

This book includes traditional sights and major attractions in Italy for young and old. But, it spotlights Parent Tips for how to get the most out of sightseeing with children in tow. It also features special places designed to delight children and their adult companions.

Having children did not quash the lure of travel for us. Over the years, we've learned to adapt (no more leaving the details to the last minute). In the sections below, we offer some suggestions for how to get the most out of traveling with children and young teens.

INVOLVE YOUR CHILDREN

The more kids of any age participate in the planning of the trip the better. Begin to read to them, or suggest for them to read, books and stories about Italy and famous Italians. Share this book with them. The **Fun Facts** we've devised are meant just for the kids. Look on a map and mark your trip – from Milan to the Lakes to Venice and Verona, then to Florence and Tuscany and on to Rome. Research Italy and things Italian on the Internet.

Have the kids pick a famous Italian – Galileo or Leonardo da Vinci, for example – read about them and design an itinerary so the kids can follow their favorite Italian's path (visit the town of Vinci; in Milan, see Leonardo's *Last Supper* and stop by the Leonardo da Vinci science museum.) For the very young, get pictures of places in Italy you will be going from your travel agent, travel magazines or on-line. Your child can make a collage of the pictures on poster board, or glue them into a little notebook.

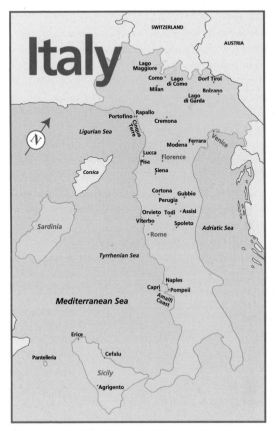

Even if your teen displays an active disinterest in your trip – ignore the disregard. They are listening. Talk up the trip and offer a set of choices so in each city, your teen has a chance to do or see something they want to do.

ON THE PLANE

This is a long trip. If you're traveling with babies and toddlers, make sure you have enough extra diapers, a couple changes of clothes, blankets, bottles, toys that distract, something to suck on when the plane takes off and lands – nursing moms, you're it!

Help older children select toys, books and other personal belongings that can fit in their own backpack that they carry. This is key, otherwise you will be schlepping around all the things they cannot carry.

Technology and teens are the ticket. Following are some different ideas of what to put in your child's pack for a trip to Italy.

For kids of all ages
- A **CD player and story tapes**. On one trip, our son listened to *The Hobbit* on tape from start to finish (see section on books and story tape ideas). Even teens enjoying hearing a story on tape. Many are delightfully read by either the author (check out the Limony Snicket tapes,) or professional actors like Patrick Stewart, Kenneth Branagh and Lynn Redgrave in *The Chronicles of Narnia*. A list of interesting audio books is found in Part II, *Planning Your Trip*.
- **Coloring books and sketch pads, crayons, markers and watercolor.** Children of all ages love to color and draw their own pictures. For the young ones, try to find coloring books that feature ancient Rome or a topic relevant to their trip – castles, the seashore or boats. Watercolor works for older kids. You can get a cup of water on the plane.
- **Chess or checkers** (travel version).
- **Origami**. Travel time is a great time to learn this fine art.
- **Puzzles**. We carried the pieces of jigsaw puzzles in a zip-lock bag. While we didn't use this on the plane, it's a great idea for a rainy day when you may be locked indoors with one or more children.

For young kids
- **Sculpty clay**. Fun, fun, fun! When our children were younger, they did everything from designing jewelry to building cities while strapped into their seats on the plane.
- **Beads**. Stringing beads can be great entertainments, but they also could end up scattered on the floor. Keep the beads in zip-lock bags.
- **Chapter books**. Instead of bringing a lot of big books for the early reader, we found that bringing chapter books saved space and weight. Chapter books are even a good idea for pre-readers. *Stuart Little* or *Charlotte's Web* can easily be read to younger children with shorter attention spans. You can just stop the story and pick it up later. Plane trips also work for read aloud time – parents reading to children, children reading to parents or, even, siblings reading to siblings.
- **Finger puppets**. Little children can entertain themselves for some time with a menagerie of little finger puppets.
- **Magnets**. We found a wonderful small box-size set of magnets in various geometric shapes that the kids used to make different designs and sculptures. It kept them occupied for quite some time.

For teens
- **iPods**. Even if you can't figure out how to download the music, they can.

- **Homework**. Oh, no. You've decided to take a trip over winter or spreak break. And, in today's world of No Child Left Behind, you have kids whining that there will be No Homework Left Behind, or, of course, it will be graded down for being late. Help your student organize what it is they must accomplish over the holidays. If you can, make copies of the pages in their book they will need – so you don't have to lug Algebra 1 and History of the U.S. throughout the hill towns of Tuscany – and encourage them to work hard on the plane ride when there's nothing much to do, so they do not have to pull out the polynomial worksheet while in Rome.
- **Journal Writing**. Travel is always a wonderful time to pick up the habit of writing. Think extended Facebook statuses. Journal writing is a satisfying way for teens to write about, who else but themselves, their trials, the vagaries of life, the catastrophe of traveling with parents or the joys of family fun abroad. Whatever their predisposition to family travel, writing about it through a journal, poetry or short personal essays not only passes the time, but builds a lifelong skill. A great time to start is on the plane.
- **Books**. For us, there is nothing better than to curl up on a long plane ride and pull out a good book. No cell phones ringing, work deadlines, dinner and snacks to prepare. Let your teens pick a few choice books to bring. Our son, who is dyslexic, always packs several long books on tape/CD – from Hemmingway to Harry Potter — acquired either from the library, store bought or from the great folks at Recordings for the Blind and Dyslexic.
- **Director of Photography**. A great way to keep teens involved in your trip is to, oh how hard it is for some of us, give them control of the videocam. Let them record your family travels – daily life in Italy. For real video buffs, let them edit their work when they return home, and you may be surprised at the outcome. Or, give your teen his or her own camera – from dispensible to digital — to shoot stills.

KIDS JUST WANT TO HAVE FUN

An art museum in the morning, peeking into an ancient church on the way to lunch at an *enoteca* to taste the local wine, with a detailed look at the city's architecture and a tour of the grand cathedral in the afternoon, may sound like a fine itinerary for you – but to a child or teen it spells disaster. As our five-year-old little girl remarked after one day like this, "I just want something to climb on!" You will not be able to see everything you want. Visits to the art museum may be shorter, or enjoyed with parents taking turns with the kids. Here are some ideas that worked for us:

Room to roam: Kids like monuments and sites where they can move around a lot. In Sirmione, our children were thrilled with the medieval castle, Scaligera Fortress, and the Roman ruins called the Grottoes of Catullo. Ancient Rome was a big hit. The walkway above the walls of Lucca was great fun to ride bikes and play. Italy's major cities have especially lovely public gardens; Rome's Borghese Gardens, for example, has bicycle rentals, a zoo and pony rides for little ones. Break up your touring with enough outside active adventures to help kids burn up some energy.

Make art museums active: Art museums are doable if you make them a creative, active experience for children. Go early in the morning or late in the day to avoid lines and crowds. Bring a sketchbook and pencils or crayons. Most museums allow children to draw and color, as long as they work quietly. A group of children from our neighborhood school visit an art museum on days off, led by one of the moms who is an art historian and curator. Since they were in first grade and even now as they're pushing 14, she talks to them about the art and gives them enough time to sketch and color. Some kids try to copy the masterpieces, others are inspired to draw original work, some scribble. But all of them, including many rambunctious, sports-minded boys, happily spend at least an hour in an art museum.

Postcard treasure hunt: Another idea is to head straight away to the gift shop and buy several postcards of art on exhibit in the museum. Go on a treasure hunt in the museum, where your children will try to find the painting/sculpture on the postcard.

Play counting games: Bored in the umpteenth church we entered one day in Assisi, our daughter at age four began counting how many candles were burning. She decided to keep a record so she could compare how many were burning in different churches. We had a little extra time to see the church while she busied herself counting all the burning candles!

Challenge the inner critic: For older kids, who are critical by nature, ask them to critique each art museum they visit, either in a journal, in a hand-held mini-tape recorder, videocam or verbally. Was the exhibit interesting? Why or why not? Were there too many pieces of art? How does that affect you as a visitor? What was your favorite painting or sculpture?

Why? Modern art museums, like the Peggy Guggenheim in Venice, can lead to questions of interpretation. Why did the artist choose that color or design? What did he or she mean by their artwork? Does the title match the scene? What would you title the piece? **Look for things that are gory (yes, gory!) and spooky.** The Bridge of Sighs, leading to the prison in the Doge's Palace in Venice, intrigued our children. The weapons rooms in Verona's Castlevecchio and in the Doge's Palace were another big hit. Even Galileo's middle finger, elegantly displayed (groan, groan), in Florence caught their eye, causing a burst of wails and giggles when they were older. Plan your day's itinerary to include sites your children want to see. Let the kids know what awaits them at the end of their visit through the art in the castle or palace – the weapons rooms and other gory items usually are at the end.

Science Rules. Go to the library and get a couple of Bill Nye the Science Guy tapes to get kids psyched about science, if they're not already. Include the science museums when you are traveling in Italy. Our kids, who continue to be fascinated with outer space and with inventions, love the science museums. Galileo's telescopes (Florence) and Leonardo da Vinci's inventions (Vinci and Milan) were trips enjoyed by all, especially our son who we had trouble getting out of the museums.

History comes alive in Italy. For children who are history buffs, this is a land of sheer delight. To help them put things in perspective, see the timeline we've included in the introduction. Check the bibliography for history books and stories of the life and times of famous people. Visit your local library before the trip, and save space in your suitcase for extra books you may want to bring back. Let them document their walk through history either by camera or videocam, blog, or by recording it in a journal (see below).

Keep a journal. Kids like to tell their own story and traveling is a great time to keep a record. Either buy a journal in your hometown, or wait until you get to Italy and purchase a beautiful, albeit more expensive, journal in any of the Italian cities' paper shops. For pre-readers, they can draw pictures of their trip, with stories dictated to parents. Journals also are a great way for kids to share their travel adventures at school. For our kids, journals preoccupied them on long train trips across Italy while we dealt with the administrative side of traveling – getting tickets at train stations, long bank lines, etc.

Camera Ready. Children of all ages love to take photographs. Let them use yours, or buy them a less expensive disposable camera. Encourage them to plan their shots, keeping an eye on how many they have left.

The Food Critic. One of our son's middle school carpool friends and his family traveled to Cinque Terre, hiking from village to village. Family members selected one food item, like pizza, that they tried in each village. They picked their favorite, talked about what made it so special and not only enjoyed the food, but a wonderful family conversation, as well.

Give them time to play. One day, we woke up later than our kids to find them quietly playing with little toys they brought along with them. This was week two of our three-week visit when they were five and seven. Neither wanted to venture outside for an action-packed day of sightseeing, but preferred to spend the morning playing with their toys. We acquiesced, brought cappuccino and pastries to the room and sat on our hotel balcony to enjoy a quiet moment together. Ahh!

Okay, so you try all these nifty ideas and your kids are staring at you with that "you-must-be-crazy" look. You can:

1. Force them to enjoy art (good luck);

2. Negotiate ("Now if you give us a few minutes of peace here, we'll take you to the Naval Museum, or playground or get you a double-scoop of your favorite gelato" – that works for awhile);

3. Pass out those gameboys/iPods;

4. Give up and split up. Throughout our book, we try to alert parents to where one of them can go with the kids while the other gets more time in the museum. Sometimes this is simply the best option. Just plan ahead so you know who wants to see what the most. Family living, like politics, is the art of compromise.

3. ROME

All roads lead to **Rome**, or *Ro-ma*, as you soon will be calling it. And certainly no trip to Italy is complete without a visit to the capital of the Republic of Italy. The Eternal City gracefully entered the 21st century with a sparkling new look. Buildings gleam after being spruced up in anticipation of the Jubilee – the Catholic Church's year 2000 pilgrimage and celebration, which drew millions of visitors from around the world. Ancient Rome has never been more ready for a New World.

Many applauded the efforts of Rome's former mayor, Francesco Rutelli, for crafting the city's major facelift – from excavating the emperor Nero's huge Golden House to the restoration of the Colosseum. Perhaps Rutelli's former life as an architect and a founding member of Italy's Green Party provided the foundation for such an undertaking – but whatever the reason – hope springs eternal for Rome and the tons of tourists who descend on the city.

We especially appreciated the mayor's decision to ban automobiles from about 100 piazzas, including the Piazza del Popolo and the Campo dei Fiori, where dodging cars, picking fruit and minding the children was too much for even the best multi-tasking parent.

Rome is the capital and largest city of both Italy and of the region of **Lazio**. It is situated in the west-central part of the country near the Tyrrhenian Sea. If you picture the boot shape of Italy, Rome is where the laces tie. The city is built on seven hills and is home to more than 6 million souls. The **Tevere** (Tiber) **River**, which splits the city in half, is Italy's third longest, though it is hardly mighty – it has an average width of less than 120 meters (400 feet).  Surprisingly, the Tiber is nearly invisible to most tourists, except to cross over to get to Vatican City and some other less visited neighborhoods of this sprawling city.

Safety Tips

Purchase the **Roma Pass Card**, which allows you to visit museums and monuments of Rome and skip long lines. You also can travel free on public transportation. The pass is valid for 3 days and the first 2 sites are free, others are half off. Cost: €28.70 or €30.70 for the Roma Plus Card, which provides urban and provincial transportation.

SO MANY SIGHTS, SO LITTLE TIME!

Consider it a mission impossible to make a meaningful visit to Rome in one or two days. Rome is not Florence or Venice, where most major sights are crowded into a compact central tourist district within walking distance. Just getting from one place to another, with children in tow, is a daunting task. It is difficult to overstate how much more sprawling, chaotic and confusing Rome is compared to any other Italian city – or even compared to Paris, London or New York. But, if a few days are all the time you have, just follow the first two days below in our Five-Day Itinerary; in two full days you can at least get a sense of the ancient and sacred that mix to make Rome a living museum.

Remember: Even by taxi it can take 30 minutes or more to travel between most of these major sights, all of which are described in greater detail later in this chapter.

Day 1: Ancient Rome

Plan on a full day to take in the **Roman** and **Imperial Forums**, the **Colosseum**, and surrounding sights. The fragments of ancient Rome scattered across the immense Roman Forum were the highlight of our children's visit – both as youngsters and as young teens.

Trevi Fountain (before or after dinner): Our kids loved throwing coins in the fountain. Save room for the excellent *gelato* nearby at world-famous San Crispino.

Day 2: Sacred Rome

Vatican City (4 hours or more): **St. Peter's Basilica** and the **Vatican Museums** are awesome whatever your religious background. The Sistine Chapel was a high-point of our children's visit. They marveled at how one man – Michelangelo — could possibly have lain on his back for most of a year painting the famous ceiling frescoes.

Catacombs (2 hours). Kids love both the mystery and history of these cool underground burial mazes. Our children enjoyed the visit to **Priscilla**

Catacombs because it was a small, personal tour (just us) that did not go on endlessly. (They are also convenient to the Borghese Gardens, Rome's central park, which is a nice break – see below).

Piazza Navona (evening): Our kids delighted in the "street performers" and sketch artists in this lively piazza filled with fountains, sculpture and sidewalk cafes. At Christmas time, they were delighted with booth after booth of sweets and small toys, as well as a visit from La Befano, the Christmas witch who brings toys to all the good children.

Day 3: Rome Old & New

The Pantheon (1 hour): Kids are awed that this pagan-temple-turned-church is nearly 2000 years old.

Capitoline Hill (2 hours or more): A short walk from the Pantheon, the **Piazza del Compidoglio**, overlooking the Roman Forum, is an architectural wonder and home to the **Capitoline Museums**. Kids love the gigantic head and foot from a statue of Constantine, the towering equestrian statue of Marcus Aurelius and the amazing view down to the Roman Forum.

St. Paul's Outside the Walls (1 hour): Second only to St. Peter's, this impressive basilica is built over the tomb of St. Paul.

Or, alternatively:

Church of the Bones – Santa Maria della Concezione: Near the entrance to the Borghese Gardens, in a crypt below the church, lies the strange spectacle of the bones of 4,000 Capuchin monks arranged into altars, friezes and chapels.

Campo dei Fiori (1 hour or more): A taste of more ordinary Roman living at this lively outdoor food and flower market (open daily, except Sunday, until 1pm). Kids love to pick out their own breakfast or lunch. For a complete meal, **La Carbonara** is a good bet for a classic sit-down lunch (listed with restaurants later in this chapter).

Borghese Gardens (2 hours or more): This is Rome's central park, a very quiet, safe and entertaining place for a picnic lunch, bicycling and afternoon fun. Two art museums also grace this enormous public park, notably the **Galleria Borghese**. Parent Tip:Any sightseeing expedition you can follow by a visit to the **Borghese Gardens** will earn major brownie points with your kids. Tiny bumper car rides, ponies, bicycles and family peddle-carts to rent – plus lots of paths and grass to run in. A great way to end (or break up) the day! Take your teens here to toss a Frisbee or kick around a soccer ball. This picturesque public park is home as well to one of Rome's top art museums – Galleria Borghese – which at least one adult can sneak off to see while the children play.

Spanish Steps (before or after dinner): The **Piazza Di Spagna** is a favorite hangout for people of all ages. With children it is best visited in the afternoon or early evening, when the musicians, artists and Italian families are at their most entertaining. The 137 steps are located just below one exit from the Borghese Gardens, so the two can be seen in tandem.

Day 5: Day Trip from Rome

Cervetri (6 hours or more, including travel): Before the Roman Empire, the great Etruscan culture dominated the Italian Peninsula around present-day Rome and up through Tuscany. While Egyptian pharaohs were erecting pyramids, the more democratic Etruscans were constructing their *necropoli* – cities of the dead – with fascinating burial mounds of varying sizes. The best of these are in Tarquinia and Cervetri, with the latter the closest – about an hour by train from Rome and well worth the trouble.

Tivoli Gardens (4 hours or more, including travel): Tivoli is where the wealthiest Romans built their summer villas – and it remains home to the **Villa D'Este** and its world-famous fountains. The gardens, hedge maze and whimsical fountains are great fun for kids and wondrous for adults – particularly at night during May through September when the monumental sculpted fountains are floodlit. Tivoli is 40 minutes by train or car from the city center.

GETTING AROUND TOWN

Quick. Someone invent a Star Trek-like transporter to beam families from sight to sight. This highly charged city makes New York seem calm in comparison. Driving can be hazardous, buses crowded and taxis difficult to find when you really need one. None of which may be a problem for traveling without children, but can cause some families to become apoplectic.

Here's our advice:

Don't drive yourself. While Italian drivers are not nearly as insane as rumored, navigating unknown streets with children who may be a wee bit disagreeable and able to distract parents enough to turn a pleasant outing into a scene from Dante's *Inferno*, is not recommended. Also, non-residential cars are not allowed in the historical city center.

Do use the buses. At times they may be crowded, especially on routes that terminate at the Vatican on holy days. On our last trip, our Speilberg-wannabe 10-year-old son filmed from inside a jammed-packed tiny bus our brief excursion from the Borghese to the Capitoline Museums. His footage, filmed zooming through the front window, showed the harrowing scene of pedestrians ambling through the streets while the bus prodded them out of the way – with inches to spare! We love the bus because it gives us a true feel for Rome.

Do use taxis, just don't count on finding one late on weekend nights or holidays. Cabs are expensive in Rome, but offer the easiest way to get

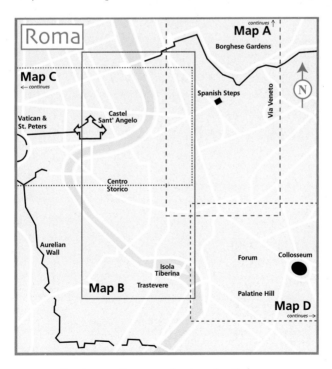

See the next four pages for these detailed maps

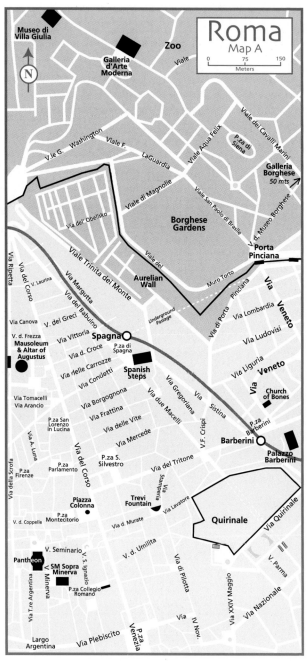

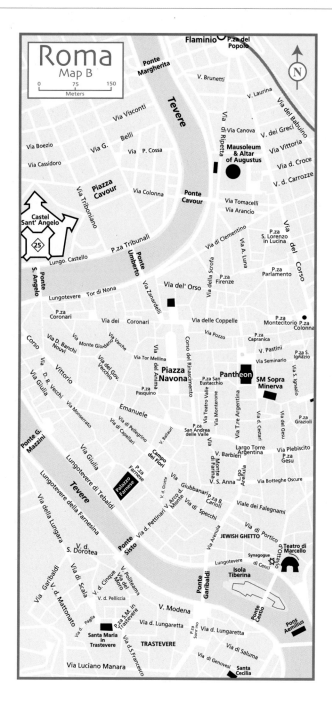

Roma
Map B
0   75   150
Meters

Flaminio   P.za del Popolo

Ponte Margherita

V. Brunetti
V. Laurina
Via del Babuino
Via Visconti
Via di Ripetta
Via Canova   V. dei Greci
Via Boezio
Via G.   Belli
Via P. Cossa
Via Vittoria
Via Cassidoro
Mausoleum & Altar of Augustus
Via d. Croce
V. d. Carrozze

Piazza Cavour
Via Colonna
Ponte Cavour
Via Tomacelli
Via Arancio
P.za S. Lorenzo in Lucina
Via Triboniano

Castel Sant' Angelo
25
Lungo. Castello
P.za Tribunali
Ponte Umberto
Via di Clementino
Via A. Luna
P.za Parlamento

Ponte S. Angelo
Lungotevere   Tor di Nona
Via del' Orso
Via della Scrofa
P.za Firenze

P.za Coronari
Via dei   Coronari
Via delle Coppelle
P.za Montecitorio P.za Colonna
Corso
Via D. Banchi Nouvi
Via Monte Giordano
Via Vecchie
Via Pozzo
P.za Capranica
Vittorio
Via del Gov. Vecchio
Via Tor Mellina
Corso del Rinascimento
V. Pastini
Via Seminario
P.za S. Ignazio
Via D. B. Vecchi
Via del Anima
Piazza Navona
P.za San Eustacchio
Pantheon
SM Sopra Minerva
Via Giulia
Via Monserato
P.za Pasquino
Via Teatro Valle
Via Monterone
Via T.re Argentina
Via d. Cestari
Via del Gesu
P.za Grazioli
Ponte G. Mazzini
Emanuele
Via di Pellegrino
Via di Capellari
V. Baltauri
P.za San Andrea delle Valle
Largo Torre Argentina
Via Plebiscito
P.za Gesu
Campo del Fiori
V. Barbieri
V. Monte di Farina
Via Botteghe Oscure
Via Giulia
P.za Farnese
Palazzo Farnese
V. d. Grotte
Giubbanari
V. Arco d. Monte
V. S. Anna
Lgo Arenula
Lungotevere di Tebaldi
Tevere
P.za B. Cairoli
Via di Specchi
Viale dei Falegnami
Lungotevere della Farnesina
V. d. Pettinari
Via Arenula
Via di Portico
Lungotevere della Lungara
S. d. Dorotea
Ponte Sisto
Via d. Pettinari
JEWISH GHETTO
Teatro di Marcello
Synagogue
Lungotevere di Cenci
Via Garibaldi
Via di Scala
V. d. Mattonato
V. Politeama
V. del Moro
V. d. Cinque
V. d. Pelliccia
Ponte Garibaldi
Isola Tiberina
Ponte Cestio
Pons Aemilius
V. Modena
V. d. Paglia
P.za S.M. in Trastevere
Santa Maria in Trastevere
Via d. Lungaretta
P.za Sonrino
Via d. Lungaretta
Via di Saluma
Via Luciano Manara
Via d.S.Francesco
TRASTEVERE
Via di Genovesi
Santa Cecilia

Tevere
N

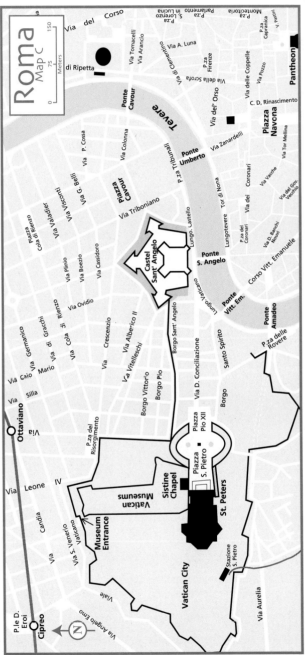

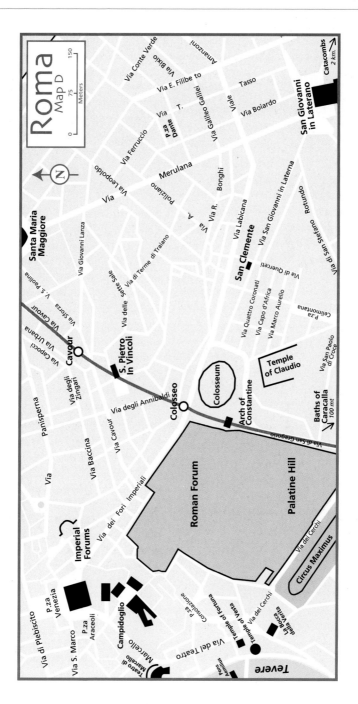

around with the family in tow. But beware of turning into Cinderella without a coach to take you home (see sidebar below). Cabs can become scarce, especially on Saturday and holiday evenings.

Cinderella's Taxi

One night we dawdled at the Piazza Navona, soaking in a wonderful Roman evening gazing at Bernini's famous fountains and enjoying the late-night antics of performance artists strutting their stuff. It was 10pm, and our young daughter fast asleep in the jogger stroller. We decided to hail a cab for the hotel. If it were only that easy. At the taxi stand, people were jockeying for position and no one cared if we had *bambini* with us or not. We made the fatal mistake of walking to another cabstand, only to find a similar situation. On we marched, piazza after piazza, dodging scooters that screeched through the streets like unguided missiles. Finally, after midnight, with our son marching in a zombie-like state, Barbara cajoled a taxi driver who had just let some people off at their hotel to take us home. (He was not very interested, complaining that the traffic was so bad that night – a holiday night.) Our little boy was asleep before the cab door shut. So wait at that first taxi stand or head home a bit earlier on those holiday evenings.

Do use the Metro. The *metropolitana*, or Italian subway system, is a quick and convenient way to get between certain sights, such as the Vatican and the Spanish Steps. It also offers a true, sometimes colorful picture of the real Rome. Stations are marked with a big white "M." Both lines (*Linea A* and *Linea B*) meet in the lower level of Rome's central train station (*Termini*). At any station you can buy a 75-minute ticket, from the booth or vending machine, for almost €1. To validate the ticket you have it punched by inserting it into one of the bright orange machines. If you get on again within 75 minutes, just stamp the ticket again and you are good to go. Also, children under 10 ride free. Visit *www.romebuddy.com/givesadvice/trains.html* for more information on the metro. See metro map on next page for details.

Do choose to walk. Although Rome is too large a city to walk to every sight with the family, it is possible to organize your daily itinerary to get around largely by foot. Try to turn each day's travels into a walking tour, using city street maps and planning to veer off course to at least glimpse secondary sights. Walking is always the best way to get a feel for Rome. Remember that the flimsy, light-

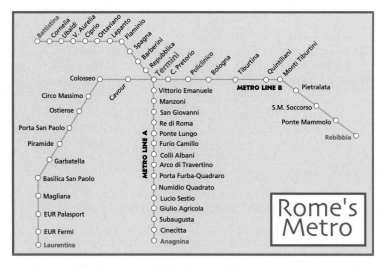

weight strollers that carry so nicely onto airplanes won't work well on Rome's bumpy pavement (or anywhere in Italy); there's no such thing as a handicap ramp at corners or curbsides. If you enjoy walking, the best bet is a small jogger stroller – the urban dune buggy of strollers.

FINDING YOUR WAY AROUND ROME

Rome is built on seven hills – Capitoline, Palatine, Aventine, Esquiline, Quirnale, Caelio and Viminale – which have shrunk over the years due to flooding and extensive build up of the valley floor by eras of construction. The first two hills are most familiar to tourists. Capitoline Hill contains Rome's City Hall – the Campidoglio – on the site of ancient Rome's temple of Jupiter. Palatine, located next to Capitoline, is the seat of Ancient Rome, a collection of palaces of emperors and temples to the gods.

Even the best of maps left us at times lost and bewildered as we trekked through Rome's labyrinth of narrow, web-like streets. While we continue to refer to maps, we prefer to orient ourselves by relying on main streets.

Here are several main thoroughfares and the tourist sites located nearby:

• **Via Del Corso** runs from the Piazza del Popolo south to the Piazza Venezia. Along the route, on the eastern side, you will pass or come quite near to the Spanish Steps and the Trevi Fountain, which intersects with **Via Dia Del Tritone**.

• Nestled between the Via Del Corso on the east and the Via Del Plebiscito and Corso Vittorio Emanuele II on the south and southwest

respectively, in a spider-web of streets, are the **Pantheon**, **Piazza Navona** and the **Campo dei Fiori**.
- Rome's most elegant shops are located along **Via dei Condotti** and the **Via Borgognona**, streets that fan out from the Spanish Steps.
- Continue south from the Piazza Venezia on **Via Dei Fori Imperiali** and you will head into the Colosseum.
- The **Via Vittorio Veneto**, made famous in the film *La Dolce Vita,* travels from Piazza Barberini, host to Bernini's Fountain of Triton, up the Pincian Hill to the Borghese Gardens and art gallery.

WHERE ARE WE GOING NOW?

Rome was not built in a day, so be prepared not to be able to see all of it during a brief stay. Kids will absorb the grandeur and especially the history if you organize your visit thematically.

For example, an entire day exploring aspects of Ancient Rome and a separate day visiting the relics of Sacred Rome may be more satisfying, in retrospect, than a helter-skelter whirlwind of looking at unrelated but "famous" sights.

Ancient Rome

Visiting ancient Rome is like traveling back in a time machine, according to our children. They found the vastness of the **Roman Forum** and **Colosseum** shocking. "How were these monuments built in the days before cranes?" is a question they pondered throughout our trek through the ruins. The impact of antiquity did not rescind as they strolled through the site as teens.

Parent Tip: To get oriented, visit the **information center** on Via dei Fori Imperali (at the corner of Via C. Ricci), about halfway between the Capitoline Hill (Piazza del Campidoglio) and the entrance to the Roman Forum (at Via Cavour). Guided, English-speaking tours are available every day at 9:20am, 11:55am, 1:35pm. Maximum number on the tour is 15. *Tel. (06)397-46-2221; E-mail: Tech@closeup.it; Fax (06)3751-271.*

THE ROMAN FORUM

Via dei Fori Imperiali, at Via Cavour. Tel. (06)699-0110. Web: www.capitolium.org. Open 9am until one hour before sunset. Closed May 1, December 25 and January 1. The Roman Forum and Palatine Hill are inside the same archaeological site; ask for a combined ticket with the Colosseum if you are seeing it all. Maps and self-guided audio tours are available in the little gift shop behind the ticket booth.

According to tradition, Tarquinius Priscus, the fifth king of Rome, drained Rome's valley by building a grand sewer that collected the stagnant water from the marshes and directed it into the Tiber River. The valley became known as the Forum because it was an open place outside the inhabited areas. Over time it became the main piazza of the city. It reached its glory during the Republic when elegant buildings dotted the pathways, boasting to the world of Rome's power and wealth. The Forum was a lively and bustling gathering place for the people and administrators of the world's greatest city. Official announcements and news were broadcast – by voice – to citizens.

After the fall of Rome, as the Empire lost its luster, the Forum was used less and less. The buildings fell into ruin and people pillaged the abandoned structures for materials to construct other buildings. The Forum gradually surrendered to nature and became a meadow – a pastureland for cows, to be exact. About two hundred years ago, archaeologists discovered the ruins and they continue to excavate the area today.

Parent Tip: With children in tow, it will be nearly impossible to stop at every structure in the Forum. Here's a must-see list for you and the kids.

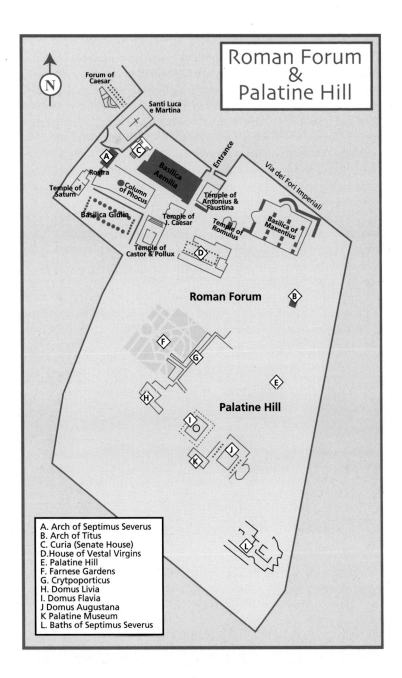

Roman Forum
&
Palatine Hill

N

Forum of
Caesar

Santi Luca
e Martina

Entrance

Via dei Fori Imperiali

A

C

Basilica
Aemilia

Rostra

Column
of Phocus

Temple of
Saturn

Temple of
Antonius &
Faustina

Basilica of
Maxentius

Basilica Giulia

Temple of
J. Caesar

Temple of
Romulus

Temple of
Castor & Pollux

D

Roman Forum

B

F

G

E

H

Palatine Hill

I
O

J

K

L

A. Arch of Septimus Severus
B. Arch of Titus
C. Curia (Senate House)
D. House of Vestal Virgins
E. Palatine Hill
F. Farnese Gardens
G. Crytpoporticus
H. Domus Livia
I. Domus Flavia
J Domus Augustana
K Palatine Museum
L. Baths of Septimus Severus

Even these stops, spread out as they are, will take about two hours. Maps and more detailed descriptions – including English-language audio tours – are available in the gift shop behind the ticket window at the entrance on Via dei Fori Imperiali.

Via Sacra: The main road through the Roman Forum is the Via Sacra. Spectacular processions advanced down this street to herald another victory in battle for Rome. The victorious commander was paraded down Via Sacra in a gilded carriage drawn by stunning white horses. Processions typically ended at the Temple of Jupiter with a sacrifice to the gods and a display of treasures plundered from the enemy. At the end of the procession came the defeated captain, who was publicly put to death.

Comitium: The Comitium was the seat of political and judicial decision-making. Decisions made here had to reach agreement in the Senate, which met at the nearby Curia. The soul of the Comitium continues to live in the words, if not the hearts, of today's Roman politicians. Politicians who speak to the public from a podium are said to be holding a *comizio*.

Fun Facts

• On every December 17, the Saturnalia, one of Rome's most fun and unique festivals, was celebrated. For three days the social classes switched roles – servants bossed around masters and masters bowed to their servants' beck and call.

• Concordia means "of the same mind." It is where we get the word concord, which can mean agreement or treaty. Eventually the Temple of Concordia became a museum of treasures taken from the defeated enemy.

• Vesta was the goddess who protected the domestic hearth, which explains the round shape of the temple – ancient Roman huts also were round. A sacred fire was required to burn constantly inside the temple. If the flame expired, evil would befall Rome. The king's daughters were placed in charge of the fire during the Imperial Age. But from the Republic on, the solemn duty was entrusted to the vestals who quite conveniently lived in the house next door.

Curia: This is the home of the Senate, often rebuilt throughout the ages and eventually turned into a church in the 7th century AD. In those days, only old men with years of experience could be elected to the Senate – a word derived from the Latin word for elderly. The ceiling inside the Curia is quite high, especially compared to the size of the building. One reason given is it allowed a speaker's voice to be amplified since this was a time before microphones. Notice the two bas reliefs found in the center of the Forum. They depict antiquity's version of the New Deal – one represents abolition of debt of the poor and the other the creation of the dole through grants to the poor.

Arch of Septimius Severus: Win a war, build an arch. This arch, built in honor of Septimius Severus and his sons Caracalla and Greta, celebrates the victory over the Parthians and the expansion of the Roman Empire. After his father's death, Caracalla killed his brother in order to become emperor and even washed out Greta's name on all the monuments in hope that he would be forgotten. You can still see the erasure on the arch today.

Lapis Niger: The oldest Latin inscriptions (6th century BC) ever found were discovered under this black stone – or *lapis niger* in Latin. Written in an archaic language, the inscriptions threatened damnation to anyone who should violate the area. A small room is located under the rock, with an altar and the tablet on which the inscription was written. Some believe Romulus, founder of Rome, was worshipped at this spot.

Temple of Saturn: The remains of several temples are visible behind the **Rostra**, built by Julius Caesar for orators to address the multitudes since they were no longer using the Comitium. Eight gray granite columns on the left of the Rostra mark the remains of the Temple of Saturn. Built between the period of kings and 498 BC, this temple is were Romans kept the state treasure.

Temple of Vespasian and Titus: Three columns mark the temple dedicated to Vespasian and his son Titus.

Temple of Concordia: Only the base remains of this temple, not surprising since the foundation was laid in 367 BC. This temple was constructed to celebrate the cessation of struggles between patricians and plebeians.

Turn around to breathe in the flavor of the Forum. From here you could address the crowds on political topics. Or you could wander down the avenue reciting recently written poetry.

Look down the road slightly beyond the fig and olive trees and you will see a fenced-off area on the right with entrances to underground tunnels. It is likely that gladiators used these tunnels because the games were held here, in the Forum, before amphitheaters were built.

Temple of Vesta: Located on Via Nova, which runs parallel to Via Sacra, are the remains of the beautiful rounded Temple of Vesta. The temple, quite old, was rebuilt after the fire of 191 AD.

The House of the Vestals: Several statues of vestals are situated around the central courtyard of the house. You can see the remains of several small rooms at the sides of the courtyard. Vestal Trivia: Six vestals were selected from the children of patrician families. These girls had to serve for 30 years, during which time they could neither marry nor have children. They were honored and treated like royalty, often carried about the environs in carriages. The best seats in the amphitheater were reserved for these girls. And, if a condemned man passed a vestal on the way to his execution, he was pardoned of his crime.

Temple of Romulus: Back to the Via Sacra, moving toward Palatine, is the Temple of Romulus. Don't get confused. This is not a temple to the founder of Rome, but to emperor Maxentius' son who died young. Some archaeologists argue that the temple actually was dedicated to Jupiter Stator and the Household gods, which in combination with Vesta protected home and family.

See the bronze door. It is the original door – about 1,700 years old – with a lock that still works! They don't make them like they used to.

Arch of Titus: Keep walking up Via Sacra. To the right, toward Palatine, you will reach the Arch of Titus. In 71 AD, Vespasian and his offspring Titus dealt a blow to the holy city of Jerusalem, sacked it and razed its temple to the ground. They also walked off with many treasures, including the seven-branched candelabra and the silver trumpets, two revered Jewish religious symbols. You can see these symbols carved in the arch. The second relief shows Titus advancing on Jerusalem, along with the goddesses Roma and Victory.

Temple of Venus & Roma: A great temple once stood here, dedicated to the goddesses who protect Rome – Venus and Roma. The temple was completed during Hadrian's reign in 135 AD. Today, the church of San Francesca Romana is located in one part of the huge temple, with a museum in the monastery of the church. The museum contains many items found in the Forum.

Walk across the lawn to the valley of the Colosseum, where the emperor Nero built his gargantuan palace, Domus Aurea, on the entire area in front of you.

PALATINE HILL

Open daily 9am until one hour before sunset. Enter Palatine Hill either from inside the Roman Forum (from the main entrance on Via dei Fori Imperiali, at Via Cavour), or from a separate entrance across from the Colosseum, up from the Arch of Constantine (a combined ticket with the Colosseum is available here).

One of the Seven Hills of Rome, Palatine looks down over the Forum, which its residents once ruled. It is the place where the fabled Romulus founded Rome in 754 BC. For a millennium it was the most exclusive address in Rome – home to Emperors and the wealthiest families. Although the ruins – much of it recently excavated – are not as evocative as the Roman Forum, it is a natural playground for kids, and a shady, quiet and scenic resting spot for adults.

As the story goes, Romulus chose the Palatine Hill as the ideal spot to build his new city. Remains of a wall and moat have been discovered beneath this hill, which some scholars claim are the remains of the boundaries of the original Rome. Traces of shepherds' huts also have been unearthed at the summit of the hill.

Augustus was born here and built his new house here to live in the same quarter, as did Romulus. After the fall of the Western Roman Empire, many kings visiting Rome resided in the luxurious homes on the hill. In 1550, Cardinal Alessandro Farnese purchased the Palatine Hill, built a grand villa and cultivated a beautiful garden, creating the world's first botanical garden, still partly preserved.

The Hut of Romulus: At the bottom of the gardens (with your back to the Forum), descend a steep staircase and step into Rome's most ancient monuments. Past the ruins of the Temple of Cybele or Magna Mater, you will come to a balustrade. Down below are huts from between the 9th and 7th centuries BC. One hut appears more prominent than the others, and some Romans believe it to be the Hut of Romulus.

The House of Livia & Her Husband, Augustus: Return to the top of the staircase, turn right at the 7th–6th century BC cisterns and you will walk into the house of Livia, wife of Augustus. Further along is her husband's complex. Augustus' house was divided into two parts: a large, public area and a smaller, private area decorated with splendid paintings. Augustus had a temple with porticoes, libraries and treasures built next to his home, which was plain next to the ostentatious palaces created by Rome's more extravagant future leaders. A peak at the immense ruins of Domitian's imperial palace, Domus Flavia, hints at the opulent lifestyles led by Rome's rich and famous of the time.

Domus Augustana & Stadium: The emperor actually resided here, the private part of the palazzo. The facade overlooks the Circus Maximus. As you walk through the ruins, you come upon the stadium, a long narrow passage once used for horse races.

THE COLOSSEUM

Piazza del Colosseo. Tel. (06) 700.5469, (06) 399.6770 reservations. Tuesday through Sunday, 9am to 7pm. Admission €8.

The Colosseum symbolizes Rome, just as surely as the Eiffel Tower is Paris and the Statue of Liberty New York. It opened in 80 AD with a celebration lasting 100 days. Getting a good seat in the Colosseum was as difficult as getting a ticket to a Lakers' game. And similar to the Lakers, celebrities occupied the choice seats. A web-like series of corridors and rooms inside the Colosseum were used as storerooms and as cages for wild beasts. These corridors were covered by a huge wooden stage on which the events – gladiator fighting gladiator, gladiator fighting wild beast, wild beast fighting wild beast – took place.

For the first time in centuries – 15 to be exact – the Colosseum is open for performances. In this millennium, you can see theater – the first performance was of *Oedipus Rex* – or hear musicians like Elton John, Paul McCartney, and other "classical" artists. Tickets cost about $25.

Although the Colosseum is not very impressive as architecture, even its ruins can give kids a sense of what an engineering feat it must have been nearly 2,000 years ago. It also was fully elliptical and more glorious in the days of Roman Empire – with each column covered in marble and each portico sporting a marble statue of some ruler, nobleman or other notable.

Parent Tip: The Colosseum is the place to play count the cats! After hours marching around the Forum, our kids were numb to any more ancient splendor – but they loved spotting and counting some of the hundreds of cats that call the Colosseum home. The cats especially like the alcoves behind the fence around the outside.

Gladiator Games: What did a Roman emperor do for fun? Call for the games to begin. But these games were deadly. **Gladiator fights**

took place at the Colosseum, stirring the crowds to frenzy. Gladiators often were slaves or prisoners of war who had little hope for the future. They were trained at schools to learn the "art" of combat. On game day, they paraded with much fanfare into the Colosseum. As they approached the emperor's platform they shouted *"Ave Caesar moritur te salutant!"* or "Hail emperor, those ready to die salute you!" (Sounds strikingly similar to Star Trek's Klingon warrior hail, "It's a good day to die.")

A blast of a trumpet signaled the start of the ruthless battle. But hope lived on for some defeated gladiators. Fallen, and prepared to die, the defeated gladiator waited for a sign from the crowd. If he were valiant in his pursuit of the now victorious gladiator, the crowd would shout, *"Mitte!"* – "Spare him." However, if he disappointed the fans with a mediocre job, the audience gave him a "thumbs down" sign, and he was killed on the spot. While no endorsement deals existed, winning gladiators did reap a windfall of profits. Some even gained their freedom, after years of worthy, but bloody battle.

THE ARCH OF CONSTANTINE

Anchoring the Piazza Colosseo is the grandest and best-preserved triumphal arch in Italy. Victorious armies would return from their campaigns and parade to the arch, which marked the end of the ancient Triumphal Way. It was erected in 312 AD to commemorate the emperor's victory over Maxentius at the Ponte Milvio (the oldest bridge in Rome and still standing).

IMPERIAL FORUMS

Via dei Fori Imperiali. Entrance is allowed only to the Forum of Trajan and the Trajan Markets. Go early to avoid waiting in lines at the ticket office. Forum of Trajan is open Tues-Sat. 9am to 6:30p.m. (closed Monday). Sundays and holidays 9am to 1pm. Closed May 1, December 25 and January 1. Web: www.capitolium.org/english.htm.

To see the Imperial Forums in chronological order, start from the Piazza Venezia, walk down Via dei Fori Imperiali on the right side in the direction of the Colosseum. Pass the statue of Julius Caesar to Via del Tulliano. The Forum of Caesar will be on your right.

The Forum of Caesar: Caesar purchased the land to build his Forum, yet did not live to see it completed. His dream was to build a Forum to commemorate himself and his family ties to the gods (Caesar believed his family was directly descended from Aeneas, son of the goddess Venus). It was begun in 54 BC, finished in 44 BC and was the first Imperial Forum.

A statue of Venus, by the famous ancient artist Arcesilao, was located in the Forum's temple dedicated to the goddess.

The Forum of Augustus: Walk back to the Via dei Fori Imperiali toward the Colosseum. Cross the street and find the statue of Augustus. Look down and view this ruler's Forum.

Complaining of the small size of the other Forums, Augustus paid for his Forum from treasures awarded after victorious conquests. It took 40 years to build the Forum of Augustus, which was constructed around the time of Christ's birth. The piazza was rectangular. This Forum commemorates the deaths of Brutus and Cassius – who killed Augustus' kin, Caesar.

At the bottom rose the temple to Mars the Avenger, faced in white marble. Statuary of *"summi viri,"* great heroes of Roman legend and history, dotted two covered porticoes, many paeans to the Augustus family.

The Forum of Trajan: Via dei Fori Imperiali. Tel. (06)670-0048 Forum of Trajan and Trajan Markets open weekdays 9am to 6:30pm (closed Monday); Sundays and holidays 9am to 1pm. Closed May 1, December 25, January 1.

Trajan had his Forum – the last and most grand of the *fori* – built between 107 AD and 113 AD. When he realized that little space existed for him to create an everlasting monument to none other than himself, he relied on the creativity of a world-famous architect, Apollodorus of Damascus, to save the day. Apollodorus's design involved cutting through a hill connecting Quirinal and the Capitol, thus giving Trajan a vast space to adorn himself. The architectural masterpiece was completed in six years, 112 AD. In the following year, the incredible Column of Trajan was erected.

In 801 AD, an earthquake struck and destroyed most of the buildings in the Forum of Trajan. Excavations in the early 19th century, under the orders of the Napoleonic Government, discovered many of the Forum's splendors. More recent excavations have unveiled even more understanding of life in the once bustling Forum of Trajan.

The Trajan Markets: Put your back to the Column and go past the Basilica. On the left at the bottom is a small door in an arch. Through the door, you are in the Forum of Trajan, opposite the Trajan Markets.

Find the stairs that lead to the market and move upward. All sorts of activity transpired here: Food stores run by the Senate, flower-fruit-vegetable stands and even a fish house. Administrative offices also were located here.

Exit the Trajan Markets to Via Quattro Novembre. Keep going up until you reach Largo Magnanapoli, turn right into the Salita dell Grillo. Here, to the right you see the Trajan Markets. In Roman times, the buildings on the left would have been the Subura, a neighborhood of low-income tenements. If you arrive here on Sunday morning around 11:00am, you can descend to the Chapel of John the Baptist.

Notice the bricks. They are squared travertine blocks, a way of building that was called *opus quadratum.*

Turn around in Piazza del Grillo and walk down the street along the gray stone wall on the right. Behind it stand the remains of the Forum of Augustus. You can see entrances that in ancient times led into the Forum. Continue to the end of the street, and you are back where you started.

THE CIRCUS MAXIMUS
Buses 15, 90, 94. Metro: Circo Massimo.

The Tarquin kings who, after draining the valley used wood to construct the arena and added spectator seats, built the *circus* (racetrack). This circus was maximus! It held nearly 200,000 people, more than most modern sports arenas. It is 620 meters long and 118 wide, in the shape of an elongated rectangle. In the middle, running just about the full length, was the *spina* – a low wall, eventually built in masonry and marble – around which raced the chariots or runners.

Today, all that remains of the *spina* is a slight hump. If you don't have time to walk over here, there are great views of the Circus Maximus from Palatine Hill at the ruins of Domus Augustana.

NERO'S GOLDEN HOUSE (Domus Aurea)
Via della Domus Aurea. Tel. (06)399.67700. Adm., Tuesday through Friday, 10am to 4pm.

And, golden it is – or, at least what's left of it. Built between Rome's

> ### Fun Fact
> Chariot races were preceded by extensive pomp and circumstance. Each chariot team was divided into stables distinguished by their colors: russata (red), albata (white), veneta (light-blue), prasina (green), purpurea (purple), and aurata (gold). Chariot drivers were dressed in their faction's color and the horses were adorned in matching colors. The driver who made it – alive – around seven laps was the winner. Rules? Forget it. A driver could dash his opponent's chariot into the side of the spina or try to knock over his competitor (think Star Wars' pod-racing on horses).

Great Fire and Nero's suicide, this extensive villa was filled with gold leaf, stunning frescoes and stucco ceilings enhanced by semi-precious stones. The villa was built as an opulent place to party, and Nero lived up to his reputation as a party animal. After his death, Rome officials, embarrassed by the excesses of the Domus Aurea, stripped the villa of its' many treasures, covered it with dirt and built over the party palace. In the 15th century, a young man accidently fell through a cleft in the hillside and re-discovered Nero's Golden House. Since then, architects, artists and others have reclaimed what is left of the villa. Visit *www.historyforkids.org/learn/romans/architecture/goldenhouse.htm* for more history for kids on Nero's Golden House.

Political Rome

CAMPIDOGLIO

Although Romulus chose the Palatine Hill to build Rome, Capitoline Hill emerged as the religious and then political seat of Rome. The Piazza del Campidoglio forms the northwest boundary of the Forum and includes the Capitoline Museum, Senatoral Palace, the Palace of the Conservatori, the Church of Santa Maria D'Aracoeli (formerly the Temple of Juno Moneta), and a bold bronze statue of Marcus Aurelius. The Administration of the Commune of Rome has its main office at the bottom.

Ascend up to the piazza by way of the *cordonata* – a staircase with steps wide enough for horses to mount – to fully appreciate this muscular public space. Pause on the top step and take in the stunning Renaissance design, the genius of Michelangelo. Although the master did not live to see his design completed, the Piazza is a blending of architecture and sculpture at its most monumental. Taking center stage is the spectacular and recently cleaned copy of a statue of Marcus Aurelius (the original, plated in gold, is now in the adjacent Capitoline Museum). At the top of the steps, perched on the parapet, are the statues of Castor and Pollux, the two mythical twins of Jupiter. At either side of the twins are two reliefs that caught the eye of our children – the piled up arms of defeated enemies, trophies of Marius.

With your back to the steps, directly behind Marcus Aurelius is Rome's City Hall, the **Palazzo Senatorio**. Notice this grand building's bell tower and stairway, at the base of which is a statue of Minerva, the allegorical goddess of Rome. At the rear of this grand building is the best view out over the Roman Forum. After completing your visit atop the Campidoglio, descend the steps to the left to access the Roman Forum; the entrance is a few hundred yards further along down the **Via dei Fori**

Imperiali.

As you stand in the center of the Piazza del Compidoglio – and if the kids haven't already pointed it out – ask if they notice Michelangelo's studied sense of symmetry. This is particularly evident as you approach the twin Palazzi that house the **Capitoline Museums**. Be sure to check out the Palazzo dei Conservatori, on the right, and its matching building across the square, the Palazzo Nuovo, which together make up the Capitoline Museums.

THE CAPITOLINE MUSEUM

Piazza del Campidoglio. Tel. Information and reservations (06) 67102071. Hours: Open Monday through Saturday, 8:30 am to 7:30 pm, Sunday 9am to 6 pm. Web: www.en.museicapitolini.org. Admission. Buses: Via del Teatro di Marcello: 44, 63, 81, 95, 160, 170, 175, 204, 628, 715, 716, 780, 781. Via dei Fiori Imperiali: 84, 85, 87,175, 186, 810, 850. Via del Plebiscito: 46, 62, 63, 64, 70, 80, 81, 87, 186, 492, 628, 640, 810. Metro: Line B/Colosseo stop.

The Capitoline Museum is actually two museums, in twin palaces facing each other across the Piazza del Campidoglio. Claimed to be the oldest museums in the world, founded by Pope Clement XII in 1734, the museums focus on ancient society and culture. Even if you have been here before, take a second look. The Capitoline Museums underwent a substantial renovation and were reopened for the Jubilee.

While this is a stunning museum for those keen on antiquity, it can be torturous for high-spirited children. Here are some highlights for a quick visit:

Hall of Gladiators: No, it's not bloody warfare, but exquisite sculptures, many donated in the 1700s by Pope Benedict XIV.

Hall of the She-Wolf: She is located in the center of the room; the symbol of Rome. The female wolf is attributed to a fifth century BC

workshop in Etruria or Magna Graccia, the twins were added around the 16th century.

Hall of the Geese: The geese are cute, but Bernini's statue of Medusa with all those snakes is the reason to visit – that and the bust of Michelangelo.

Hall of Hannibal: The frescoes of the Punic War, including Hannibal on an elephant are intriguing. The museum notes that this is the only room that preserves the original 16th-century decoration of the frescoes.

When the going get rough, head for the huge room with the equestrian statue of the emperor Marcus Aurelius. There are bleacher type seats for the weary and a comfortable place to color or read.

Need some fresh air? Amble to the outside courtyard where your kids will squeal over the enormous fragments of a colossal statue of Constantine. Head, feet arms and a hand with one finger pointing up are arranged on the right side of the courtyard.

Be sure to use the tunnel connecting the three main buildings of the Capitoline – it is a fascinating journey for little ones and their imagination. It was built in the 1940s, but closed for the past 30 years. Its recent opening allows visitors to see the Tabularium, the first century BC Roman state archive constructed above the Roman Forum. From the Tabularium, there is an amazing view of the ruins below. Let your kids give a ringing speech to their subjects milling about below in the Forum.

Parent Tip: Kids are hungry? Visit the Capitoline Café, located on the terrace of the Palazzo Caffarelli. The lovely café offers breakfast and lunch/dinner items, scrumptious pastry, gelato and a good selection of wine. It's open from 9am to 8pm, with extended hours during the summer.

THE PANTHEON

Piazza della Rotonda. Tel. (06)6830-0230. Web: www.great-buildings.com/buildings/Pantheon.html. Open daily 9am-6:30pm, except Sunday (closes at 1pm). Regular mass at 10am Sundays. Buses 70, 81, 87, 90.

As you head down the Via Della Minerva to Piazza della Rotonda, the first surprise is the lively, festival-like atmosphere in the piazza surrounding this ancient structure. This one-time pagan temple is unbelievably preserved, in large part because it was converted into a Christian church 14 centuries

Fun Fact

What holds the cupola up? The cupola is made of materials that get increasingly lighter the higher up you go. Volcanic pumice stone is the uppermost material, which is exceedingly lightweight.

ago. The original Pantheon was built around 25 BC by Agrippa and rebuilt by the emperor Hadrian.

Inside, the building is even more astonishing, and is one of the coolest spots in Rome on a blazing-hot summer day.

The *cupola* on top of the building is the biggest built in the ancient world – surpassed later only by Michelangelo's design for the dome atop St. Peter's. At one time, beautiful bronze tiles covered the cupola, but the Byzantine emperor, Constant II, pillaged them. One thousand years later, Pope Urban VIII, a member of the Barberini family, took off with the bronze beams of the portal to use for Bernini's massive altarpiece at St. Peter's Basilica and for cannons for Castel ant'Angelo, the Pope's military stronghold. "What the barbarians didn't do, the Barberinis did," is an old but apt Roman saying. On the other hand, if it had not been converted into a Catholic church, this ancient pagan temple might have ended up just another Roman "ruin."

Sacred Rome

VATICAN CITY

No visit to Rome is complete without leaving Italy to enter Vatican City (*Citta del Vaticano*), officially an independent state since the 1929 treaty between the Holy See and the Kingdom of Italy. Home to the Pope since 1377, the Vatican has its own money, railway, radio station and police — the brightly garbed Papal Swiss Guard. It also has its own postal service, with stamps more striking and delivery more efficient than the famously feeble *Posta Italiano*.

Plan to spend most of a day here, especially if you want to do more than glance inside St. Peter's and race through the Vatican Museums that house, among other treasures of ancient and Renaissance art, Michelangelo's glorious Sistine Chapel. Here is a quick overview; note that several very cool side tours – the Vatican caves, the audience with the Pope and the Vatican Gardens – require special advance reservation: *Tel. (39)(06)6988-4857, Fax (39)(06)6988-5863.*

Parent Tip: Mail your postcards at the Vatican if you expect them to arrive home before you do. Cards mailed from elsewhere in Italy to North America often take three weeks or more!

Planning the Vatican

Before your vacation, visit the Vatican's website: *www.vatican.va/museums/index.htm.*

When you arrive, stop first at the **Pilgrims and Tourists Information**

Office, located on the left side of the beautifully colonnaded St. Peter's Square (*Tel. (06)6988-4466 or (06)6988-4466, open daily 8am to 7pm*). If gardening is sacred to you, this is the place to arrange – preferably several days in advance – a guided tour of the **Vatican Gardens**, Rome's most beautiful park. The two-hour tour is daily at 10am (Admission) and includes a look inside the Casino of Pius IV, a remarkable Renaissance villa. (Open May-September except on Sundays; once a week October-April.)

The **Vatican Post Office** is located on the other side of the square (great stamps for collectors and a highly efficient service for mailing your beautiful Vatican Museum post cards). A branch is also located in the Vatican Museum, near the **cafeteria** (which is probably the most convenient and reasonable place to eat around the Vatican.)

St. Peter's Basilica is generally open 7am to 7pm, but closed to the public when there is a special mass or an official ceremony in the piazza. Papal guards, in street clothes, bark out requirements for attire – no shorts (men, too), short skirts or sleeveless dresses – and they mean it.

Inside, in addition to the soaring architecture and sacred art, you can plan to see:

• **Holy Vatican Grottoes** (Tombs of the Popes): Entrance from the right transept (*closes an hour before the church*).

• **Dome** (Michelangelo's cupola): Ascend this architectural wonder of the world by stairs or by elevator; walk out on the roof for an unparalleled view over Rome. (*8am to 6pm, admission*). The line forms on the left just inside the church's main entrance.

• **St. Peter's Treasure** (church museum): Entrance from left of nave (*9am to 6:30pm, admission*).

• **Vatican Museums and Sistine Chapel tours** (2 hours): *March-October: Monday-Friday at 10:30am, noon, 2:00pm; Saturday 10:30am and 11:15am. From November-February: everyday but Sunday at 10:30am. Admission: €21.50 or €17.50.*

• **Vatican Gardens** (2 hours): *March-October: Tuesday, Thursday and Saturday at 10:00am. November –February: Saturday at 10:00am. Admission: €12 or €8. To book in advance, for individuals: Tel. (39)(06)6988.5100. For groups: Tel. (39)(06)6988.3578*

The **weekly papal audience** is quite exciting for youngsters and adults alike. It is typically held each Wednesday at 10am in the piazza (May-September) or in the Nervi Auditorium (October-April). You must apply in advance for the free tickets to the Papal Prefecture, either by mail or in person – look for the bronze door in the colonnade on the right side of St.

Peter's Square. (*Mail: Papal House Prefecture, 00120, Vatican City, or call (06)698-3017.*)

The **Vatican Caves and Necropolis** (*Grotte Vecchie*) require reservations. Underneath the tomb of St. Peter, archeologists discovered in the 1940s a street of Roman and early Christian tombstones, sarcophagi, fresco fragments and mosaics. Admission to the *Grotte Vecchie* is by written, advance request to the North American College in Rome (*Via dell'Umita 30, Tel. (06) 672-256 or 678-0184*), or by filling out a request form at the Vatican Excavations Office (*Uffizio degli Scavi*), located to the left of St. Peter's, after the Bells Arch. Specify a date, number of people, language and the hotel and/or phone number where you will be staying in Rome. Do it early: only 15 visitors per day are permitted. The entrance is off the Square, to the left of St. Peter's, where the Swiss Guards are posted. Admission.

The Vatican Museums: The entrance is on Viale Vaticano, on the north side of St. Peter's (furthest away from the Square), near Piazza Risorgimento. *Tel. (06)6988.3333. Hours: weekdays from March 1 to Oct. 29, daily 8:45am to 3:45pm (except Saturdays, 8:45am to 12:45pm). From Nov. 1 through Feb., from 8:45sm to 1pm. Closed all Sundays and major Catholic holy days. Admission, except on the last Sunday of every month, when it's free but closes at 12:45pm, as on Saturdays.*

ST. PETER'S BASILICA

Open daily April-September 7am to 7pm, Oct-March 7am-6pm. Dome open October-March 8am-5pm, April-September 8am-6pm. St. Peter's Treasury open daily 9am-6:30pm. Sacred Grottoes open Oct-April 7am-5pm, May-Sept 7am-6pm. Web: www.vatican.va.

The Square

The monumental ambition of St. Peter's Square (*Piazza San Pietro*) rivals that of the Colosseum, which could fit almost precisely inside of it. Tens of thousands flock to St. Peter's Square on religious holidays, so make sure you hold onto little ones. Just in case, we had a meeting place visible at the four-foot eye level – a gilded fountain by Maderno. Across the way is another stunning fountain by Fontana.

Bernini's **Colonnade** (1656) engulfs the square, with 284 enormous columns and 140 saints perched atop. While the Vatican obelisk initially appears minor compared to others throughout the city, it's story is fantastic. Caligula brought this obelisk from Egypt in 37AD. It is from the city of Heliopolis, founded as a capital by Akhenaton, who is credited with founding the first monotheistic religion. The obelisk, with four bronze lions encircling its base, originally was planted in the circus of Nero. Sixtus V moved it to St. Peter's in 1586.

Walk past the obelisk, up a gentle slope to the foot of St. Peter's, the world's largest church (although, in fairness, Milan's cathedral is longer). The Basilica was built over the spot where St. Peter is entombed.

In 324, **Constantine** ordered the erection of a church in honor of St. Peter. Charlemagne and Frederick II received their imperial crowns in this first church (long before separation of church and state became a rallying cry!) By the 15th century, however, the church was in tatters, and then the merry-go-round of popes and artists commenced.

First, Pope Nicholas V, in about 1450, decided to build a bigger and better church. He commissioned Bernardo Rossellino to design the new building. Work stopped upon the death of Pope Nicholas V, only to be resurrected (the building, not the pope) in 1506 by none other than Pope Julius II, with the assistance of Bramante. Bramante died in 1514 and his successor was Raphael, who died four years later before he could complete it. The sack of Rome (1527) delayed things quite a bit until, finally, in 1546, the 72-year-old Michelangelo took over and modified Bramante's plan for the dome. Upon his death, a succession of artists, including Fontana and Maderno (who also produced the beautiful fountains in the Piazza St. Pietro) completed the facade. On November 1, 1626, Urbano VIII dedicated the Basilica, 302 years after it all began!

The Facade

Everything about St. Peter's is immense, starting with the facade. If the intent was to make man remember his smallness in the universe, the designers succeeded. On either side of the staircase leading through the main gate to the church, stand the statues of Saint Peter (DeFabis) and Saint Paul (Adamo Tadolni). Nine balconies grace the facade. The Pope offers his Christmas and Easter benedictions from the central one.

The Interior

The enormity of the church strikes visitors immediately. For parents with active children, here are the most important aspects of St. Peter's that you will want to see before dashing back outside to play hide-and-seek among the colonnades:

• **Charlemagne's Crowning**: Upon entering, turn right and the Pieta is behind the crowd you see dead ahead. On the way, look for a disk of red porphyry on the floor, marking the precise spot where Charlemagne was crowned Emperor of the Holy Roman Empire by Leo III on Christmas Day in the year 800.

• **Michelangelo's Pieta** – Ahead is one of history's most emotional marble carvings. Gaze at the elegant, albeit grief-stricken Mary with her dead son lying across her lap. The Pieta has been restored and now resides behind a glass wall. Michelangelo was only 24-years-old when he sculpted the Pieta and made his mark in the art world. Look for his name that he etched on the band around Mary's dress.

• **St. Peter's statue** – By the far right pew is a bronze statue of St. Peter that has been touched on the foot by so many millions of tourists and worshippers that it is worn almost through at that spot.

• **Michelangelo's dome** – Just past St. Peter's statue is the grand dome (*cupola*) designed by Michelangelo. It remains quite literally the crowning architectural feat of the Renaissance. The largest freestanding dome at that time, it serves well its purpose to lift eyes toward heaven. Ascending the dome is a big hit for kids of all ages, but the line often is long. With little ones, you may want to spend an extra Euro or two and take the elevator (from the Pieta toward the high altar, just before

the Altar of St. Wenceslas). From the top, you can look down over the impressive church or walk out onto the roof and choose an equally stunning birds-eye view over the Eternal City.

• **Baldacchino** – Under the cupola but above the high altar rests Bernini's Baldacchino, or Grand Canopy, made from bronze pillaged from the Pantheon.

• **Chapel of Confessions and Tomb of Saint Peter** – Maderno made the Chapel of Confessions, located in front of the altar. Around the chapel are 95 perpetually lit lamps that mark the Tomb of Saint Peter.

• **Sacred Grottoes** (Tombs of the Popes) – Numerous popes are buried here in the foundation of the earlier St. Peter's. The most popular tombs are that of the simple monument to Pope John XXIII and Pope John Paul II. More ornate is the bronze tomb of Sixtus IV, in Renaissance style. Entrance is from the right transept (*hours: 7am-6pm*).

Parent Tip: St. Peter's and the Vatican Museums are long days for most children. But there are great places to split up, with one adult lingering over the art while the other watches the children scamper about outside. The **Piazza** is a good place to shepherd the children – lots of room to run and make noise. Also, check out the **courtyard garden** into which you emerge after touring the Vatican Museums, next to the gift shops and restaurant – which is very convenient for a light lunch or snack given the paucity of reliable restaurants near the Vatican.

VATICAN MUSEUMS

Viale Vaticano. Tel. (06)6988-4466. Web: www.vatican.va/museums/index.htm Admission. Closed Sundays and major religious holiday, except the last Sunday of each month, when admission is free. Hours: Monday through Saturday, 9am to 6pm, last admission is at 4pm. Closed Sunday, except last Sunday of month, open 9am to 2pm, last admission is at 12:30pm (admission is free, lines are longer).

Unless your children are art historians, better promise lots of gelato after this visit. This must-see museum, one of the world's greatest, is an exhaustive (and exhausting) treasure trove of ancient and Renaissance art – including rooms of frescoes by Raphael and the incomparable Sistine Chapel painted by Michelangelo. This is an immense museum – technically a series of interconnected museums – with room after room of stunning art, sculpture and artifacts. It is impossible to enjoy all this museum has to offer in one visit, so cut your losses and organize your visit by stopping only in the rooms that most interest your family.

Our advice, particularly in summer or near Easter, is to go either when the museum opens or an hour before the doors close, since this is when the lines to enter are shortest. Lines can be blocks long and, just when you think you are in, you have to trudge up several sweltering flights of stairs (no air conditioning, of course) to begin the tour. Beware: although closing time is advertised as 4:45pm, you must be admitted prior to 3:45pm.

Are the kids staging a sit-down strike, refusing to go into yet another art museum? Or, no time at all to take in the splendors of the Vatican Museums? We suggest you march through all the rooms until you make it to the Sistine Chapel. Even the most exasperated child will wonder at how Michelangelo painted on the ceiling. The other good news: someone else will urge your children to be quiet. *"Silenzia"* booms from a tape at intervals throughout your visit to this amazing chapel. You can't leave Rome without viewing Michelangelo's spectacular frescoes in the Sistine Chapel.

Here are some other **must-see rooms** in the Vatican Museums:

Egyptian Museum: An incredible collection of Egyptian sarcophagi, wooden mummy cases, mummies of animals and a collection of papyri with hieroglyphics are housed at this museum. Children love this room, and it is sometimes hard to get them out. Plan to spend a little extra time here. For those not able to visit Cairo, this exhibit is the next best thing.

Etruscan Room: We had trouble getting our children out of this room, but knowing how much more there was to come made it imperative that we shoo them along. The ancient tools and jewelry of this pre-Roman civilization on display bedazzled the children. They enjoyed trying to figure out how things worked.

Rooms of Raphael: If the Sistine Chapel were not here, Raphael's complex frescoes would probably be the museum's top exhibit. The *School of Athens* (*photo below*) provides a chance to challenge older kids to name the famous Greek philosophers, mathematicians and thinkers: Aristotle,

Plato, Socrates, Euclid and Pythagorus are among the featured greats. Look for clues, such as the globes held by Ptolemy and Zoroaster. Since this is, after all, the headquarters of the Catholic Church, Raphael compensates for this secular theme with a series of religious themes that are equally striking.

Enjoy the *Dispute of the Holy Sacrament* and the wonderfully lit *Liberation of St. Peter*.

The Loggia of Raphael: A big hit with everyone in our family. Our children especially liked the *Creation of the World*, and with paper and colored pencils sketched their own interpretation, while we took turns visiting other rooms. This loggia is divided into 13 arcades with nearly 50 scenes from the Old and New Testament, so be sure to gauge your child's endurance – you don't want to rush through the Sistine Chapel. Don't miss these paintings: *Creation of Eve, Jacob's Dream, Moses Receiving the Tablets of Law* and *King David*.

Parent Tip: If your kids like to draw, consider bringing sketchpads and pencils along. It gets kids off their feet and gives the adults a chance to double back for a closer look at a favorite artist. The Raphael rooms are particularly well suited for hanging out a while – our kids struck up conversations with American college students who were doing their own drawings.

Pinacoteca Vaticana: We are fans of **Giotto** – perhaps most famous for his depictions of St. Francis of Assisi – and this is the room to see some of his greatest work: *Il Redentore* and the *Martyrdoms of Peter and Paul*. Overall, the paintings collected here provide a remarkable sample of Renaissance art. Look for Raphael's last painting, the *Transfiguration of Christ*, and Leonardo da Vinci's *St. Jerome*. Other artists include Lippi, di Pietro and Fra Angelico. Madonnas, with and without Child, pour forth from the walls of this room

Pius Clementine Museum: Sculpture lovers will want to find their way to this room. The museum founded by Pius VI and Clement XIV also contains beautiful mosaics, including The *Battle between the Greeks and the Centaurs*, created in the first century. Also, journey to the Octagonal Court where some of the most important statues are housed. *The Cabinet of the Laocoon* portrays the revenge of the gods on a Trojan priest who had warned his countrymen not to admit the Trojan horse. Not pleased with Laocoon's defiance, the gods directed two mighty sea serpents to kill Laocoon and his sons.

Vatican Library: Numerous popes contributed to produce this exquisite library founded by Sixtus IV, who also was responsible for the Sistine Chapel. Over 500,000 volumes and nearly 60,000 ancient manuscripts reside in the library.

Sistine Chapel: The splendor of the Sistine Chapel makes the long lines and the never-ending march through the Vatican's exhaustive art collections all worthwhile. Michelangelo, who found painting secondary to sculpting, nevertheless produced this glorious and monumental series of frescoes for the Pope's private chapel. Together they tell the Bible stories of the creation of the world, the fall of man and the last judgment.

Imagine. Michelangelo had to be cajoled to work on this room. Pope Julius II begged and prodded, finally forcing the sculptor to temporarily abandon his work on the tomb of Julius II to paint this "barn of a building." What motivated Michelangelo to turn this unwanted assignment into an epoch masterpiece continues to puzzle art historians – especially considering he spent much of the time on his back, nose to the gigantic ceiling. He completed the work in four years, from 1508 to 1512. Adults who have not visited in many years will be thrilled to see how well the recent restoration has resurrected the lively and sometimes surreal color scheme that had been obscured under centuries of grit and grime.

Fun Fact

Situated just below the Lord is the Apostle Bartholomew, who is dangling a skin meant to symbolize his martyrdom. Look closely at the skin. Rather than bearing a resemblance to the martyred saint, it is a sardonic portrait of Michelangelo that some historians interpret as the artist's confession of his own guilt and unworthiness.

Michelangelo returned to the Chapel 22 years later – when he was over 60 years old – to paint the *Last Judgment* (1534-1541). At the time he began working on the *Last Judgment*, Michelangelo was past 60 years of age. This awe-inspiring fresco covers the entire rear wall and includes a grim self-portrait of the artist himself. The *Last Judgment* reflects the changing mood of the world, brought on by the spiritual and political crisis of the Reformation. Contrast the high spirits and the radiance of the ceiling with the somberness of the *Last Judgement*. Controversy swirled around Michelangelo's decision to paint nude figures. He was charged with obscenity and, in 1564, the painter Daniele da Volterra was directed to paint drapery over the naked bodies of St. Catherine and St. Blaise. But Michelangelo may have had the last laugh. Biagio da Cesena, Master of Ceremonies at the Vatican court and one of the strongest critics of the painting, is portrayed by Michelangelo as Minos, with the addition of two large donkey ears.

Most tourists crane their necks to take in the all-too-familiar *Creation of Adam,* which occupies the very center of the ceiling. (We confess to having purchased a reproduction of this scene years ago when traveling through Italy without children.) It is splendid, evoking primal emotions and the wonder of man's origins. Adam reaches out to accept the spark of life – physical and spiritual – from the finger of God the Father. But don't forget to look around. Even the "lesser" paintings on the lower walls – Botticelli's *Exodus,* Signorelli's *Moses Consigning His Staff to Joshua* and Perugino's *Donation of the Keys* – would, hanging in a traditional art museum, appear more outstanding than they do surrounded by the genius of Michelangelo.

Also, force your eyes downward before you leave. Our daughter, five-years-old at the time, showed equal interest in the unique design of the floor. This inlaid work is called *intarsia* and represents a style that grew popular in Rome during the Middle Ages. *Intarsia* can be executed in wood, though here it is in marble.

CASTEL SANT'ANGELO, OR THE MAUSOLEUM OF HADRIAN
Open Tuesday-Sunday, 9am-7pm. Tel. (06)681.9111. Web: castelsantangelo.com. Admission: €5.

The popes did not always rule by faith alone, as this fortress near the Vatican suggests. Designed by Hadrian himself three years before his death, the Castel Sant'Angelo has worn many masks throughout her history. For 80 years it stored the cremated remains of Rome's imperial rulers. During the Middle Ages, as the papacy carried out its grandiose plans next door (St. Peter's), the Mausoleum of Hadrian metamorphosed into a fortress for the popes. Given the perpetual state of strife during these early years, the popes frequently crossed over from the Vatican to take refuge in the heavily fortified castle. Since then, it has been used variously as a prison, a residence for popes and princes, and has even served as a military barracks.

Children may enjoy the unique collection of armaments from the Stone Age to the present day. It also is a great resting place after your 'assault' on St. Peter's and the Vatican. The café on the 4th floor has great views from the roof terrace, which adds to its charms.

CATACOMBS

Web: www.catacombe.roma.it/welcome.html. International Catacomb Society: http://catacombsociety.org/visiting_Christian.html.
Catacombs of San Callisto, *Via Appia Antica 110; Tel. (06)513.01580. www.catacombe.roma.it. Open March to January, Thursday through Tuesday, 9am to noon and 2pm to 5pm.*
Catacombs of San Sebastian, *Via Appia Antica 132; Tel. (06)78.50.350, info@catacombe.org, www.catacombe.org, Open 9am to noon and 2pm to 5pm. Closed Sundays, 22 Nov. to 20 Dec. and Christmas and New Year's Day. €8. Reduced price for children age 6 to age 15, €5.*
Santa Domitilla, *Via di Sette Chiese 282; Tel. (06)511-0342.*
Catacombs of Priscilla, *Via Salaria 430; Tel. (06)862-06272.*
Both are Closed Mondays. Discounted tickets for children age 7 to age 15. Children under age 6 admitted free.

The Via Appia Catacombs

South of Rome around Appia Antica are these catacombs, which are the most frequently visited among Rome's major catacomb sites open to the public. Most children find the catacombs eerie and mysterious, yet not too scary. The Via Appia Antica (don't confuse it with the Via Appia Nuova, a modern road) makes for an interesting journey in itself. Once known as Rome's "Queen of Roads," it passes beneath the Aurelian Wall at Porta San Sebastiano, a well-preserved gate. You can stop there and visit the **Museum of the Walls** (open Tuesday-Sunday 9am until one hour before sunset), which provides history about the campaigns of conquest that paraded eastward down Via Appia and also offers access to an intact section of the 4th century wall itself.

The catacombs were simple cemeteries – sacred burial ground. One reason may have simply been that the soft porous rock, called tufa, made it easy to dig. Ancient Romans, in contrast, followed the ways of the Etruscans and built their necropoli outside of the city center. There are also Jewish catacombs from the same era, including one adjacent to the Priscilla site.

Catacombe di San Calisto (Saint Callistus) is a kilometer further on. It is home to the "Crypt of the Popes," a major tourist attraction. Popes of the 3rd and 4th centuries are buried here. You will see some precious frescoes and inscriptions. A short distance to the west is **Catacombe di Santa Domitilla,** which have some very interesting paintings.

The **Catacombe di Priscilla** are in an entirely different part of town, east of the Borghese Gardens. Our kids enjoyed these smaller catacombs, which are out in a residential area. Although it's best to call ahead, we just showed up and arranged a one-hour guided tour for our family alone. Although perhaps not as historic as San Calisto, the Priscilla Catacombs have some very old and unusual frescoes. One is believed to be the oldest known image of the Virgin Mary.

ParentTip: While visiting the catacombs, walk along the via Appia antica, the old Roman road built when the ancient Romans constructed their acqueduct system. It is believed that this road was the first to be made with layers of cemented stone over a layer of small stones, crowned with drainage ditches on both sides, with dirt pathways as sidewalks. Talk a short jaunt up and down the road around the catacombs and stop into the delightful **Appia Antica Café**, past the tombs (*Via Appia Antica, 175, Tel. 338-346-5400, closed Monday*). Cool down with icy drinks in the lovely, tree-shaded garden. Great lunchtime menu. You can rent bikes here, but the owners caution that the cobblestone roads are dangerous for little ones. Carriage rides also are for hire at the café.

OTHER CHURCHES

You and your kids might enjoy visiting one of the following churches:

Church of the Bones – Santa Maria della Concezione

Bottom of Via Veneto. Hours: 9am-noon, 3pm-6pm; Admission: Free. Buses: 52, 53, 56, 58. Metro: Barberini. Web: eternallycool.net/2007/10/spooky-rome-the-cappucin-crypt.

One of Italy's strangest religious sights – but one of endless wonderment for all but the youngest children (who may be freaked out) is the "Church of the Bones." Here you can view the remains of some 4,000 Capuchin monks, their bones neatly arranged and sorted to create macabre friezes and altars. The bones are in the **Capuchin Crypt**, below the church. Spines, skulls and pelvic bones are used as decorations throughout. Mummified heads stare out at you from shadowy chapels with names such as the "Crypt of the Pelvises" and the "Crypt of the Leg Bones and Thigh Bones." You might wonder if this is all an elaborate parody of the medieval Catholic custom of mummifying and displaying saints. Not at all, says Friar Alberto, the caretaker. "The object of the journey here is the dramatic presentation of the final end of human existence rising out of the soil." Okay. But it's still a little creepy.

Saint Paul's Outside the Walls

Via Ostiense, 186. Tel. (06)541-0178. Open 7am-6pm. Cloisters open

9am-1pm and 3pm-6pm; Metro: San Paolo (from Piazza Porta San Paolo take bus 23 or 673 from the top of Via Ostiense).
Second only to St. Peter's in size, St. Paul's Outside the Walls was built by Constantine in 314 AD, enlarged by Valentinian and Theodsisu and finally completed by Honorius.
St. Paul is said to have been beheaded nearby. Originally built in the countryside, the basilica is now located amidst Rome's vast industrial sprawl. Along with St. John Lateran and Santa Maria Maggiore, it is one of the Patriarchal Basilicas that have existed since the earliest days of the Roman pilgrimage.
St. Paul's has suffered bad luck through the centuries. The Norman sack of 1084, several earthquakes and a horrendous fire in the 19th century has left little of the original church. What remains is an 11th-century door constructed in Constantinople, a magnificent 13th-century Cosmatesque cloister, which contains remnants of ancient inscriptions and sarcophagi from the early Christian period and 5th-century mosaics over the arch of triumph located in front of the apse. The Gothic *baldacchino* (canopy) over Paul's tomb (Arnolfo di Camio) is stunning. The church also houses the crucifix that is said to have spoken to Saint Bridget in 1370. Buried here is St. Ignatius de Loyola who established the Jesuit religious order.

Santa Maria Maggiore
Piazza di Santa Maria Maggiore; open 8am-7pm; near Termini station, Metro: Via Gioberti.
A vision of Mary shared by a wealthy Roman and Pope Liberius supposedly led to the creation of this church in about 352. Both visionaries found the site when a bizarre August snow shower led them here. This is the largest church in Rome dedicated to the Virgin Mary. Inside are some of Rome's best 5th-century mosaics and beautiful frescoes. The *campanile* (bell tower) is also the tallest in Rome. But the church's prized possession is the Christ child's manger from Bethlehem, arranged in a little shrine in front of the altar.

Santa Maria Sopra Minerva
Piazza della Minerva (behind the Pantheon); open 7am-12pm and 3pm-7pm; buses 70, 81, 87, 90.
Built on the site of the pagan temple to Minerva (hence the name Saint Maria above Minerva), this church contains the tombs of many notable persons, including Saint Catherine of Siena. Also featured are works of art by Michelangelo (statute *of Christ Carrying the Cross*) and a delightful

elephant with an obelisk on his back (*Il Pulcino*) designed by Bernini and sculpted by Ercole Ferrata.

Other Fun Museums

MUSEO DELLE TERME – THE NATIONAL MUSEUM
Baths of Diocletian, Viale di Terme. Web: www.roma2000.it/ zmunaro.html. Closed Mondays; open 9am-2pm except Sundays and holidays until 1pm. Admission.

Sculptures 'R Us at the Museo Delle Terme – an outstanding collection of classical Greek and Roman works, early Christian sarcophagi and other bas-relief pieces. This is a full-day visit museum, so with children in hand, you may want to start with the best. Begin in the Hall of Masterpieces, where you will find the *Pugilist*, a bronze sculpture of a seated boxer, and the *Discobolus,* a sculpture of a discus thrower.

Another must-see is the *Great Cloister*, an architectural wonder. It is a square space surrounded by an arcade of 100 Doric columns. Some scholars believe Michelangelo designed and built this visually delightful space, while others argue he was too busy at the time (1565) to have taken on this commission.

MUSEO E GALLERIA BORGHESE
Villa Borghese, Piazza dell'Uccelliera, 5. Tel. (06)632-8101. Web: www.galleriaborghese.it/borghese/it/default.htm. Closed Mondays; open 9am-9pm, except Sundays until 8pm and holidays, 9am-1pm. Open until midnight Saturdays. Admission €8.50. Underground: Spagna. Bus: 95, 490, 495, 910.

One of our favorite museums in Rome. Located in a beautiful old villa and situated in the midst of the grand Borghese Gardens, it is a very child-friendly environment. The museum is small enough to enjoy with children and to give them a taste of the art world. However, its location in the park gives families many options. One parent can easily entertain little ones – playing, bicycling, riding the ponies or even visiting the Borghese's pathetic zoo – while the other enjoys a tranquil visit to the museum.

The ground floor consists of sculptures, with Bernini's *David and the Slingshot* (1619) the most notable highlights. It is a self-portrait of the artist. Masterpieces by Caravaggio, Raphael and Bellini adorn the walls of the second floor.

MUSEO DELLA CIVILTA ROMANA

Piazza G Agnelli, 10. Viale della Civilta Romana; Tel. (06)592-6041. closed Mondays; open 9am-7pm, except holidays until 1:30pm. Undergroundo: EUR Palasport (Marconi). Admission €6.20.

The art is less remarkable in this museum. The reason to come here is the **scale model of ancient Rome** on display. If the kids really got fired up over the Roman and Imperial Fori, this is a way to imagine what ancient Rome looked like when it was less "ruined." Called the *Modello Plastico* (plastic model), the replica depicts Rome during the height of empire in the 4th century BC.

Relaxed Rome

Some of our family's most memorable moments were hanging out at one of Rome's famous and lively piazzas, eating gelato, chatting with other tourists and native Romans, or just watching the parade of characters stroll by – from "Armani men" striking a pose, to performance artists begging for attention (and a few Euros, of course). Here are some of the "in" places to see and be seen in Rome:

PIAZZA NAVONA

"This is like a carnival," squealed our youngest child, as she gazed out on all the caricaturists, artists, performers and craftsmen. All the while, her gelato flowed like a sticky river down her hand as it melted in the baking July sun. After a day of traveling back through ancient Rome, the kids had a grand time enjoying modern-day ice cream and watching the carnival of activity at Piazza Navona.

Bernini also designed the **Fontana del Moro**, at the southern entrance

to the piazza. At the northern end is a 19th-century sculpture of Neptune battling a sea monster.

Evening is the best time to soak up the atmosphere at the Piazza Navona. We particularly enjoyed the outdoor café closest to the Fountain of of Four Rivers (immediately to the right as you face Santa Agnese). Unlike many piazza cafes, **Ai Tre Tartufi** served restaurant-quality food at reasonable prices. A tip from the child-friendly waiter: go inside to order your gelato. It's a lot cheaper.

Kids are in for a treat if you visit Rome between Christmas and the Epiphany when the piazza hosts a toy fair. Candy booths tempt you with sweets and dolls, puppets and more dangle from strings overhead. Celebrate the arrival of **La Befana**, the witch of Christmas, on the eve of January 6 in Piazza Novana.

PIAZZA DI SPAGNA – SPANISH STEPS

Fun Fact

We all got a great chuckle from Bernini's fantastical Fontana Dei Quattro Fiumi (Fountain of Four Rivers). Look at the figure representing the Nile. See his hands raised as if to shield his eyes? Some art historians believe Bernini sculpted this figure to look as if he is trying not to cast a glance at the "ugliness" Bernini found in the facade of the church his fountain is facing, Santa Agnese in Agone. The facade was designed by Bernini's rival, Borromini. The four rivers represented in this magnificent sculpted fountain are the Nile, Danube, Ganges and the Plata.

Picture perfect. The Spanish Steps have a long tradition of serving as a gathering point for tourists, artists, musicians and world travelers. Allegedly, you are no longer permitted to linger too long on the steps, certainly you are not allowed to eat or drink wine there anymore. But we've joined the throng of folks sitting and watching the Roman world pass

before us, including a bride taking her wedding pictures on one of the world's most spectacular staircases!

The stairs were constructed in 1725, and are named after the old Spanish Embassy that occupied the site. If your kids (and pocketbook) can handle a very expensive restaurant, the glassed-in terrace of the Hotel Hasler offers a panoramic view down the Steps and over much of Rome. Also at the top of the steps is the church of Trinita dei Monti by Carlo Maderno (early 16th century).

Back at the bottom, the fountain in the middle of the piazza is known as the *Barcaccia*, designed by Bernini in 1628. Adjacent to the steps, at the bottom, is the famous tearoom, **Babington's**. Spread out in all directions from the bottom of the steps is Rome's fashion district, a tempting distraction from the rigors of being a tourist! For a very satisfying and reasonably priced family restaurant, we recommend nearby **Pizzeria Le Grotte** (see the Rome section of the *Sleeps & Eats* chapter).

TREVI FOUNTAIN
Toss a coin into the fountain and you are destined to return to the Eternal City – so goes an ancient tradition. We did. And it worked! Like the Piazza Navona, nighttime is the best time to visit the Trevi Fountain, although on a clear day it's beautiful as well. It is bustling with activity – music, vendors, tourists and Romans alike congregate here to live *La Dolce Vita*, at least for one night.

The floodlit fountain is spectacular, and makes a dramatic backdrop for evening gatherings. It was commissioned by Clement XII and built by Nicola Salvi in 1762, using a Bernini design. Neptune gallantly rides his chariot drawn by marine horses and preceded by two tritons. The four statues up top symbolize the seasons and the crest is of the family of Clement XII, the Corsini. To the left, in the niche, is a statue depicting Abundance and to the right, Health.

THE BORGHESE GARDENS

Fun, fun, fun for kids. There's something for every child in the gardens, which has large open expanses, picnic sites, ponds and snack wagons. The entrance at the end of Via Veneto is close to the little bumper cars, small amusement rides and rentals. Round and round the track our kids spun, while we sat back, relaxed (for a change) in Rome. As teens, we traveled back to this small amusement center, and both kids squeezed into those tiny cars for another spin around the track, laughing at all the fun they had ! In season (after April 1), pony rides and a little cartoon theater (in Italian) are here too. Bikes are for rent, including the family-style pedal cart with a canopy and seats for four. We took this to shuttle ourselves to the Galleria Borghese, one of Rome's premier art museums. You can also rent boats and row in the park's lake. A small open-air tram runs through the park, and is a pleasant diversion for younger children.

The gardens are located just outside the ancient walls of Rome. You can enter either at the bottom of Via Veneto – which is a nice walk, lined as it is with fine restaurants and boutiques – or by way of the Piazza del Popolo, where you exit through the olds walls to reach the park. Coming this way, the Borghese Gardens are across the Piazzale Flaminio, straight ahead and to the left.

Want to know more about the horticulture? Ask for Beth, who went to college in Barbara's hometown, Pittsburgh.

Rome's **zoological park** also is located in the Gardens, although our children left more sad than happy. Avoid this unless you are desperate to see a zoo. While it looks as if the animals are well cared for, their space is quite small. Open daily 8am until two hours before sunset.

Parent Tip: A visit to the Borghese Gardens is the best way to end – or to break up – a long day touring Rome. It is a real treat for the kids and a reward for good behavior!

PIAZZA DEL POPOLO

Some of the best views of Rome can be seen from this stunning piazza. The **Egyptian obelisk** is over 3,000 years old, brought to

Rome from Heliopolis by Augustus. Its first home was at the Circus Maximus, but Pope Sixtus V moved it here. Two baroque churches rest at the south end of the piazza: Santa Maria dei Miracoli (1678) and Santa Maria in Monesanto (1675).

CAMPO DEI FIORI

Get your fresh flowers, fruit and vegetables in this bustling, Roman market open every morning until 1pm. One of the liveliest and most local scenes you are likely to see, this market square is a taste of an older Rome. Its history, however, is not so pleasant. In this camp, heretics were burned at the stake and criminals were hanged. A monument to Giordano Bruno, a philosopher who was burned at the stake in 1600 for advancing Copernican theories, reminds us of the *campo's* more gruesome past.

Now it's a typically chaotic Roman marketplace, where vendors hawk their wares and the locals loudly and dramatically negotiate for bargains. The kids enjoyed the scene, even as they scrunched up their faces when they heard of its past. The market provides a nice late-morning snack after your morning tour; or, for a more substantial meal, the excellent **La Carbonara** restaurant overlooks the action.

Day Trips from Rome

CERVETRI

Cervetri was built atop of the Etruscan city of Caere. Not until the 18th century did people uncover the buried city and its *necropoli*. Etruscans buried their people in mounded huts pretty much above ground. The *necropoli* were laid out like an Etruscan city of the living, so we now have a good sense of what an Etruscan village may have looked like.

This is an outdoor activity, with long lanes for children to run and skip through. While you must respect the burial grounds, children and adults are allowed to climb down the stairs into the crypts and even climb up on the mounds of the huts. A day-trip here, besides an incredible history lesson, is a great energy burner.

A museum (*open Tuesday-Sunday, 9am-7pm*) is on the land of the **Banditaccia Necropolis**, one of the four Etruscan burial grounds. Pick up a guide to the museum and *necropoli* from one of the vendors outside the necropolis. Visit www.mysteriousetruscans.com/index.html to discover key facts about the Etruscans. Click on Etrucscan Tombs and find out more about Cervetri.

Getting There
From the Lepanto terminus in Rome you can catch a bus to Cervetri. Or you can hire a cab to bring you there. The concierge at the Lord Byron set up our trip to this Etruscan necropolis.

Tourist Information
Pro Loco. Piazza Risorgimento, Tel. (39)(06)994-3706.

TIVOLI GARDENS
Tivoli the city is haggard, and even the gardens are starting to show their age. Cardinal Ippolito d'Este created the gardens in 1550. Enter through the musty old villa, where Franz Liszt lived from 1865 until his death in 1886. The gardens and fountains are spectacular. Walk around to find the *Fountain of Glass* by Bernini, the *Fountain of Dragons,* the *Fountain of the Owl and Birds* and other shining examples of past beauty.

The kids had the best time playing hide and seek in the mazes of bush and shrubs. This is a great break from the typical tourist routine and terrific photo opportunities. Bring snacks.

On the way to Tivoli, stop off at the **Acquapiper**, a water park off the road between Rome and Tivoli. The park features a smaller pool for younger children. Older kids can take off on some long, fast slides and enjoy the wave-machine pool. There are picnic areas, a restaurant and the omnipresent video games. *Via Maremmana Inferiore, km 29. Guidonia. Tel. (0774)326-538. Web: www.aquapiper.it. Take the COTRAL bus to Palombara. Car SS5 to Guidonia. Open May-September 9am-6pm Monday through Friday and 9am-7pm weekends. Admission €12, under 4 free.*

Getting There
By Bus: COTRAL buses can take you to Villa d'Este and the Tivoli Gardens. They depart from the bus station every 15 minutes.

By Car: About 30 kilometers from Rome, take the A24 straight to Villa d'Este, exit Tivoli.

By Train: Roma-Pescara Line to Stazione Tivoli.

Tourist Information
Largo Garibaldi. www.villadestetivoli.info/storiae.htm. Tel. (0039)0445.230310. Email: villadestetivoli@telekottageplus.com. Hours: Tuesday through Sunday 8:30am to one hour before sunset. Closed: All Mondays, Christmas and New Year's day and May 1. Admission €10.

WHICH ONE IS MY ROOM?

Rome offers a wide range of accommodations for your family, most quite pricey, even by Italian standards. Unlike the smaller towns, you may want to be more attentive to location. Remember, Rome is one of the largest and most hectic cities in Europe.

If you can afford it, the best hotel location for families is near the **Borghese Gardens**, or in the vicinity of the **Spanish Steps** and **Trevi Fountain**. The Borghese Gardens offer expansive running room and amusements for active kids of all ages (see above).

Very Expensive
HOTEL LORD BYRON ***** *Via G. de Notaris 5, 00197 Rome. Tel. (39)(06)322-0404, Fax (39)(06)322-0405. Web: www.www.lordbyronhotel.com.*

Plush, intimate, relaxing and extraordinarily kind to children is an apt description of this elegant five-star. The hotel is nestled in a quiet corner of Rome, near the Borghese Gardens and across from the embassy of Belgium. Entering this world-class hotel we held our breath, wondering if our two young and energetic children would be welcome in such a quiet environment, draped with exquisite paintings and antiques. Surprise! Perhaps the solitude helped the kids unwind, or maybe it was the mirrored sliding doors in our ultra-modern suite (which they used to play out secret Star Wars intrigues), but the little ones stayed in line. Since then, we returned with teenagers, the hotel is re-decorated and even more stunning.

For the ultimate in parental privacy and relaxation, ask for one of the suites with enclosed connecting double rooms. The staff is incredibly helpful. Ask them to help with side trips, including to the Etruscan

Hotel Prices

Very Expensive – over €400/night
Expensive — €250-400/night
Moderate – €150-250/night
Inexpensive – under €150/night

necropolis at Cervetri and to the nearby Priscilla catacombs. Expect all modern conveniences, including fax and laundry service. The hotel also boasts an excellent restaurant, Sapori del Lord Byron, and a well-known piano bar, Il Salotto, which evokes a romantic mood of reverie. For dinner, get a babsitter for young children to fully appreciate the extraordinary cuisine and service. "Hospitality is like an exquisite flower, it must be surrounded by a thousand delicate attentions," is the hotel's motto. And, it lives up to its standard.

HOTEL EDEN ***** *Via Ludovisi, 49. Tel. (39)(06)478-121. Fax (39)(06) 482-1584. Web: www.edenroma.com.*

Enter Paradise. Guests can expect pampering at Hotel Eden, one of the "Leading Hotels of the World." The hotel is decorated in antiques, but with all modern conveniences. Each room has video players, computer and telefax links, two telephone lines and a minibar. The award-winning restaurant, La Terrazza dell'Eden, offers fine Mediterranean cuisine in a spectacular setting. All guests have complimentary use of the gym and other sports, including golf, are located nearby. Geared more for the business traveler, the hotel makes an effort to accommodate families, even advertising its babysitting service. Eden has over 100 rooms and several suites. Check out the gossip section on their website. This is where the stars – from Nicole Kidman to Robin Williams – come out to play.

HOTEL RAPHAEL **** *Largo Febo, 2 (Piazza Navona). Tel. (39) (06) 68 28 31. Fax (39) (06) 68 78 993. Web: www.raphaelhhotel.com.*

At Piazza Navona, this is an ideal location for discovering many of Rome's spectacular monuments and sites, with the Pantheon and Trevi Fountain also nearby. The ivy-covered Hotel Raphael exudes elegance while still welcoming the younger traveler. The hotel offers 73 rooms (five

are non-smoking), six suites (some with private terrace) and 10 deluxe apartments. Its 15th-century decor, accentuated by Renaissance art, offers a striking mix with modern conveniences, including air conditioning, color TV, direct-dial phones and a minibar. Room service is available. Don't miss the authentic Pablo Picasso ceramics on display in the lobby. Traveling with older children who miss the gym, or feeling the guilt of succulent dining without your health club or Y nearby? Enjoy the hotel's Fitness Center and Finnish sauna.

HOTEL HASSLER-VILLA MEDICI ***** *Piazza Trinita dei Monti, 6. Tel. (39)(06)699-340. Fax (39)(06)678-9991. Web: www.hotelhassler-roma.com.*

Adjacent to the Trinita dei Monti church, this 85-room, 15-suite, hotel is perched atop the Spanish Steps, a world-renowned location. It exudes elegance and sophistication, decorated with antiques but awash in modern amenities. Some rooms have glorious views, while the Rooftop Restaurant offers a bird's-eye view of Rome. Reservations are necessary. The Sunday brunch: heavenly. Spa and beauty services available.

Expensive

HOTEL DELLE NAZIONI **** *Via Poli, 7. Tel. (39)(06)679-2441. Fax (39)(06)678-2400. Web: www.hoteldellenazionirome.com.*

Situated just around the corner from the Trevi Fountain, the Hotel Delle Nazioni originally was a patrician palace. Recently remodeled and decorated with modern paintings and furnishings, the hotel offers a nice location next to the infamous Italian Parliament and only a stroll from the chic and fashionable boutiques along Via Condotti (Rome's most elegant shopping street). It has 87 rooms, with eight connecting double rooms for families. Rooms are equipped with satellite television (a plus for sports-addicted teens curious about European "football") and air conditioning. Note the golden replica of *David* in the hotel's Donatello bar.

ROMANTIK HOTEL BARACCO **** *Piazza Barberini, 9. Tel. (39)(06)487-2001. Fax (39)(06)485-994. Web: www.www.hotelbarocco.com.*

This 28-room hotel, located in the center of Rome near the Via Veneto, was built during the Art Deco era of the 19th century and reflects  a modern look throughout, marked by wonderful marble bathrooms. The hotel was restored by Roman architect Bruno Begnotti. It is an intimate and sophisticated hotel, but welcomes families looking for connecting doubles. Rooms are air-conditioned and insulated from the noise of the city below. A breakfast room is situated on the ground floor, or you can have breakfast served in your room. Check out the special offers on their website.

HOTEL LOCARNO *** *Via della Penna, 22. Tel. (39)(06)361-0841. Fax (39)(06)321-5249. Web: www.hotellocarno.com.*

We like this hotel because it is located slightly off the beaten path, offering a peaceful atmosphere after a hectic day of touring throughout Rome. Yet it is still close enough to all Rome's attractions. Situated between the Piazza del Popolo and the Tiber River, Hotel Locarno opened its doors during the art-deco period, in 1925. It has 48 rooms, suites and apartments, with modern amenities, including TV and  air-conditioning. There is a pleasing breakfast served seasonally in the main garden or on the rooftop garden. The hotel offers guests free bicycles.

Moderate

HOTEL SANTA MARIA *** *Vicolo del Piede, 2. Tel: (39)(06)58-4626. Fax: (39)(06)589.4815. Web: www.hotelsantamaria.info.*

Our favorite moderately priced hotel in Rome! Tucked away into a corner of the bohemian (lots of students and art galleries) Trastevere section of Rome, Hotel Santa Maria is a gem of a hotel. Enjoy breakfast in a garden with lovely orange trees, delicate flowers and Mediterranean plants. All rooms lead into the garden; this hotel is on one level. The rooms are simple and charming. Our teens, reading over my shoulder as I write this, give a big thumbs up to the two-level arrangement of the senior suite. We stayed in the winter and didn't get to enjoy the free bikes available for guests. There is Internet service (a big deal for kids wanting to stay connected with friends back home.) And, the staff is so welcoming and thoughtful, serving us cappucino and scones before we left, at 6:00am, for a flight home. We learned of Hotel Santa Maria from a family we met at Hotel Casci in Florence. This hotel was not on our itinerary, but we took the chance, making arrangements while traveling through Tuscany, and we are so glad we did.

HOTEL GENOVA **** *Via Cavour, 33. Tel. (39)(06)476-951. Fax (39)(06)482-7580. Web: www.hotelgenovarome.com.*

Walking distance from the main train station, Termini, Hotel Genova is a plain but comfortable hotel. It is located close to the Roman Forum and the Colosseum. The hotel's 91 rooms feature air-conditioning, phones and television. Guests can expect an adequate breakfast served in a newly appointed breakfast room.

HOTEL TREVI *** *Vicolo del Babuccio, 20/21 A, Tel. (06)678.9563, Fax. (06)699.41407, Web: www.hoteltrevirome.com/en.*

Steps away from the Trevi Fountain, this refined but warm hotel is a good find for travelers who enjoy living in the center of the party. Some rooms run a bit small, but are clean and crisp. Weather permitting, take your cappuccino at the roof garden and spy down on the city below.

HOTEL MEMPHIS **** *Via degli Avignonesi, 36-36A. Tel. (39)(06)485-849 or 482-7955. Fax (39)(06)482-8629.*

Great location for families. Although a nondescript hotel, Hotel Memphis is a stone's throw from the Trevi Fountain and Spanish Steps. Its 24 rooms all have a private bath and most modern comforts: television, phones, air conditioning and mini-bar. A real draw is the advertised babysitting service.

HOTEL VILLA FLORENCE ROME *** *Via Nomentana, 28 (Piazzale Porta Pia). Tel. (39)(06)440-3036. Fax (39)(06)440-2709. Web: www.hotelvillaflorencerome.com.*

In 1860, Hotel Villa Florence was a noble country house, located just beyond the hustle and bustle of Rome's center. Today the air of tranquility remains. Guests gaze on glimpses of ancient Rome throughout the hotel, with sculptured heads and warriors peeking from the hotel's garden. All rooms are air-conditioned and secure parking is available. Breakfast is served in a pretty room, adjacent to a cozy living room. Ask about Room 9, which is quiet and large enough for a family of four.

HOTEL SEILER ** *Via Firenze, 48. Tel. (39)(06)485-550 or 488-0204. Fax (39)(06)488-0688. Web: www.www.travel.it/roma/seiler/index.htm.*

Located a few short blocks from both the Roman Forum and the *Termini* station, the Hotel Seiler is very basic but reasonable. Along with its nearby sister hotels – the Acropoli and Galeno – the Seiler is geared toward tour groups and students. For that reason, it has quite a few multi-bedded rooms. This part of town, near *Termini*, is a bit ragged and hectic.

However, you are within walking distance of many major sights – and Seiler is in a better location than the Acropoli and Galeno.

HOTEL GENIO **** *Via G. Zanardelli, 28. Tel. (39) (06)683-3781. Fax (39)(06)654-7246. Web: www.venere.com.hotel.*

Near the banks of the Tiber River sits Hotel Genio, a charming hotel with 61 rooms, complete with air conditioning and minibars. Plush Persian rugs adorn the floors of the common areas and many of the rooms. The hotel also is a short walk to the Piazza Navona. Eat breakfast at the rooftop terrace and you'll catch a bird's-eye view of the Eternal City.

CAMPO DE' FIORI ** *Via del Biscione, 6. Tel. (39)(06)688-06865. Fax (39)(06)687-6003.*

It could be the best buy in town IF you are willing to walk up flights of steps – there is no elevator in the six-floor building. There also is no air conditioning, which makes it tough on muggy, summer days. But the rooftop view is one of the best in the city and the staff is quite friendly. Rooms are small but comfortable.

HOTEL ABRUZZI ** *Piazza della Rotunda, 69. Tel. (39)(06)679-2021. Web: www.hotelabruzzirome.com.*

A great location, good price, but no private bath — which can be difficult for families with young children. However, Abruzzi is a comfortable *pensione*, with many large rooms to relax in. The location is grand. Some rooms have views of the  Pantheon. Your wallet will sing a song of joy at this friendly hotel.

Inexpensive

HOTEL LUXOR *** *Via A. Depretis, 104. Tel. (39)(06)485-420. Fax (39)(06)481-5571.*

Family-friendly, 27-room Hotel Luxor is located in the city-center, steps from Rome's main street, Via Nazionale, and near the central train station (*Termini*). The famous Spanish Steps are in walking distance, as are the must-see Trevi Fountain and the Colosseum. The recently renovated building is neo-Gothic, with beautiful archways, high ceilings and pleasant art, typical of a Venetian-style palace, as the hotel management is quick to point out. One four-bedded room even has a frescoed ceiling. Modern conveniences include television, air-conditioning, a mini-bar and telephone, as well as 24-hour desk service. The rooms are large and comfortable and the staff friendly. Our family enjoyed staying at this hotel, although you must be prepared for the late-night and early-morning buzz of the omnipresent Vespa motor scooters.

HOTEL ANGLO AMERICANO **** *Via Quattro Fontane, 12. Tel. (39)(06)472-941. Fax (39)(06)474-6428. Web: www.angloamericanohotel.com.*

Tired of ancient or Renaissance art? Craving a more modern high-tech environment? Look no further than Hotel Anglo Americano. This lovely four-star, located in the center of Rome near Via Veneto and the Trevi Fountain, is bedecked with black leather chairs, marble floors, and wood furnishings. Lovely flower and plant displays pepper the common areas and your room. The hotel offers all modern conveniences, including air conditioning, color television, radio, mini-bar and private garage. This hotel is handicap accessible.

HOTEL COLORS ROME *Via Boezio, 31. Tel. (39)(06)687-4030. Fax (39)(06)686.7947. Web: www.colorshotel.com.*

This brightly colored, plain and simple, but lovely hotel and hostel is located just north of the Vatican. It is run by Enjoy Italy and the staff all are native English speakers, able to help you arrange tours and give suggestions on what to do and see in Rome.

ARENULA** *Via Santa Maria dei Calderari, 47, Tel. (06)687.9454. Web: www.hotelarenula.com.*

A fantastic bargain, quite close to the Piazza Camp de Fiori and Piazza Navona and the Trastevere, situated in the area called the Ghetto. This is a no-frills hotel, but kept clean and comfortable, by the Patta family. If traveling in the summer, make sure to ask for air conditioning. Also, keep in mind that there are four floors and no elevator. The convenience and the price make this a good bet for families. (Ask for one of the four-bedded rooms).

HOTEL PANDA** *Via della Croce, 35. Tel. (06)678.0179. Web: www.hotelpanda.it.*

Kids love the panda logo! And, Hotel Panda prides itself on being a family-friendly place. It is surprising that a hotel is this inexpensive located as it is near the Spanish steps and one of the most chic shopping areas in Europe. The rooms are plain and simple – wrought iron and terra cotta, but they are clean and the hotel is quiet, despite its location. A good choice for families.

HOTEL ADLER** *Via Modena, 5. Tel. (06)484.466. Web: www.hoteladler-roma.com.*

Bright and light, this small pensione (8 rooms) is a family-run business that is great for families. Six of the eight rooms can sleep three, four or five people. Style is basic, but it is top-of-the-line in cleanliness and helpfulness. Breakfast is available on the charming terrace.

THE BEEHIVE** *Via Marghera, 8. Tel. (06)447.04553. Web: www.the-beehive.com.*

The Beehive has a dorm room with bunk beds that can sleep eight. What more can a family ask for! – except private bathrooms which are not offered. Run by an American couple, Steve and Linda, with children of their own, the Beehive is an economical and eco-friendly place to stay near the Termini station. Enjoy breakfast and Sunday brunch, a reading room and a cute garden. The look is modern, the feel is cozy. Also note that Steve and Linda run *cross-pollinate.com*, which connects you with B&Bs, guesthouses and apartments in Rome and Florence.

I'M HUNGRY!

Remember, each region in Italy offers its own unique cuisine. The concept of generic "Italian" food is unheard of, and unwelcome, in Italy. Nevertheless, many Roman restaurants – particularly those aimed at tourists – offer more regionally diverse menus than most Italian restaurants in North America. As Italy's capital and largest city, Rome is a sort of a culinary melting pot for the distinctive regional styles. Pesto and marinara sauce, ravioli and risotto, cannoli and tiramisu are often all found together on the same menu. This may be appalling to many Italians, rooted as they are in the divergent traditions of Italian cuisine, but it can work to the advantage of a family with varied tastes (not to mention fickle young appetites.)

Another advantage of Rome's size and cosmopolitan character is that you can find very good restaurants with food from around the globe. Tired of Italian food every meal? Then Rome is your best opportunity to hunt out a good Thai, Chinese, French or other type of cuisine. Ask your hotel concierge about nearby options.

Restaurant Prices

$$$ – about $25-55 per person
$$ — about $18-24
$ – about $7-17

Near The Spanish Steps

PIZZERIA LE GROTTE $$ *Via delle Vite 37. No telephone. Credit Cards accepted. (Moderate) Metro-Spagna. Closed Mondays.*

Hearty food in a rustic setting. A good meal at a good price, although the service was not as keen as in years past.

Wood beams, brick archways and alcoves painted with frescoes make this Roman hideaway a perfect place for lunch or dinner. Italian families with lots of children frequent Pizzeria La Grotte, just a few blocks from the Spanish Steps. Despite the exhaustive choice of restaurants in Rome, we keep coming back to Le Grotte – perhaps the best food and atmosphere for a moderately priced restaurant in central Rome. A wood-burning oven makes the pizza particularly tasty for the kids, but this is no pizza joint.

A number of fresh fish choices are offered daily. We love the risotto with black squid ink (*seppe nero:* it's terrific, really), the *penne alla arrabiata* and the pizza Margherita. Le Grotte is also known for its chicken dishes; try the spit-roasted chicken (*pollo arosto*). The antipasta bar can be a meal in itself – a cornucopia of Italian delights. Try sitting at one of the tables tucked into an alcove with frescoes on the wall – ask for it when you enter, since as of this writing they were not taking reservations by phone.

BABINGTON'S TEA ROOMS $$$ *Piazza di Spagna, 23. Telephone: (06)678-6027, Credit Cards accepted. Closed Thursday. Metro: Spagna; Web: www.babingtons.net.*

When in Rome, do as the British do – have a spot of tea – at Babington's, a tea room located just a few steps from the Spanish Steps. Babington's may lie at the foot of the Spanish Steps, but it is indisputably neither Roman nor Iberian. It is an oasis from the hustle-bustle of Rome. Housed in a centuries-old establishment made famous by its staid decor and weighty furniture, this Roman tribute to all things British makes for an interesting diversion for some real British tea. The mornings are marked

by large breakfasts of scones, English shepherd's pie, and other delicacies. A tea room since 1893, Babington's offers 13 types of tea, including their own special blend of Ceylon, Darjeeling and China tea. Coffees, wine and other drinks are available. Babington's also offers a special brunch of juice, egg Benedictine, pancakes and tea or coffee. They have great cookies and treats. Our kids gobbled them up AND drank tea.

Near The Vatican

BORGO NUOVO $$ *Located across from Porta Angelica Gate to Vatican City (104 Borgo Pio). Tel (06)689-2852. Web: www.borgonuovo.org.*

Surprisingly good quality amid tourists galore. Exhausted after a tour of the Vatican Museum, with children's halos sadly drooping in the (on sweltering heat, we searched for the closest restaurant to satisfy our hunger. A weakened state typically puts tourists in a vulnerable position, subject to fraud, deception or at least way-too-high prices for a mediocre meal. But heaven's gates remained opened a bit longer for us as we stumbled on this delightful restaurant just outside

the Porta Angelica Gate of the Vatican the way between St. Peter's Square and the entrance to the Vatican Museums.) Borgo Nuovo is a delightful restaurant, with yellow tablecloths and fruit and flower paintings dotting the yellow-pastel walls.

The food is well prepared. A good selection of meat and fish, including fried *calamari*, swordfish and veal Milanese, is featured on the menu. Try the macaroni with asparagus in a too-die-for cream sauce. The *tiramisu* – scrumptious! Service was even more heavenly than the food. Our waitress delighted in sharing culinary tips. And the indoors is air-conditioned for those simmering, summer days.

Piazza Navona

QUINZI & GABRIELI $$ *Via delle Coppelle 5. Tel. (06)687-9389.*

Q & G is a great find near the Piazza Navona. The fish at Q & G is so fresh there is no printed menu. Instead, the chef gears his menu to whatever treasures the fishermen catch that day. Fresh. You bet. Raw shrimp, crayfish and *calamari* sweeter than you

The Scoop on Gelato

Hands down: The best and most unique gelato in Rome is found at San Crispino. An Australian couple we met in Florence turned us on to San Crispino ("Even your *New York Times* thinks it's great.") and it became our Roman mission to find the shop. Actually, there are three: City Centre, Fontana di Trevi (open noon-12:30am, from noon until 1:30am on Sat.); Appio, S. Giovanni (open 11am to 12am, closed Tuesday) and Collina Fleming (hours the same as the Trevi Fountain location.) *Web: www.ilgelatodisancrispino.com.* Enjoy!!

ever tasted. Many of the pasta dishes are prepared at your table. Try the Spaghetti with lobster sauce.

AI TRE TARTUFI $$. *Piazza Navona.*

This is a great spot for people-watching. Established in 1896, this delightful outdoor café allows you and your family to feast your eyes on the comings and goings of the Piazza Navona. Choose from a small but tasteful selection of primi and secondi piatti. We usually order pizza, soup and salad. A long list of drinks, both hot and cold, including liqueurs and beer rounds out the menu. Try the house wine. It's quite good. The café is the one nearest the Fountain of Four Rivers – immediately to the right as you face St. Agnese. And here is a tip from the waiter at a *geletaria* with outside seating: Order your gelato inside. It's much cheaper.

Via Veneto

IL PEPERONE $-$$ *Via Veneto (near American Embassy).*

We resisted eating here. Too touristy. A glass bubble on a busy, noisy street. No way. One day, the kids were starving and we were exhausted. We had no choice. To our surprise, we walked away delighted with our meal. Make sure you start with the *bruschette*. The cheese and artichoke is especially mouth-watering. And the *insalata caprese* is one of the freshest we tasted. The menu is quite diverse – something for everyone. We recommend the *puttenesca* – fresh, spicy pasta.

Il Peperone is peppered with families – Italians and tourists. EuroRock music rules, although your older children will be tempted by the Hard Rock Café across the street or the nearby Planet Hollywood.

HARD ROCK CAFÉ $-$$$ *Via Veneto 62, Tel. (06)420-3051. Open daily.*

Always open, always rocking; a Roman spin on the usual American menu.

Near The Pantheon

LA ROSETTA $$$$ *Via de la Rosetta 8. Tel. (06)686-1002.*

Fish is the specialty at La Rosetta, one of Rome's finest fish restaurants located near the Pantheon. The fish dishes are simple but heavenly.

MYOSOTIS $$ *Vicolo della Vaccarella 3, Tel. (06)686-5554. Closed Sundays.*

Homey, family-run restaurant with a traditional menu specializing in meat and fish dishes.

'GUSTO $$$ *Piazza Augusto Imperatore 9. Tel. (06)322-6273.*

Want to break tradition? Try the cuisine at 'Gusto. How does spaghetti cooked in a wok with stir-fried vegetables sound? Or Italian shrimp and vegetables tempura-style? Few traditional dishes can be found on this menu. A downstairs pizzeria, while tempting you with braids of buffalo mozzarella entwined with tuna and *rughetta*, also offers pizzas the old-fashioned way.

Campo dei Fiori

LA CARBONARA $$ *Campo dei Fiori, 23. Tel. (06)654-783. Closed Tuesdays. Web: www.la-carbonara.it.*

If you're near this lively Roman market square and want to do more than nibble on produce, La Carbonara handles all the classic dishes with aplomb. The house specialty is *pasta alla carbonara,* prepared to perfection in a rich sauce of egg, cheese and bacon. The *spaghetti alla vongole verace* (spicy clam sauce) is among the best renderings of this dish in town, as is the *fritto misto* (batter fried mixed vegetables) – as it should considering the restaurant is cheek to jaw with the best source of fresh produce in Rome.

Monte Gianicola
ANTICO, Arco $$ *Piazzale Aurelio 7, Tel. (06)5 15-274. Closed Mondays.*

If you don't mind the trip up Monte Gianicola, Antico Arco offers informal chic matched by creative cuisine. Hip and hipper. Treat older children and yourself to this hot spot for young Romans. And while your soaking in the scene, enjoy the creative twists on Italian cuisine. A big plus – a non-smoking room – shocking for Rome!

SPORTS & RECREATION
Bicycles

There are several places to rent bikes at the **Borghese Gardens**, the only place to ride with kids in Rome, including **Bici Pincio**, *Viale della Pineta, Tel. (06) 678.4374.*

Here are some options, though *for older teens and adults:*
Bici & Baci *(Via del Viminale 5; Tel. (06)482-8443; www.bicibaci.com), two blocks west of the Stazione Termini.*
Danilo Collalti *(Via del Pellegrino 80/82; Tel. 06-6880-1084).*
Top Bike Rental, *Via dei quattro Cantoni 40, 00184 Rome Italy, Tel. (06)48.82.893, www.topbikerental.com/Index.php.*

CyberCafes

Easy Internet Café, *Via Barberini 2, just off Piazza Barberini. Near the Piazza di Spagna. Open: 24/7.*

Bibli, *Via dei Fienaroli 23 (Trastevere), Open: 11am-midnight.*

Freedom Traveller Internet Point, *Via Gaeta 25 (near the main train station. Open daily 9am to midnight.*

Hackers, *Via Sebastiano Veniero 10-16 (near the Vatican).* Order pizza while you check your Facebook and email.

Internet Café, *Via Salaria 170 (Trieste) Open: Monday-Friday 10am-2am, Saturday and Sunday 4pm-2am. Price: until 4pm and Via dei Marrucini 12 (San Lorenzo) Open: Monday-Friday 9am-2am, Saturday and Sunday 5-2am. Price: until 9pm.*

Kaos, *Via Cartoni 125 (Monteverde) Open: 9am to 2pm, Sunday 4am to 2am, closed Friday.* Serves sandwiches and salads.

Rimaweb, *Via del Portico d'Ottavia 2/a (historic center), Open: 9am to 7:30pm daily.* Great staff.

The Netgate, *Piazza Firenze 25, Open: 10:30am to 9pm daily.* Offers discounts at Planet Hollywood.

Library

Biblioteca Centrale per I Ragazzi (children's library), *Via San Paolo alla Regola, 16, Tel. (06) 454.60391, E-mail: centralragazzi@bibliotechediroma.it. Hours vary.* Good selection of English books that you can read but not borrow. Great rainy-day activity.

Parks

Borghese Gardens. *Entrances: Piazzale Flaminio, Porta Pinciana, Via Mercadante, Via Aldrovandi, Viale delle Belle Arti.* The most fun of all the parks. Bicycling, boating, children's cinema, playground, pony rides and horseback riding, zoo and scooter rides.

Botanical Gardens. *Trastevere. Entrance: Largo Cristina di Svezia.* Plants and playground

Gianicolo. *Entrances: Porta Cavalleggeri, Salita di Sant'Onofrio, Porta San Pancrazio, Via Garibaldi.* Permanent puppet theater and fairground games every Sunday.

LunEUR (formerly called Luna Park), *Via delle Tre Fontane, Tel. (39)(06)592-5933. Web: www.luneur.it/. Open October through April, 3pm-8pm Monday, Wednesday and Friday and 3pm-1am Saturday, Sunday 10am-1pm and 3pm-10pm. May through September 5pm-1am Monday through Friday, 5pm-2am Saturday and 10am-1am Sunday. Admission free, pay for each ride.* This amusement park is losing the race with time but still

is a fun treat for kids. Look for a cool house of mirrors, and fun rides for the littlest travelers.

Monte Mario Park. *Web: www.agri-net.org/parco_en.asp?idparco=55 Entrances; Via della Camilluccia, Via DeAmicis, Via del Parco Mellinni*. Nature park with a plant and animal reserve. Lovely nature walks

Puppet Shows

Teatro Verde, *Circonvallazione Gianicolense, 10, Tel. (39)(06)588-2034. In Trastevere*. Call for show times. Puppet shows are in Italian. Visit the prop workshop before the show begins.

Gianicolo. See above under parks.

Swimming

Piscina delle Rose, *Viale America, 20, Tel. (39)(06)592-6717. Open mid June to September. 9am-7pm. Children under 1 meter free*.

Foro Italico, *Tel. (39)(06)396-3958. An indoor (open June to September) and outdoor pool (open November to May)*.

Tennis

Circolo Montecitorio, *Via Campi Sportivi, 5, Tel. (39)(06)875-275*.

EUR, *Viale dell'Artigianato, 2, Tel. (39)(06)592-4623*.

Tennis Belle Arti, *Via Flaminia, 158, Tel. (39)(06)360-0602*.

Water Parks

Aquapiper, *Tel: (0774)326-536. Web: www.aquapiper.it. Via Maremmana Inferiore, near Tivoli*.

Hydromania, *Vicolo Casal Lumbroso, 200. Web: www.hydromania.it*.

4. TUSCANY & UMBRIA

FLORENCE

Both in architecture and sculpture, the cold marble and cool cobblestones of **Florence** provide the perfect outline for the warm hues of **Tuscany** by day and for the blue and blood orange sunset

that ushers in night. As Rome is Empire, Florence is Renaissance. In Florence – *Firenze* – and in a half-dozen hill towns within an hour's drive are located perhaps the most dense and admired collection of artistic achievement in human history.

Tuscany is at once high culture, soothing pastoral beauty and a chic playground for sophisticated visitors and expatriates from around the world. Florence in particular is a living museum of endless educational value for families with children. Come here to feel a connection with mankind's break with the barbarism of the medieval world, to see the artifacts of the dawning of secular enlightenment and to witness Europe's awakening to the artistic and scientific potential of individual freedom.

WHERE ARE WE GOING NOW?

The brilliance of the *David*, the vast treasures of the **Uffizi**, the dreamy drift of the **Arno** – all make Florence a mecca for romantics. Yet inside the stone city there also are many fun-filled adventures for families. Trekking through a real palace, a famous art museum, or a beautifully designed Italian garden gives young children great opportunities to burn energy, absorb history and enjoy the aesthetic of *Firenze*.

For science fans, many of Galileo's original instruments, including one of his own ten digits, can be found marvelously preserved at the History of Science Museum, located just behind the Uffizi. And remember, you can top off every day with a gelato from world-famous Vivoli's!

Palaces, Piazzas, Churches, Statues & More

PIAZZA DELLA SIGNORIA

This is ground zero for families visiting Florence. What makes this huge public square so memorable – and unmistakable – are the huge sculptures that rise above the crowd, looming over the mosh-pit frenzy of tourist season. It's a great place to play or grab a gelato, since most major sights are within a kilometer of here.

In the **loggia** resides Cellini's Mannerist masterpiece, *Perseus* (1545). Cast your eye on Giambologna's *Rape of the Sabines* (1583), where the volatility of the act is cast in cool, fluid marble. A copy of the *David* looks right at home among its sister statuary in the sprawling piazza – where the original stood for hundreds of years – unable to overwhelm the way it does showcased alone inside the Accademia.

Then there is Ammanati's *Neptune Fountain* (1575), dubbed *Il Biancone* (Big Whitey) by the locals because of the god's rather bland appearance. The kids were intrigued with this fountain, although art critics express a less favorable view. Giambologna created another colossal sculpture that resides in the piazza, the *Equasterian Monument to Cosimo I*. Our son, seven at the time, after taking in all the piazza has to offer, looked up at us and said, "I want to move here and study art." Not a bad place to start!

> ### Fun Fact
> In June, the Piazza della Signoria is flooded with sand and stadium seats are erected for fans and visitors to enjoy the Calcio in Costume, a game of soccer played in Renaissance garb. Similar to Siena's Il Palio, minus the horses, the Calcio pits one Florentine neighborhood against another. It began as a ballgame, perhaps similar to rugby, to keep young men in shape to serve in the citizens' militia. The event unfolds over three weekends. Ask your concierge for tickets – but ask far in advance.

PALAZZO VECCHIO

Open Monday-Friday 9am-7pm and Sunday 8am-1pm, closed Thursday. Admission for upstairs galleries.

Stone upon stone, climbing higher to the dramatic if not harsh Arnolfo's Tower, rises the Palazzo Vecchio (or **Palazzo della Signoria**). Work on the palazzo began in the 13th century and initially housed the Priors and Standard-bearers of Justice, who made up city government (called the *Signoria*). Eventually it became the home of Cosimo de Medici before the family settled into the **Pitti Palace**. Famous prisoners were housed in a tiny room at the top of the tower, called the *alberghetto*, or little hotel. From there they could cast an envious eye on daily life in the piazza far below. Savonarola spent his final days captive here before his execution. Today, the building is home to Florence's municipal government.

Walk up the steps to the platform at the top. Orators addressed public assemblies often with fiery speeches from this perch called the *arringhiera*, or oration terrace – hence the word 'harangue.'

Sitting royally in front of the palace is the **Marzocco**, the lion that is featured on the city's coat of arms. The name Marzocco comes from Mars, god of war and protector of Florence during Roman times. The original Marzocco was ruined, replaced by a new one by Donatello, which now sits in the National Museum. Donatello also sculpted the second statue in front of the palace, Judith and Holofernes (the original is inside the Palazzo Vecchio.)

Stride inside to the courtyard as if you were a Medici – the building is palatial and a paean to the Medici family. The courtyard was designed by Michelozzo in 1453 and elaborated on in 1565 to celebrate the marriage of Francesco dei Medici and Joan of Austria. Across the courtyard, up the stairway on the right is the entrance to the palace.

The courtyard is a good meeting place if your family needs to separate to see – or not see – the museum. Following are highlights of the museum:

Inside the Palazzo Vecchio

If you have limited time in this museum, the most important room to see is the imposing **Salone dei Cinquencento**. Glide up Vasari's spectacular staircase to this room, noted for its pendulum-swinging history. Work was begun on the room after the expulsion of the Medici's from Florence in 1495. Savonarola created a new form of government to give more power

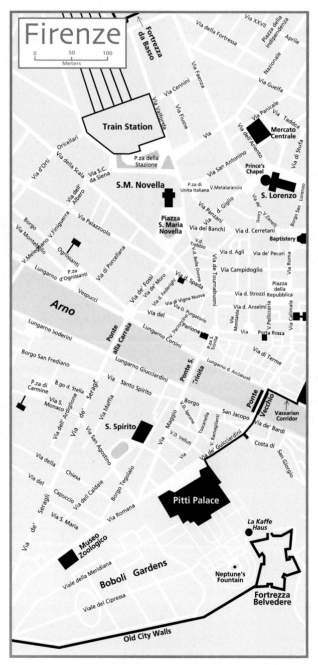

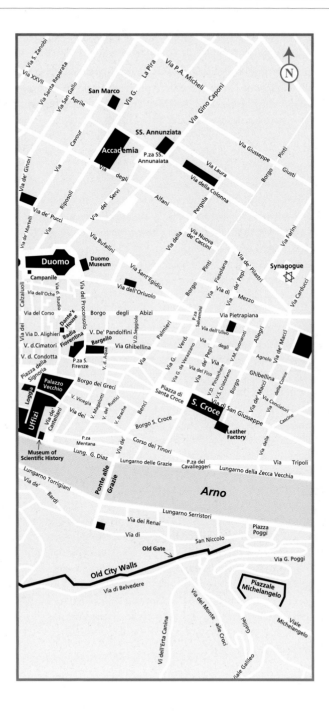

to the people and this was the people's room, replete with benches for the Consiglio Maggiore, the people's assembly.

When Cosimo I regained power, he scrapped the benches of the people for his throne. Then, he called for the room to be decorated with frescoes depicting his family's history – oh, and as an afterthought, that of Florence as well. Look skyward and you will see Vasari's painting called *Stories of Florence and the Medici*. Also, make sure you examine Michelangelo's unfinished piece, *The Genius of Victory*, which was designed for the tomb of Pope Julius II.

Don't miss these rooms:

• **Francesco I's studiolo.** Designed by Vasari in 1572 for Cosimo's son, the tiny closet-of-a-room is where the boy enjoyed a reclusive life of study.

• **Quartiere di Eleonora di Toledo.** These rooms were all frescoed by the Flemish artist Giovanni Stradaro (1523-1605) for Cosimo's wife, Eleonora. They offer a well-deserved relief from the pomposity of the Medici. Rather than depict one family member after another, Eleonora's frescoes honor women of strength and courage – from the Sabines to Penelope, wife of Ulysses. Past her room is the chapel of the Priors, a tranquil place for prayer and mediation.

* **Sala dei Gigli (Room of the Lilies).** Look for the sculpture, *Judith and Holofernes*, which once occupied a place of honor in the Piazza Signori until it was displaced by Michelangelo's *David*. At this point, Judith went inside to the palace!

• **Guardaroba.** Here you can see a "wardrobe" painted with maps depicting the world at the time (1563). The artist is Fra Egnazio Danti.

• **Cancelleria.** Machiavelli's office when he served as secretary and diplomat of the Florentine Republic (1498-1512). He was out of a job once the Medici returned to power and, for a while, thrown in prison. Surprisingly, he dedicated his book, *The Prince,* to a Medici – Lorenzo, Duke of Urbino – perhaps in a last ditch attempt to curry favor with the rich and famous. It didn't work. He died not knowing the fame – or infamy – his writings would bring him.

• **Apartment of Pope Leo X (1475-1521).** Newly opened to the public, this stunning room was the office of the mayor of Florence until 2005 . The kids thought it a hoot that in this magnificent room, with paintings describing the siege of Florence (which led to the overthrow of Savonarola), was the modern desk of the mayor, with family pictures still there. Let us know if the mayor finally got around to removing his photos!

Parent Tip: A rite of passage for our children is purchasing an Italian made journal to write or sketch in about their travels in Italy. It was Carravita's turn during our last trip. While the boys in our family waited in line at the Uffizi, off we trotted to search for her journal. We found a lovely one – it was a hard decision – at **Carte, Etc.** (*Via de' Cerchi, 13r, Tel./Fax (39)(055)268-302, www.carteetc.com*). The store features the ancient art of **bookbinding** and **hand-made marble paper**. Besides beautiful journals, you can purchase photo albums, adress books, desk sets and items related to calligraphy. The manager was quite helpful and thrilled to help Carravita make her big decision, as he explained much about the history and art of bookbinding and papermaking in Florence.

PONTE VECCHIO

Many times the bloated waters of the Arno grabbed at the Ponte Vecchio, seeking to pull it down into its muddy waters. But each time, the little old bridge withstood the onslaught of water only to rise more strong and solid than before. In 1944, it survived the Nazis' bombing of bridges, with Hitler ordering only the old bridge to be saved.

The Ponte Vecchio, or old bridge, spans the Arno at its narrowest point. It began in the 1st century as a tiny wooden bridge (though some argue that a bridge may have existed at this spot even during Roman times). In 1345, it was replaced with the present covered bridge, including the three stone arches. At that time, butchers, fishmongers and other food vendors monopolized the bridge. But in the 1500s, Cosimo ordered the food market gone and he replaced it with the purveyors of fine jewels. So it is today. Goldsmiths and jewelry shops line the Ponte Vecchio, hawking their wares much the same as their ancestors hundreds of years earlier.

Photo Op

Take a picture at the center of the bridge during one of Florence's splendid sunsets, when the muddy river awakens, wrapping itself in golden sunlight that will dazzle your eye even more than the precious gems sold in the shops. Interestingly, the Arno river actually did turn to gold in the 1960s, when a raging river caused much of the goldsmiths' wares to be washed away.

PIAZZA DEL DUOMO

Don't worry, you can't miss the Duomo. This remarkable structure looms high over the city, the Iron Giant of medieval times. Truth be told, it is somewhat eccentric, with its green, white and red striped marble. "It looks like a carnival tent," squealed our little daughter, echoing the innocent view shared by the child in *The Emperor's New Clothes.* Although the official name of the church is **Santa Maria del Fiore** (Saint Mary of the Flowers, which links the Madonna with the flower of Florence, christened by Pope Eugenio IV in 1436), everyone calls it "The Duomo."

Plan to spend some time: the complex includes the cathedral, **Campanile** (Bell Tower), a **museum** and the **Baptistery**, with its famous bronze doors by Pisano and Ghiberti.

The Duomo

Church open Monday through Saturday: 10am-5 pm, Sunday: 1pm to 5pm.

Work on the church began in 1296 by Arnolfo di Cambio. His goal was to make the biggest church in the Catholic world, and he busily laid the foundation for the enormous building. Unfortunately, or maybe fortuitously for him, he died before coming up with a plan to construct a cover for the huge foundation. Giotto stepped in at Cambio's death in 1301, but became more engrossed in constructing the Campanile (Bell Tower), a spectacular accomplishment. When Giotto died in 1337, Andrea Pisano took over until he left to attend to other projects. A competition in 1418 between Ghiberti and Brunelleschi over building the dome ended in a tie, with Ghiberti withdrawing. He already had beaten out Brunelleschi over the baptistery doors. Brunelleschi certainly did his homework; studying architecture and engineering feats in Rome and elsewhere.

His plan: Use a cantilevered system of bricks that supported itself while it was built upward. Workers raised the dome of the cathedral by continually adding concentric circles of brick – each row was self-supporting – marking the first time this architectural device was used. In 1436, the dome was finally finished and the church was hailed as one *"erta sopra e'ceili, ampla da coprire chon sua ombra tutti e popoli toscani."* (Translation: "raised above the skies, wide enough to cover all the people of Tuscany with its shade.") It remains one of the five highest domes in the world, along with St. Peter's and the Pantheon in Rome, St. Paul's in London, and Santa Sofia in Istanbul.

Enter the church and its enormity takes on new meaning. It is huge, and somewhat cold, with elements of Gothic architecture – enormous arches supported by behometh gothic pillars. On your way in, notice the busts of Brunelleschi and Giotto on the right-hand side. The layout is typical – in the shape of a large cross. The interior measures 150 meters long and 38 meters wide at the nave and 94 meters at the transept. The dome is 90 meters high and 45.5 meters in diameter. Frescoes depicting the Last Judgment by Vasari and Zuccari at the end of the 16th century adorn the immense dome. Statues of the apostles peek out from niches in the pillars supporting the dome.

From the entrance, walk toward the right aisle between the first and second pilasters to descend to what remains of the **Santa Reparata church**, discovered in 1965 (*open 10am-5pm, closed Sunday*). Brunelleschi, through his inventive spirit, apparently also won the right to be buried in the church and his tomb can be seen in the excavations of Santa Reparata.

Time to move on with the children? Proceed to the **dome** (*open daily 8:30am to 5:30pm, closed Sunday, admission*). Climb up the stairs, a bit claustrophobic but only slightly, to reach an amazing view of the dome.

Parent Tip: Your child is peppering you with so many questions about the building of the dome and you don't want to admit you don't have a clue? Just pull out of your pocket this nifty little book with the big title: *Brunelleschi's Dome: How A Renaissance Genius Re-Invented Architecture* by Ross King. This is a great read for teens highly interested in this topic, or a good book to read to younger kids keen on architecture, but also with long attention spans. We passed this book around our family!

The Baptistery

Back upstairs, you can revel at the Baptistery which was built in the 10th and 11th century in honor of St. John the Baptist, the patron saint of

Florence. The Baptistery was more than a religious symbol. It was the place knights were named and enemy treasures were stored. Although you may be tempted to leave after scanning the famous doors from the outside, come in to see some wonderful medieval art.

While the kids are seeking Zodiac signs, enjoy the bronze paneled doors by Ghiberti and Andrea Pisano da Pontedera. You'll find stories of the Old Testament on the east door that Michelangelo hailed as "the door to paradise." Look next to the altar to see the Angel Holding the Candlestick by Agostino di Jacopo in 1320 and to the left, the wooden statue of Magdalen by Donatello in 1560.

Parent Tip: Want to look around the Baptistery a little longer but the kids are tugging at your clothes, rolling their eyes, on the verge of major whining? Ask them to find their **zodiac sign** located on the pavement around the Baptistery. They were taken from 13th-century oriental textiles.

Giotto's Campanile
April-October, 9am-8:30pm, Nov-March 9am-6:20 pm. Admission.

Giotto's bell tower is stunning, but sadly is overwhelmed by the sheer magnitude of the dome. Although named after Giotto, the Campanile's designer, he died in 1337 before it was erected. Andrea Pisano and Francesco Talenti, whose sculpted reliefs are a highlight of the tower, actually built it. Your children may enjoy the hike to the top, where a spectacular view of Florence and the Duomo await them.

Cathedral Museum (Museo dell'Opera del Duomo)
Visit the museum to see original artwork that used to decorate the Cathedral and the Campanile. Interesting pieces include *St. John* by Donatello and the Choir Gallery with many scenes by Donatello. Our children enjoyed looking at the tools, wooden models and brick molds used to construct the Duomo. They are in the same room as Brunelleschi's death mask.

Fun Fact
While building the dome, Brunelleschi built restaurants up here to save his workers the effort of descending for lunch. The walls here are 13 feet thick. From the dome's gallery, you'll get a unique view of the stained glass by Castagno, Donatello, Ghiberti and Uccello. From the marble lantern on top, the panoramic view is nothing short of breathtaking.

PALAZZO & MUSEO DEL BARGELLO
The Bargello's past is haunting and hideous. Prisoners were held inside the cold stone walls of the

Bargello, many awaiting their execution in the courtyard. It was built in 1255, originally to serve as the home of the foreign podesta, but it soon operated as the city jail, torture chamber and execution center until 1786, when Grand Duke Peter Leopold banned torture and the death sentence. Now, it houses many of the world's most stunning sculpture. And the once gruesome chopping block and hangman's platform has been transformed into a wonderful Gothic courtyard.

Museo Nazionale del Bargello
> *Via del Proconsulo, 4. Tel. (055)294-883. Open 8:30am-2pm, except Tues, Thurs, Fri 8:15am-1:50pm; closed 2d and 4th Mondays, and 1st, 3d and 5th Sundays, of each month. Buy tickets online at www.polomuseale.firenze.it/ english/bargello.*

You can see the best of this museum's masterpieces in relatively short order – it's a wonderfully manageable and engaging museum for children because of all the dramatic sculptures. If you can't linger, head straight for the following:

Sixteenth Century Sculpture Room (Michelangelo Room): A must-see in this museum. Look for the great one's *Bacchus* (1496), a resplendent if not vulgar god of wine and pleasure. Michelangelo's genius is ever present in the innovative *Pitti Tondo* (early 16th century), where Mary's head emerges beyond the frame and the entire scene comes alive. Notice how the *Pitti Tondo* is smooth in some places, rough in others. The perfectly smooth sections reflect the light, adding new dimensions to the work. This technique is called *non-finito* and is used again in Michelangelo's *Brutus* (1540).

Benvenuto Cellini's work also is exhibited here. Of special note is his bust of *Cosimo I* (1548), his patron. Perhaps it was vanity, but Cosimo was apparently not pleased with Cellini's real-life portrayal, warts and all. It was Cellini's first work cast in bronze. Giambologna's most famous piece, a bronzed *Mercury* (1564), is here as well.

The Salone del Consiglio Generale (The Donatello Room): Although eclipsed by Michelangelo, Donatello's work is brilliant. His androgynous *David* (1430), the laughingly mischievous *Atys Amor* (Cupid) and his version of the *Marzocco* (15th century) illustrate his mastery of sculpture.

Also look for the famous competing reliefs for the Baptistery doors done by Ghiberti and Brunelleschi. Both depict the sacrifice of Issac. And the winner is …! You should also take a trip to the second floor to find some curious bronze animal sculptures, including the wildly popular **tacchino** (turkey).

Must-See Museums

THE ACCADEMIA – AND THE 'DAVID'

Galleria Dell'Accadmia, Via Ricasoli, 60. Open Monday, 815am-2pm, Tuesday-Sunday 8:15am to 7:15pm. Closed on Christmas and New Year's Day and 1 May. For reservations, call: (055)041.5200.345, or purchase on line. Web: www.gallerieaccademia.org/sito/ing_museo.html.

A very confident young man took chisel to hand and out of a colossal chunk of marble, one rejected by older, wiser artists, sculpted a figure Florence found worthy of symbolizing the city's courage and love of freedom. Michelangelo, while in his late 20s, accepted the commission granted him by the Florentine Republic in 1502 and created the *David*, the first monumental statue of the High Renaissance.

While Michelangelo certainly was influenced by Hellenistic sculpture, what he produced in the *David* transcends that art form. The *David* delicately balances between calmness and tension, demonstrating action-in-repose, a mark of Michelangelo's style of sculpture. On July 30, 1873, the *David* began its ten-day journey from its place in front of the Palazzo Vecchio to its present home at the Accademia.

The corridor that leads to the *David* possesses a group of controversial sculptures also by Michelangelo. *The Slaves* (or *Prisoners*) are four enigmatic figures struggling to free themselves from the stone that encases them. Sculpted in 1530 for the tomb of Pope Julius II, some art historians say they are incomplete. Are they? Or do they represent Michelangelo's comparison of the emerging sculpture as a prisoner of the stone, just as the soul is held prisoner in the body? Kids and teens love looking and talking about these sculptures.

The Accademia, built in 1784 for Accademia art students,

also includes huge Mannerist paintings that surround the *David*, including the *Madonna del Mare* by Botticelli. Also interesting is the **Sala Dell'Ottocento**, a gallery of plaster models and other works by students.

This is a very family-friendly museum – not at all formal and rushed like the Uffizi. It is small, with relatively few pieces of art. It's most relaxed in the evening – open late and strollers are welcome. Feel free to linger and admire the *David* from every angle. Bring your sketchpad. Our daughter at age five dozed in the stroller while her brother happily sketched the *David* – a more memorable souvenir than postcards!

Fun Fact

Ouch! Accidents and injury have haunted the *David* throughout his life. In 1527, someone inside the Palazzo Vecchio, in the heat of anger, tossed a bench out of the window that shattered *David's* left arm in three places. A poor peasant lost his life when in 1544 *David's* left shoulder disconnected and fell on top of the peasant. In 1870, Florentine leaders noticed a tilt in the *David*, who was beginning to lose his balance. That's when they packed him up and marched him on to the Accademia. In 1992, someone with an axe to grind, took his hammer and hacked at the David's foot.

UFFIZI

Piazzale degli Uffizi, 6. Tel. (055)294-883. Web: www.uffizi.com. Open Tuesday-Sunday 8:15am to 6:50pm. Closed Christmas, New Year's and 1 May. Admission.

Florence's brilliant challenge to families who love art is the world's first museum, the Uffizi. Nearly all of the nearly 2,000 works of art here are worth a close look – an impossible feat when traveling solo, let alone with toddlers (or an impatient teen) in tow. Here are some tips for getting the most out of a family visit to the Uffizi:

Purchase tickets in advance by asking your concierge, or visiting *www.florenceart.it/booking/?google-florence-museum-rete-di-ricerca* which has tickets for many of the museums in Florence, Venice, Rome and Milan. Just remember, you pay a service fee for booking online.

• **Go early or very late**. The queue (line) is always, always long – but being there first thing in the morning, or late in the day when others have moved on to other adventures, is the best strategy. Since most adults want to spend a minimum of two hours here, arriving less than two hours before closing conserves your children's patience for the art.

• **Arrange a special outing for the kids** while one adult manages the inevitable wait in line. Our kids went to – where else? – Vivoli's for a late afternoon snack. Children also could get their portraits sketched in the piazza outside the Uffizi. A short trip to Ponte Vecchio is another fun option. Some kids don't mind the wait. We saw some older children leaning against the building engrossed in a book, while others manipulated gameboys. As a teen, our son grabbed the videocam and entertained himself (and many passerbys) by filming life outside of the Uffizi.

- **Go on a scavenger hunt.** Prepare ahead of time a list of things to find in the gallery. Be specific (Rembrand't *Portrait of an Old Man*) or general (an old man). Or, go on a self-portrait scavenger hunt to see who can find the most self-portraits by famous artists (Titian, Michelangelo, Raphael, Rubens, Rembrandt and others are in the Third Corridor). Then encourage your children to draw their own masterpiece while you get a few extra minutes in the gallery.

- **Play the match game.** This game involves purchasing postcards of the paintings or sculptures you want the children to find. For example, you can probably purchase postcards of Botticelli's *Primavera* or the *Birth of Venus* and other famous paintings of the Ufizzi at your local art museum's shop or at the Uffizi's gift store. Then, give your children a handful of postcards and let them match them with the real thing. Younger children really enjoy this game.

- **Bring a sketchpad and let them draw.** We do this often in our hometown and the kids love it. One mother, an art historian, even organizes trips for kids to the museums on days off from school. Kids love it. Some try to copy what they see, others are inspired to compose their own work. It's great for getting children to think about art, and you get more time to take in the art!

- **Take a break at the delightful rooftop café.** The view of the rooftops of Florence and the fresh air makes for a wonderful respite from the Ufizzi's onslaught of art. The prices will gouge you – surprise: you're a captive audience – but the treats are all tasty.

Twenty years ago, when we first visited the Ufizzi, we were stunned by the sheer quantity of great art – and by the way one masterpiece was crowded above another with little in the way of climate control or security. On that day, a cool May drizzle drifted into one of the open windows of a corridor, gently wetting not only us, but the art, as well.

These days the art is, in some ways, more carefully displayed and the lighting improved – but the windows remain open, perhaps out of tradition. These corridors originally were open loggias without decoration.

In 1581, Francesco I closed them, added windows and began to move the Medici family collections here. On one of our earlier trips to Italy with kids, we also were disappointed to see Plexiglas placed over some art, including Botticelli's *Venus* and *Primavera*. Not only does the light bounce off the glass, but smudgy fingerprints further distort the art. (Those aren't our kids' fingerprints, are they!?) However, our latest trip found great improvements in the display of art.

Work began on the building, now the Uffizi, in 1560 by Vasari the court painter for Cosimo I. It initially was designed as an administrative building – *uffizi* simply means offices.

In 1737, the last of the Medici inheritors, Anna Maria Luisa, donated the entire gallery to the Tuscan state under the stipulation that the collections would stay in Florence. The first true art museum in the world, the Uffizi opened to the public at the end of the 18th century.

The Uffizi collection is organized chronologically, allowing visitors to better grasp art trends. If your time is extremely limited, skip directly to the following rooms (you can always double back):
* **Room 8**: Fra Fillippo Lippi – sublime Madonnas
* **Rooms 10-14**: A shrine of Botticelli works, including *Primavera* (1478) and *The Birth of Venus (see photo at right)*.

* **Room 15**: Andrea Verrocchio's, da Vinci's teacher, work is displayed here. Pay close attention to the *Baptism of Christ*. A young Leonardo da Vinci won rave reviews with his painted angel on the left. Also *Adoration of the Magi* by da Vinci (1481), an unfinished work.
* **Room 25**: *Madonna of the Goldfinch* by Raphael; *Tondo Doni* (1506) by Michelangelo
* **Room 26**: Raphael's room
* **Room 28**: *Venus of Urbino* by Titian (other Mannerist masters are in rooms 29-30)
* **Room 43**: *Young Bacchus* and *Medusa* by Caravaggio are reportedly self-portraits
* **Room 44**: Rembrandt portraits, including two revealing self-portraits

Add these works to your list, if you have more time:
- **Rooms 2-6** represent the 13th and 14th centuries
- **Room 2**: *Maesta* by Giotto (1310); compare it to the *Maesta* by Giotto's teacher, Cimabue (1285)
- **Room 3**: *Annunciation* by Simone Martini (1333) and *Presentation of Jesus in the Temple* by Ambrogio Lorenzetti (1342). Both represent 14th-century paintings from Siena.
- **Rooms 7-9** represent Early Renaissance
- **Room 7**: Masters of the early Renaissance: *Madonna and Child with Saints* by Domenico Veneziano (1448); *Portrait of the Duke Federigo da Montefeltro* (you know this painting – the man profiled in the red hat) and his *Duchess Battista Sforza of Urvino*, by Pier della Francesca (1465)

MUSEO GALILEO (formerly History of Science Museum)
Piazza dei Giudici 1 (behind the Uffizi). Open daily from 9:30am to 6pm, except Tuesday from 9:30am to 1pm. Closed 1 and 6 January, Easter, 1 May, 24 June, 15 August, 1 November, 8 December and 25-26 December. Tel. (055)265.311. Web: www.museogalileo.it/en/index.html. Visit www.museogalileo.it/en/pressroom/enews/eflorencefamily.html for information on family days at the museum.

This is a fascinating place for anyone interested in either science or history. The University of Florence founded Florence's History of Science Museum (Museo di Storia della Scienza di Firenze) in 1927. It is located on the Arno, just behind the Uffizi, in the Palazzo Castellani. The museum displays nearly 5000 original items, including many of the telescopes, lenses, globes and other scientific instruments and experimental devices used by Italy's most famous scientists, particularly Galileo – whose middle finger is famously preserved here. (Although it was a bit disconcerting when the guard enthusiastically waved her middle finger at our kids, afraid they might miss one of the Medicis' most graphic souvenirs.)

The museum is organized into 21 halls. The most fascinating items, concerning early mathematical and astronomical discoveries, are in the first six rooms, especially Hall IV. That room illustrates the extraordinary intellectual (and political) adventures of Galileo (1564-1642), who was accused of heresy by church officials fearful of his findings. Exceptional documents are exhibited here, such as the lens (broken in ancient times) from the telescope the controversial Pisan scientist used to observe – for the first time ever, in late 1609 and early 1610 – four of the moons of Jupiter (the "Medicean" planets). Galileo used the lens to confirm the craters and mountains on the moon's surface, the phases of Venus, and many other celestial phenomena. Our teens particularly appreciated the highly knowledgable docents, who patiently answered their every question about Copernicus and Galileo.

Parent Tip: A good book choice for older teens, and you, too, is *Galileo's Daughter* by Dava Sobel. Letters between Galileo and his eldest daughter give incredible insight into the genuis of the man and his struggle to maintain a balance between the Church view and his own scientific-based knowledge of the universe.

PITTI PALACE & BOBOLI GARDENS

"Come on, Eleanor. We're moving to the suburbs." And they did – Cosimo I and his lovely wife, Eleanora of Toledo found their digs at the Palazzo Vecchio too small, with not enough greenery and sunlight. They crossed the Arno, bought the Pitti Palace and its extensive gardens in 1549 and lived in sunny opulence for the rest of their lives. Few felt pity for Luca Pitti, the wealthy Florentine banker who established the Pitti Palace in 1440, went bankrupt and lost his estate. His goal of keeping up with his neighbors, the Medici, seemed all too foolish to most Florentines.

Historians believe the original Pitti Palace may have been designed by Brunelleschi. When the Medicis finally purchased the property, they called in Ammannati to enlarge the estate. Today it houses several museums, the royal apartments, costume gallery and coach museum. The lovely garden that so impressed Eleanora is the exquisite **Boboli Gardens** – reason enough to come here.

Here is what you'll find within:

Galleria Palatina

Open Tuesday–Sunday, 8:15am to 6:50pm. Tel. (055)294.883. Admission.

The most popular of the Pitti museums is the Galleria Palatina, which contains a collection of 16th- to 18th-century paintings. The most notable paintings are in the five former reception rooms that are off to the left after you enter the museum, the first of which is the **Sala di Venere**. Several works by Titian are here: *Concerto, Portrait of Pietro Aretino, Portrait of a Grey-eyed Gentleman* and *Mary Magdalene*. These paintings can be found in the Sala di Venere and Sala di Apollo.

Go to the **Sala di Giove** to see one of Raphael's greatest portraits, *Donna Velata* (1516). Most of Raphael's works are also in the **Sala di Saturno**.

Other artists represented in this collection include Rubens, da Cortona, Lippi and del Sarto.

Fun Fact

Look up at da Cortona's fabulous ceiling frescoes that weave events in the lives of the grand duke (Cosimo III) with the gods – this is the Medici family after all! In the Venus room, the fresco portrays the grand duke as a young man saved by Minerva, the goddess of knowledge, who tears him from the loving arms of Venus. In the Apollo room, Cosimo III is taking lessons from Apollo, god of the Sun and symbol of knowledge. Next, in the Mars room, our boy Cosimo is engaged in battle, guided by the light of Mars, god of war. Finally comes the reward for all the hard work. Jupiter, king of the gods, crowns Cosimo III. In the final room, the Saturn room, Mars and Prudence are taking an elderly Cosimo III to Saturn, father of the gods. For all his hard work, Cosimo is again crowned, this time by Fame and Eternity.

The State Apartments
Open daily 8:30am-6:50pm, holidays 8:30am-1:50pm. Call for appointment in the winter.

The King of Savoy occupied this dwelling when Florence, for a brief time, was the national capital.

Museo degli Argenti
Open daily 9:00am-7:00pm. Closed Monday.

Medici jewelry, vases, and other trinkets, some garish as well as expensive, are displayed in this area, which served as the Medici summer apartments. Enjoy yet another series of rooms gloriously frescoed to chronicle the Medici's personal lives of the rich and famous.

Galleria d'Arte Moderna
Same hours as Galleria Palatine. tickets on second floor. Admission.

Modern art here means 18th-19th century. The gallery resides on the second floor of the palace and is dominated by modern works from Tuscany, with some French impressionism. The paintings are organized chronologically and by theme.

Galleria del Costume
Open 8:30am-1:50pm, except closed alternating Sundays and Mondays. Admission.

Kids love looking at old clothes. Here the clothes represent garb worn from the 16th century to modern day. Take a peek at a reconstructed dress that Eleanora of Toledo was buried in – the same dress she wore in her portrait by Bronzino. Historical theater costumes, created at the workshop of Umberto Tirelli also are on exhibition.

Museo delle Carrozze

Fun for the kids. These carriages are elaborately decorated, especially the carriage owned by King Ferdinand II of the two Sicilies.

Parent Tip: The next museums, the **Galleria del Costume** and **Galleria delle Carrozze** are big hits with most children. One adult can easily take the children on to see the period garb and carriages, while the other enjoys a more casual pursuit of art.

Boboli Gardens

Open 8:15-5:30 (March), 8:15-6:30 (April, May, September and October), 8:15-6:30 (in the month of October when Daylight Saving Time ends), 8:15-5.30 (June August). Entry is permitted up to an hour before closing time. Closed on the 1st and the last Monday of each month, New Year's Day, May 1st and Christmas Day. Tel. (055) 294.883. Web: www.polomuseale.firenze.it/english/boboli.

By now, you're praising Eleanoras's maternal instinct for getting a place with space to play. After spending time in the museums, the Boboli Gardens are a child's great escape. The Gardens sprawl lazily out from the Pitti Palace. Don't be put off by the fact it's an uphill climb from the entrance. Shady groves and secret nooks provide a desperately sought respite from the burning heat of the Tuscan summer – with spectacular views over Florence and its Duomo your reward near the top.

Boboli is the quintessential Italian garden; the bushes are sculpted with the same precision and passion as the marble. Pathways with marked signs cut a course up the steep slopes to the splendid sculptures and fountain. Kids love *Pietro Barbino Riding a Tortoise*. Also look out for a Roman amphitheater ascending in tiers from the Pitti and for the magical *Neptune's Fountain*, by Lorenzi (1565).

Near the top of the steep hill you can sit back, sip cool drinks and enjoy views over Florence from the cozy **Kaffeehaus**. A bit pricey, but on a hot day it's a perfect place to cool down and grab a snack. Muster the courage to move from this piece of heaven, and it's off to the summit – to **Belvedere Fort** – and more magnificent vistas.

Bring a picnic lunch and let your children play like a Medici, romping and running in Florence's only public garden.

LA SPECOLA & THE MUSEUM OF WAXES

Via Romana 17. Open 9am-1pm, closed Wednesday. Admission.

You're desperate to keep the kids in line, or you simply want to gross them out. Welcome to Florence's House of Horrors. Past the Pitti Palace

is La Specola. Visit the zoological section to see its amazing collection of
... well, just about everything that wiggles, walks, swims or flies. Some are
rare, like the Madagascar Aye-Aye. Some are awful – case-in-point is the
wax model of a skinned cat. But the real gross-out stuff is waiting for you
in the Museum of Waxes. Apparently Cosimo III was obsessed with disease
and one of his artists, a priest named Gaetano Zumbo, expertly provided
wax models of the revolting ravishes of diseases on the human body.
There's even a wax of a rat pulling a plague victim's intestine. Gaetano must
have been to one too many exorcisms.

Parent Tip: Use your discretion whether to enter the room on
reproduction. It is rather graphic and you may not find it appropriate for
your children.

DANTE PILGRIMAGE
Via Dante Aligheri. Open 9am-noon and 3pm-7pm. Admission.
For all you Dante fans, this is your Graceland; for others, it may be
Purgatorio.

Dante's House: Beatrice will have difficulty leading Dante fans to
their paradise – the writer's real home. Instead, you will be guided to an
accurate reconstruction of Dante's life in the 13th century. Upstairs is a
museum that contains numerous manuscripts from Dante's time, including
several versions of the *Divine Comedy.*

Dante's Seat: From the Piazza del Duomo, walk east of the Loggia del
Bigallo to a stone bench marked "Sasso di Dante." Supposedly, the poet
enjoyed people-watching here as the cathedral was being built.

Dante's Beatrice: At Via del Corso no. 6 is the Portinari-Salviati
Palace, home of Dante's beloved Beatrice.

PIAZZA & BASILICA SANTA CROCE
*Open weekdays 8am-12:30pm and 3pm-6:30pm. Easter through October
open 8am-6:30pm. Sundays and holidays open 8am-1pm.*
The superstars of the Florentine Renaissance are entombed within
mammoth Santa Croce: Michelangelo, Machiavelli, Galileo and Rossini
are among the illuminati. During the Middle Ages this entire area was an
unhealthy marshland, frequently flooded by the Arno. Only the destitute
lived here. In the 13th century, Franciscan fathers settled here to preach.
Soon a monastery was erected and a school established for the children of
the city's elite. Before long, the Franciscan stronghold became a religious
center of the city and officials decided to build a larger basilica. Santa Croce
was consecrated in 1443, although the neogothic facade was erected in the
19th century.

Today the piazza is a hodgepodge of architectural styles: a medieval row of houses juts above a 19th-century statue of a curmudgeon Dante, the 16th-century church, Palazzo Serristori and, of course, the **Basilica Santa Croce** (which means Holy Spirit).

Step into the basilica and you feel like a speck in the universe. It is an immense church. Cambio made the church so wide he was forced to use wooden beams for the nave, forming a hut-shaped structure. Santa Croce is beloved by Florentines because of the illustrious men buried here. Tombs of the rich and famous are scattered throughout the basilica. On the right aisle beyond the first altar is the tomb of **Michelangelo Buonarroti** (1475-1564). When Michelangelo died in Rome, Pope Clement VII tried to have him buried in St. Peter's, but the artist's family quickly rushed his body to Florence where its citizens paid homage to him.

Continue down the aisle, and you will come to **Dante's funeral monument**. He is not buried here, but in Ravenna. Still further down the aisle is the tomb of poet **Vittorio Alfieri** (1749-1803). Next is the tomb of **Niccolo Machiavelli** (1469-1527). After a relief of the Annunciation by Donatello are the tombs of **Giioachino Rossini** (1792-1827), one of Italy's greatest composers, and **Go Foscsolo** (1778-1827), a poet.

On the other aisle, almost directly across from the tomb of Michelangelo, is the burial spot of **Galileo Galilei** (1564-1642).

Beautiful chapels abound in the basilica, including the **Peruzzi Chapel** and the **Bardi Chapel** painted by the great Giotto in the 1330s. Benedetto da Maiano's exquisite marble pulpit depicts scenes in the life of St. Francis of Assisi.

Leave the church for the cloisters and the **Opera di Santa Croce museum**. This area was seriously flooded during the flood of 1966, with tremendous damage to works of art. Look for the famous Crucifix painted by Cimabue (1240-1302), Giotto's teacher.

Be aware of any special shows that may be housed downstairs. At Christmas time, we stumbled onto a student competition of crèches. They were gorgeous, and it was fun to see the school projects of Italian kids.

PIAZZELE MICHELANGELO
Across the Arno from Santa Croce.

Hike up the steep hill if you think you and your kids can do it, or take bus number 13 from the station, **to enjoy a view of Florence and environs** (*see photo on next page*). Look over the hill you just climbed, to the right; the rising hill is the town of Fiesole. During the siege of Florence in 1530, Michelangelo ordered the hill encircled with walls to defend the city below.

Climb the long flight of steps to the right of the loggia (your back is to the city) and you will come to San Salvatore Al Monte, a 16th- century church designed by Florentine architect Simone del Pollaiolo (1457-1508). To the right of the church three roads. The one to the left leads you to the fortifications that protected the hill.

The best part of climbing up a hill, of course, is running down. Facing Fiesole, to the right are winding paths that stretch to the bottom. It's a beautiful walk down, and the kids get to burn off some steam.

THE MEDICI QUARTER – PALAZZO MEDICI RICCARDI
One block from San Lorenzo and the Piazza del Duomo.

Palazzo Medici Riccardi was for some time the largest private address in Florence. Cosimo the Elder chose the area to build his palace, but scrupulously decided against a more opulent design submitted by Brunelleschi. He didn't want to put wind to the sail of envy that already was blowing through Florence against the highly successful Medici family. Instead, he opted for the work of Michelozzi, who built the palace in 1444. Note the large stone shield on the corner that bears the Medici coat of arms. Perhaps the family chose red balls as their emblem because they represent medicine tablets. The founder of the family was a doctor, or *medico* in Italian.

The Medici eventually sold the palace in 1659 to the marquis Riccardi. Today it is the seat of the prefecture.

Here is what you'll find in this quarter:

San Lorenzo

After you leave the palace, turn right and right again and walk to the **Piazza San Lorenzo**. The **Basilica of San Lorenzo** was the family church are for the Medici and is one of the oldest in Florence. In the beginning of the 15th century, the Medicis and other wealthy families agreed to reconstruct the old church (built in the 4th century and turned into a cathedral by St. Ambrose in 393 – or so says tradition). However, the facade was never completed, despite the efforts of several great artists, including Brunelleschi and Michelangelo.

Rounded archways, a coffered central ceiling and *serena* stone (a gray stone from the Fiesole quarries) mark Brunelleschi's touch. Many paintings by Donatello are hung throughout the church. The two bronze pulpits at the far end of the central nave are the last two works completed by Donatello before he died in 1466. Cosimo the Elder is buried here – look for three grates with coats of arms and the Latin inscription *pater patriae* (father of the nation) in front of the main altar. Down below is **Cosimo's crypt.** Cosimo's parents, Giovanni de'Bicci and Piccarda Bueri, are buried in the Old Sacristy, under the table in the center of the room. Cosimo's two sons are in the tomb to the left of the entrance.

Medici Chapel
Open 9am-12:45pm and 3pm-5:15pm, Sunday 9am-12:45pm, closed Wednesday. Admission. Tel. (055)276-0340.

Purchase your ticket for the Medici Chapel (Cappella dei Magi) across the courtyard, in the garden with sculptures and large lemon trees. Cross the courtyard and go up the second staircase on the left. Only a few people are allowed in at once – and your time in the chapel is limited – so look quickly. Lorenzo the Magnificent's father, Piero il Gottoso, commisisoned Benozzo Gozzoli in 1460 to paint a fresco on the walls. The frescoes tell of the journey of the magi on their way to pay homage to baby Jesus. Many of the faces in the lively painting are Medici family members. The frescoes wrap around the tiny chapel, making you feel as if you've joined the procession. Look for Gozzoli himself in the painting – his name is printed on his red cap.

Chapel of the Princes
Piazza San Lorenzo, open Monday-Tuesday and Thursday-Saturday from 10am-1pm and 3pm-7pm; Sunday 10am-noon. Closed Wednesday.

Cosimo I commissioned this chapel in 1568 to celebrate ...what else?... but the greatness of the Medici family. The chapel is attached to the church of San Lorenzo, but the entrance is around the corner to the back of the church. Tombs of many of the Medici "princes" are found here, hence the name. Of interest are the tombs created by Michelangelo – *The Tomb of Lorenzo, Duke of Urbino* and *The Tomb of Giuliano, Duke of Nemours.* The unfinished *Madonna and Child* is another Michelangelo work. If the lines at the Uffizi and the Accademia deterred you, the Princes Chapel is an alternative to view masterpieces by Michelangelo.

Biblioteca Laurenaiana
Open Monday through Saturday 9am-1pm.
From the sacristy of San Lorenzo, go back to the first cloister to get to the Laurenziana library. Michelangelo's prowess at architecture is made clear in the vestibule, where it "broke the bonds and chains of ...common usage," according to Vassari. The staircase tumbles downward and outward, like a plummeting waterfall of stone. Enter the library to see thousands of priceless works, including a 5th-century Virgil text and the original copy of Cellini's autobiography.

PIAZZA & CHURCH OF SANTISSIMA ANNUNZIATA
Turn left out of San Marco along Via Battisti. Continue until you arrive at the Piazza Santissima Annunziata. Open 7am-7pm.
Travel back to Renaissance Florence by entering this piazza. It is a quiet refuge from hectic Florence; no cars allowed. In 1419, the Silk Guild decided to build a hospital for abandoned babies and Brunelleschi was called on to design the building. The **Ospedale Degli Innocenti** (Hospital of the Innocents) continues to work on children's issues today.

The hospital kicked off renovation of the square, although it was 100 years later that the friars of the order of the servants of Mary, who administered the **church of the Santissima Annunziata**, decided to build a second portico, located across from the hospital. Nearly another century passed before the facade of the church also was given a loggia. Although constructed over hundreds of years, the architecture blends together quite comfortably.

Parent Tip: If you're lucky enough to be in Florence on the evening between the 7th and 8th of September, you can participate in the feast called **Rificolona**. The feast, celebrating the birth of the Madonna, takes its name from a paper lantern lit with a candle that the Florentines carry in the street on that evening. Basically, the feast celebrates the habit of farmers who go and give thanks to the Madonna of the Santissima Annunziata, using a paper lantern to light their way.

WHICH ONE IS MY ROOM?
Every trip to Florence – both before and after children – we have been delighted with our rooms. Our hotel choices have never let us down, including a *pensione* we stayed at over 10 years ago for no more than $40 per night. Service always has been kind and informative, and rooms clean if not elegant. This is a city, unlike Rome, where you would not regret saving some money by staying at a two- or three-star hotel. Just make sure,

if your visit is in the scorching summer months and you need air-conditioning, your hotel can accommodate your needs.

Hotel Prices
Very Expensive – over €400/night
Expensive — €250-400/night
Moderate – €150-250/night
Inexpensive – under €150/night

Also, keep in mind that Tuscany is a compact area. If you have more than a few days – and especially if you rent a car – we recommend that you visit some of the other hill towns of Tuscany (and Umbria) by basing yourself in a more relaxed, child-oriented and economical location (Florence is by far the most expensive place to stay in Tuscany). For example, all of Tuscany to the west of Florence is conveniently reached as a day trip from the impressive and pleasant beach town of Viareggio. Similarly, all of southern and eastern Tuscany is accessible from the gorgeous and more rural hill towns of the Chianti country that stretches south from Florence to Siena.

Cortona, an hour southeast of Florence, is another very special place to stay (you might run into Frances Mayes, author of *Under the Tuscan Sun* and *Bella Tuscany*, as she lives here) and from there Assisi, Perugia and Lake Trasimeno are not too far. If you have a week or more, you might also consider renting a farmhouse or villa – *agritourismo* is the best way to slow the pace, absorb the culture, and yet still hop out on day trips to the sights that strike your fancy.

Parent Tip: Many hotels can make museum reservations for you. This is particularly important when it's a scorching hot day, your young children have wilted, older ones whining and the line to Uffizi is two hours long!! Remember to ask the concierge to make those reservations the day before you want to visit.

Very Expensive
HOTEL EXCELSIOR***** *Piazza Ognissanti 3. Tel. (39)(055)271.51. Fax. (39)(055)210.278. Web: excelsior.hotelinfirenze.com.*

Hotel Excelsior dominates the Piazza Ognissanti with its massive yet elegant facade. Once owned by Carolina Bonaparte, sister of Napoleon, the building certainly has withstood the test of time. It was a favorite of Charlie Chaplin and Orson Welles.

The opulent common areas call to mind the natural beauty of the Tuscan hills, terra-cotta blended with marble and finely sculpted precious woods. Chandeliers gently illuminate the lobby and the marble columns and spectacular wood-beamed ceilings. Stunning Renaissance painting and sculpture are presented to startle the visual palate. Each room is lavishly appointed with the same warm Tuscan hues. Impeccable service awaits you at Il Cestello, a top-rated restaurant in this luxury hotel. The hotel has 173 rooms and 19 suites, with wireless high speed Internet access in every room (fee), a gym and running maps of the city.

HOTEL HELVETIA & BRISTOL ***** *Via dei Pescioni, 2. Tel. (39)(055)287-814. Fax (39)(055)288-353. Web: helvetiabristol.warwick hotels.com.*

Part of the worldwide Charming Hotels chain, this is one of the premier hotels in Florence. Antiques abound, with each of the 52 rooms

and suites taking on its own character. The rooms are anointed in plush fabrics. Step from your relaxing Jacuzzi bath (the kids are with your partner, right?) and onto the cool marble floor. You also can enjoy dining at the hotel's restaurant serving authentic Tuscan cuisine. Renowned musician Stravinsky was a frequent guest here. Oh yes, there is tennis and a pool nearby.

HOTEL REGENCY ***** *Piazza Massimo d'Azeglio 3. Tel. (39) (055)245-247. Fax (39) (055)234-6735. Web: www.regency-hotel.com.*

The Hotel Regency's homey quality is deceiving. Indeed, this is an intimate 33-room hotel, less pretentious and more cozy than your typical 5-star. A garden separates the two wings, while comfortable parlors comprise the common areas, where guests can plan the day's itinerary amidst antiques and bouquets of fresh flowers. Yet, the Regency remains very much a luxury hotel in the heart of Firenze's tree-shaded "London Square." Utmost attention is paid to service and the rooms are spacious and well appointed.

A ten-minute or so walk to the heart of Florence, but what it lacks in proximity it makes up in tranquility. Note the private garage, a near-necessity for crowded Firenze. Wi-fi is available.

GRAND HOTEL VILLA MEDICI ***** *Via il Prato 42. Tel. (39)(055)238-1331. Web: www.villamedicihotel.com.*
Kids love the swimming pool sunk into a lush, private garden of this luxury hotel. It has 88 rooms, 15 suites, and is near the city center,

overlooking the Arno River. The bathrooms are sleekly designed with Carrara marble (Michelangelo's favorite marble).
HOTEL LUNGARNO **** *Borgo San Jacopo 14. Tel. (39)(055)272-61 Fax (39) (055)268-437. Web: www.lungarnohotels.com.*
Owned by the Ferragmos family, the Lungarno is just steps from the Ponte Vecchio, with nothing separating it from the Arno but the Tuscan air. Seventy-three rooms and 12 suites decorated in blue and white cushioned headboards and marble bathrooms make up this modern hotel accentuated by a medieval tower. Enjoy the marvelous balconies.

Expensive
HOTEL CONTINENTAL **** *Lungarno Acciaiuoli, 2. Tel. (39)(055)272-62. Fax (39) (055)283-139. Web: www.lungarnohotels.com/ en/firenze-continentale/hotels-accommodations-38.*
The decor is now modern and chic. Light wood highlighted by white drapes and modern lighting. And the views! Spectacular 180-degree views of Florence can be enjoyed from the rooftop terrace, the Sky Lounge. Sunsets in Tuscany, when the sun dances and playfully alters the colors of the hills from daytime brightness to the depth of blue and nighttime purple – all yours at the hotel's terrace. Choose a room overlooking the bustling Ponte Vecchio, or catch a glimpse of Giotto's tower. All 43 rooms (and one penthouse) are smartly appointed and include air-conditioning, direct-dial phone, fax, modem line and satellite TV. The Continental is one of the lovely, albiet expensive, Lungarno hotels in Florence.
TORRE DI BELLOSGUARDO **** *Via Roti Michelozzi, 2. Tel. (39) (055)229-8145. Fax (39) (055)299-008. Web: www.torrebellosguardo.com.*
This 16th-century hotel is nestled in the rolling hills immediately outside Florence – a five-minute taxi ride or relaxing 15-minute smell-the-

jasmine-walk to town. Impressive first impressions are the frescoes in the entrance, works of the Baroque master Poccetti. Each room in this hotel is fairly unique, especially the two-level tower suite, but note the absence of television: a plus for most of the adults, but a possible drawback for the kids. There is a beautiful garden terrace with a pool for the kids to enjoy, as well as a spa and fitness room.

HOTEL BEACCI TORNA-BUONI **** *Via Tornabuoni, 3. Tel. (39)(055)212-645. Fax (39) (055)283-594. Web: www.hotelbea ccitornabuoni.com.*

Located in the center of the city near the Piazza Santa Trinita, the Beacci Tornabuoni comprises the top three floors of a wonderful 15th-century Renaissance palace, Palazzo Minberti Strozzi. Each room has air conditioning and a minibar, although we much prefer the roof terrace with its nice view.

Moderate

HOTEL BOTICELLI *** *Via Taddea, 8. Web: www.hotelbotticelli florence.it.*

This is a pretty hotel, tucked into a centrally located corner of Firenze. The pale yellow breakfast room, with tapestries hung about and gentle sconce lighting is a pleasant place to organize your plans for the day. Our teens bolted, however, for the Internet in an adjacent room, but just after they gave two thumbs up for the hot chocolate. Our family suite was most comfortable; a modern, clean line, and the location makes walking to all sites a breeze. The staff are most helpful. A great sign of a good hotel is if you meet interesting and friendly fellow travelers, which we did at the Hotel Boticelli.

HOTEL IL GUELFO BIANCO *** *Via Cavour, 57. Tel. (39)(055)288-330. Fax (39) (055)295-203. Web: www.ilguelfobianco.it* Prime location, lovely staff and rooms that please the eye. What more can you ask for? The hotel has only 39 rooms, so book early. Enjoy breakfast, weather permitting, in the outside courtyard.

HOTEL BALESTRI *** *Piazza Mentana 7 (Lungarno Diaz) Tel. (39)(055)214-743, Fax (39)(055)239-8042. Web: www.hotel-balestri.it.* Location, location, location. This hotel occupies a choice spot – on the bank of the Arno, near the Ponte Vecchio – a mere 150 yards from the Uffizi Gallery. Ask for a room with a river view where you can write postcards or record your travel musings at the small wood table while gazing out of the room's window archway at the ebb and flow of the Arno. Hotel Balestri was founded in 1888 and has been owned and operated since then by the Balestri-Wittum family. All 100 rooms are air-conditioned, with satellite TV and direct-dial phones. A breakfast buffet is served. While the hotel is set up for business conferences, the friendly staff makes families feel right at home.

LE DUE FONTANE *** *Piazza SS. Annunziata, 14. Tel. (39)(055)210-185 or 294-226; Fax(39)(055)294-461. Web: www.leduefontane.it.* Piazza SS. Annunziata is a tranquil square, yet you can see the Duomo hovering overhead only 200 meters away. The interior of this neoclassic palace was recently renovated. Common areas are beautifully austere, with marble floors and light wood trimmings, dotted with fresh plants and flowers. Some rooms are more modern, while others capitalize on the hotel's neo-classical past. All rooms are air-conditioned, with phones, TVs and a minibar. Bus transfer to the train station or airport is available. So is a Jaguar car for "ceremonies or affairs"! Does a trip to Pinocchio Park count?

HOTEL VILLA CARLOTTA **** *Via Michele di Lando, 3. Tel. (39) (055)220-530, Fax(39)(055)233-6147. Web: www.villacarlottaflorence.com.*

This beauty of a small hotel is tucked into the tiny Piazzale Michelangelo. The 26 rooms, all recently refurbished, offer a great place to stay if the hustle and bustle of Florentine living is not your idea of a vacation. Located about one kilometer above Porta Romano among lovely wooded avenues, its garden and glassed-in veranda are wonderful. Noted for its restaurant, Il Bobolino, as well.

Inexpensive

HOTEL CASCI ** *Via Cavour 13, Firenze. Tel. (39)(055)211-686, Fax (055)239-6461. Web: www.hotelcasci.com.*

One of our favorite hotels in all of Italy! The Lombardi family's warm hospitality makes this bright and shiny two-star hotel a heavenly experience.

If you are looking for a very affordable and centrally located hotel, Hotel Casci cannot be beat. Situated in a 15th-century palace with some of the original frescoes intact, our daughter (classical-music-'R-us) was thrilled to hear that Rossini lived here four years before he left for Paris. The recently refurbished hotel is ideally located — close to the train station, the Duomo and the Accademia. The lobby has Internet access and is a great hang-out place for kids and their families. We met a wonderful family from Florida here when we noticed they were reading our *Open Road's Italy with Kids* guide! Their children and ours met in the lobby to play dominoes, Jenga, puzzles, chess and other games. A buffet breakfast is served in the lively dining area, adorned with frescoes and Renaissance paintings. Mr. and Mrs. Lombardi and their son, Paolo, always make our visit more than pleasant.

Their lovely dog, Spunky, has passed on, but a portrait of the happy pup hangs in the lobby.

ALBERGO FIRENZE ** *Piazza Donati 4. Tel. (055)214.213. Web: www.hotelfirenze-fi-it.*

Dante's wife, Gemma Donati, lived in the medieval tower house just next door to this hotel, which is steps away from key sites. It is simple, convenient and clean and they serve breakfast in a charming, bright room. Triple and quad rooms are available for families, and the price is quite right for being so close to the Duomo and the center of Florence.

ALESSANDRA ** *Borgo Santi Apostoli, 17. Tel. (055)283.438. Web: www.hotelalessandra.com.*

Tucked in between the Ponte Vecchio and the high-end shopping district. This is a 26 room, one suite and one apartment hotel that puts you and your family in the center of Florence. Some of the rooms have shared bath, but all are clean and sparkling. Suite Baccio sleeps four and has a living room, bedroom, bath and study, as well as a private balcony where you can enjoy breakfast.

HOTEL MARIO'S *** *Via Faenza, 89. Tel. (39)(055)216-801. Fax (39)(05)212-039. Web: www.hotelmarios.com.*

Friends turned us on to Mario's, and it's a good thing. Upon first blush, your heart trembles with the possibility of disappointment. So hurry up the stairs and into the warm and cozy lobby, set against a rustic backdrop. The 16 rooms are small but modern, fresh and tidy. Reserve a room in the back, as the front of the hotel is noisier with street sounds. We loved the old country wooden desks and chairs and other antiques in each room. But the best thing about Mario's is Mario (the owner). Located a block from the train station and close to the central market.

BELLETINI ** *Via de' Conti 7, Tel. (39)(055)213-561. Fax (39)(055)282-980. Web: www.hotelbellettini.com.*

Nice for the price and located near the Medici chapels. Decor is typical Florentine. Service is great. A good alternative to Hotel Casci if it is booked up.

LA SCALETTA ** *Via Guicciardini 13. Tel. (39)(055) 283-028 or 214-255. Fax (39)(055) 289-562. Web: www.lascaletta.com.*

Another good bargain, La Scaletta is a 12-bedroom pensione within a 15th-century palace and located between the Ponte Vecchio and the Pitti Palace. The rooftop terrace offers grand views into the Boboli Gardens. Note that not all of the bedrooms have a private bath, and some rooms sleep up to four people. Service is quite friendly and helpful.

I'M HUNGRY!

Parent Tip: Does one of you want to try cooking classes? Or, perhaps, you and your teens are interested in learning the ins and outs of Italian cooking? Search no more. Judy Witts Francini, founder of **Divina Cucina**, is in Florence and ready to help you learn how to prepare the best Italian food. Check out her web site for more information: *www.divinacucina.com.*

TRATTORIA ANTICO FATTORE $$ *Via Lambertesca, 1/3r Tel. (39)(055)289-975 Web: www.anticofattore.it.com Closed on Sunday.*

During the 1920s and 1930s, Trattoria Antico Fattore was the go-to place for the city's artists, musicians, journalists and actors. The artist community came to talk freely of new ideas while enjoying exquisite food and good wine. Today, the cuisine continues to hold true to the high standards of yore. We found delicious the riboletti soup, crepes florentine and risotto. And the kids voted the gelato the best from a restaurant. We had lemon, vanilla with caramel and chocolate with nuts! It is an inviting restaurant, wood-beamed ceilings, cream-colored table linens and interesting sketches and paintings, where families can feel quite comfortable and where you can count on competent and friendly service.

TRATTORE ROBERTO $$ *Via Castelloni, 4r. Tel (39)(055)921-8882.*

We stumbled onto Trattore Roberto on a cold, winter day after leaving the Science Museum intent on not walking too far for food. Situated directly across from the museum, Roberto's is a warm, cozy place filled with locals. The food is plain, simple and well-prepared. Emphasis is on fish. We especially enjoyed the brushette, gnocchi sorrentino and, Michael's favorite, risotto nero (black ink from squid). Trattore Roberto is our best bargain pick!

ACQUA AL 2 $$ *Via della Bigna Vecchia, 40/r. Tel.(39)(055)284-170. Web: www.acquaal2.it/*

Good place to impress an older teen – it's quite chic. Very hip waiters, a young professional crowd. Yet, families also are made comfortable. The restaurant is dimly lit, but warm and the menu – a contemporary twist on traditional Tuscan food. Try the samplers – amazing. Visit their web site for great recipe ideas.

I GHIBELLINI $$ *Pizza S. Pier Maggiore, 8-10. (39)(055)214-424 Closed Wednesday.*

Fifty types of pizza – say no more. Even your fussiest eaters will find something here. The homemade pasta is perfect and the tiramisu top-rate. There is a wonderful salad bar, as well. The atmosphere: Cozy country, with wooden tables and placemats you can draw on (bring out those crayons!) The back room, however, is Euro chic – very sterile, clean line, lots of metal, with music videos running on the TV. Can't say enough about this restaurant for families.

TRATTORIA GARGA $$-$$$ *Via delle Belle Donne, 3 Tel/Fax: (39)(055)211-396, Web:www.garga.it/trattoria-1.html.*

Artistic, unique, a contemporary version of the best of Florence's past. Garga is owned by Sharon Oddson and Giuliano Gargani (Garga) and their high view of food and art is evident by the personal touches throughout the restaurant — from the multi-hued walls with contemporary paintings produced by Oddson, Gargani and other artists, to the excellent Insalata Garga, to the lovely table setting, a solitaire candle with one pink rose. The staff are hip and friendly. Do try the Insalata Garga. An excellent choice for salad lovers. We also enjoyed the risotto con asparagi (almost as good as Michael's say our children!!) Sharon's cheescake – the best. Wonderful restaurant choice for families.

Check out the web site or call for information on cooking classes offered at the trattoria.

LA LOGGIA $$$ *Piazzele Michelangiolo. Tel. (39)(055)234-2832.*

An elegant restaurant, but the outdoor dining and live music on warm summer evenings makes it easier to handle with young children.

CIBREO $$$ *Via dei Macci 118R. Tel. (055)234-1100; Closed Sundays and Mondays.*

The restaurant continues to serve traditional Tuscan cuisine – *ribollita* and *polenta* made tasty with a spattering of herbs and succulent slices of Parmesan cheese. Why the name Cibreo? It's the name given to a traditional Florentine dish in which the, um, er, organs of a rooster are cooked, somehow, in a way I wasn't interested in delving into. Anyway, they will still make the dish for you, if you give them – and I guess they give the rooster – a couple weeks notice. It also offers a nice view overlooking the market of Sant'Ambrogio.

RIVOIRE CAFFE PASTICCERIA $$ *Piazza della Signoria Tel. (39)(055) 214.412*

This is why you came here, right? You are in one of the world's most spectacular squares, inhaling the same grand art and sculpture enjoyed by tourists for centuries. And now you're tasting some of the most scrumptious pastries, and, maybe, just one of course, a little of the pasticceria's to-die-for homemade chocolates. All the while, you're sipping the best cappuccino this side of Starbucks and your kids are happily playing in the open-air square, where the throngs of passersby drown out any whining or shouting that

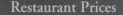

Restaurant Prices

$$$ – about $25-55 per person

$$ — about $18-24

$ – about $7-17

eventually may escape from their little mouths. Sit back. Sigh. Ahhhhhhh. You're living *La Dolce Vita*. **ALL'ANTICO RISTORO DI'CAMBI** $$$ *Via Sant'Onofrio 1/R. Tel. (39)(055) 217-134. Open Mon-Sat for lunch and dinner.* Originally an *enoteca*, you can't beat the wine list and olive oil selection at this *trattoria*. We like the location – in the midst of the artisans quarter known as San Frediano. Enjoy mouthwatering specialties including porcini mushrooms, *ribollita* and one of the best *pappa al pomodoro* in a delightfully rustic setting.

OSTERIA DEL CINGHIALE BIANCO $$$ *Borgo San Jacopo 43/ R. Tel. (39)(055) 215-706. Open Thurs-Mon for lunch and dinner. Reservations required for dinner.*

Strozzapreti, an incredibly light spinach dumpling, is one of the house specials. If you're daring, try the *pappardelle* (homemade egg noodles) in wild boar sauce. The atmosphere is intimate yet child friendly.

SOSTANZA $$$ *Via Della Porcellana 25/R. Tel. (39)(055) 212-691. Closed Saturdays and Sundays.*

Down home Tuscan cooking is offered at Sostanza. Our kids devoured the *zuppa alla paesana* (vegetable soup) as we surrendered to the homemade *tortellini*. The crowd at Sostanza, an authentic *trattoria*, is young, international and buzzing with excitement. Any adventures happened upon by your children while dining will blend into the lively atmosphere.

ANGIOLINO $$$ *Via Santo Spirito, 36/R. Tel. (39)(055)239-8976.*

Pasta, meat and vegetables cooked in traditional Tuscan style are featured at this wonderfully Old World *trattoria*. The friendly staff specially prepared plain pasta with butter, sprinkled with Parmesan cheese for the kids. We savored the homemade pasta and fried artichokes.

RELAIS LE JARDIN $$$$ *Piazza d'Azeglio in the Regency Hotel. Tel. (39)(055/245-247.*

One of the best in Florence, yet quite warm and welcoming for children. Ask to be seated in the dining room with a garden view. The homemade pasta reminds you of why you're in Tuscany. Freshness is key at Relais le Jardin and the menu changes every few weeks to keep up with the best of the seasonal produce. Reservations are recommended for both lunch and dinner.

CAFFE ITALIANO $$ *Via della Condotta 56/R.*

Caffe Italiano is more than a pastry/cappuccino bar. It offers a quick lunch, albeit from a limited menu, with tantalizing treats as a reward for eating a whole meal. The menu changes but you can always find salads, pastas and little sandwiches.

The Art of the Meal in Tuscany

It's hard to go wrong in Italy when it comes to food. Pizza is ubiquitous and most kids will eat pasta. For the more adventurous, either parent or child, here's a quick list of some of Tuscany's specialties, considered by many the most exquisite culinary delights in the world:

Try truffles, the culinary holy grail of Tuscany. They are wild mushrooms that cause businessmen in fancy suits and women perched high on stiletto-heeled shoes to dash from their cars and dive into a thicket to bring some home. To get your feet wet, try truffles shaved over pasta.

Don't forget the porcini mushrooms. We love *risotto ai funghi porcini* (rice with porcini). Many menus serve *tagliatelle ai funghi porcini* (egg noodles with porcini sauce). Risotto absorbs the flavor from a variety of ingredients – if you like fish, try *risotto di mare* (mixed seafood). These are all great dishes that we just couldn't get our kids to try!

White beans are a Tuscan staple, and one Barbara remembers her father being quite fond of. Sounds boring, right? Come on, you're saying, WHITE BEANS!! You will not try them in a car . . . or from a jar . . . But order them cooked with a dash of fresh sage and tomato (*fagioli all'uccelletto*) and it's: "Hey, I like white beans and ham. Yes, I like them Sam-I-Am," (with thanks and apologies to Dr. Seuss).

Ribollita (re-boiled) is a hearty and thick stew typically made from a base of yesterday's soup, adding cabbage, beans, potatoes and bread. It's actually quite good. *Pappa di pomodoro* is another thick soup our kids loved made from tomatoes, garlic and a generous sampling of breadcrumbs.

Bistecca alla fiorentina, a top choice grilled beefsteak, served very rare, is popular in Tuscany, as are all manner of grilled meats and roasted fowl.

The Scoop on Gelato

Everyone raves about **Vivoli** (*Via Isola delle Stinche, 7r*) and we thought maybe it was just hype, although we loved it ourselves when we biked into the city 15 years ago. But it won our kids' approval, hands down. Of course, it's the most expensive gelato in the city!

PIZZERIA ALLA MARCHIGIANA $ *Via del Corso, 60/R. Tel. (39)(055)214-961.*

The pizza can't be beat. And, you can get it by the slice. This is a great place for a quick pizza lunch or snack during a long day of touring. Remember, the pizzeria closes between 2pm and 3:30pm. Otherwise it's open from 9am until 9pm.

RISTORANTE SANTA LUCI $$ *Via Ponte Alle Mosse, 102/R. Tel. (39)(055)353-255.*

Yummy pizza made by the Neapolitan owners – Naples being the birthplace of pizza. Fresh pasta dishes also are on the menu. Surprisingly, Santa Luci is a dinner-only restaurant – an informal place to bring the family.

BIBE $$$ *Via delle Bagnese, 1/R. Tel.(39)(055)204-9085.*

We first visited Bibe ten years ago while biking through Tuscany – and it won our hearts again. Enter through the little country store; we always purchase some of the local cheeses and other treats for snacks later. Traditional Tuscan cooking is nicely done here. Try one of their hearty soups or grilled meat. Our kids were awestruck at the tank of piranha, while we enjoyed chatting about our next-day plans over coffee and a flavorful herbal liqueur.

SPORTS & RECREATION
Bicycling

We do not recommend bicycling in Florence with young children, although we did it when we biked for three weeks through Tuscany, BC (before children). The streets are narrow and harrowing, with cars sweeping within inches of your body. Bicycling out in the countryside, however – especially through the rolling hills of Chianti country to the south of Florence – is a wonderful way to experience all that is Tuscany. Just remember, they don't call them the hill towns of Tuscany for nothing. Here are some rental and tour shops:

I Bike Italy, *Tel. (055)0123.994, www.ibikeitaly.com.* Rent a bike, helmet and guide to bike the gorgeous Tuscan countryside (€50). You can also choose a walking tour (€40). Keep in mind that the countryside is quite hilly and this option is more appropriate for teens than younger children.

Alinari, *Via Guelfa 85R. Tel. (055)280-500*
Motorent, *Via San Zanobi, 9R. Tel. (055)490-113*
Florence by Bike, *Via della Scala, 12R. Tel. (055)488-992 or 480.814; Web: www.florencebybike.it.*

Bookstores/Libraries
Biblioteca dei Ragazzi Santa Croce, *Via Tripoli, 34. Tel. (055)247-8551. Open Monday, Wednesday, Friday 9am to 1:30pm and Tuesday, Thursday 2:30pm to 5:30pm.* A charming library of books, CDs, videos and magazines for children from 2 to 16.
Naturae, *Via dello Studio, 30R. Tel. (055)265-7624. Tuesday to Saturday 10a. to 1pm and 3:30pm to 7:30pm, and Monday and Sunday from 3:30pm to 7:30pm.* Buy science toys, experiments, optical illusions and outdoor gear.

CyberCafes
Internet Land, *Via degli Alfani 43r (center of Florence), Tel. (055)2638220*
Internet Train, *Via Guelfa 24/r, Tel. (055)214794 Via dell'Oriuolo 25/r, Tel: 39-055-2638968*
Netgate, *Via Nazionale 156/r, Tel: (055)2347967; Via Sant'Egidio 12/r (near the Duomo), Tel: (055)2347967; Via Cavour 144/r, Tel: (055)210004; Via dei Cimatori 17/r (near Piazza Signoria), Tel: (055)219491*
Netik Internet Point, *Via dell'Agnolo, 65r, Tel. (055)242645*
WWW.Village, *Via Alfani, 11/13r, Tel. (055)2479398*

Hiking/Walking
Club Alpino Italiano, *Via dello Studio 5. Tel. (055)239-8580. Web: www.cai.it/index.jsp.* CAI organizes all-day hikes through the striking Chianti countryside. Call to arrange a trip, or see what they have on their schedule. They also organize ski trips in the winter. Closed in August.
Mountain Travel Sobek, *Tel. 800/227-2384; www.mtsobek.com.* Sobek prefers children to be no younger than 13 and with hiking experience.
Wilderness Travels, *801 Allston Way, Berkley, California 94710. Tel. 510/548-0420 or 800/368-2794; www.wildernesstravel.com.* Prefer children to be no younger than 13 and with hiking experience.
More information on hiking and camping in Italy can be found at: *www.traildatabase.org/countries/italy.html.*

Horseback Riding

Azienda Agricola Spportiva il Paretaio, *Via Ponzano, 26. Loc. San Flippo-Barberino Val D'Elsa. Tel. (055)805-9218. Fax (055)805-9231.*

Centro Ippico di Bracciatica-Associazione Sportiva Equestre, *Via di Bracciatica 22. Lastra a Signa. Tel. (055)872-9223.*

Rowing

Societa Canottieri di Firenze, *Lungarno de'Medici, 8. Tel. (055)282-130. Web: www.canottierifirenze.it. Open Monday to Saturday 8am to 8pm and Sunday 8am to 1pm.* Experienced rowers and canoeists can take out a one-month membership. You will need two passport-size photos and a medical certificate or proof that you have health insurance. Try:

Ponte San Niccolo, May to September. Rent rowboats.

Lido, *Lungarno Pecori Giraldi, 1. Tel. (055)234-2726.*

Swimming

The Indoor Club, *Via Bardazzi, 15. Tel. (055)430-275 or 430-703. Open Monday-Saturday 10am to 11pm.* There is a gym and a sauna in addition to the pool.

Le Pavoniere, *Viale della Catena, 2. Tel. (055)333-979. Bus 17. Open May-September 10am-6pm daily. Admission. No credit cards.* Only appropriate for children who swim. Snack bar and restaurant (dinner only).

Piscina Bellariva, *Lungarno Aldo Moro, 6. Tel. (055)677-521. Bus 14. Summer: open daily, weekdays 8:30am to 11:00pm, weekends 10:00am to 6:00pm. Admission. No credit cards.* Pools for little people; separate pool for older children and adults. Lovely tree-lined grassy areas.

Piscina Costoli, *Viale Paoli, Campo di Marte. Tel. (39)(055)678-841. Bus 10, 17, 20. June through early September 10am to 6pm. Admission.* Check out the new swirling water slide.

ELSEWHERE IN TUSCANY

Exciting daytrips or overnight sojourns for families are easily found around Florence. From Pisa and Pinocchio Park in Collodi on the west, to Chianti country and Siena to the south, to Cortona and medieval Assisi to the east, there are many magical places for your family to journey to in the hills of Tuscany.

If you have only one extra day to explore – and especially if you are returning to Florence for the night – the best bets are nearby towns such as **Fiesole** (a suburb), **Vinci** (Leonardo's home town) and the hill towns of

Chianti (Greve, Castellina). Otherwise, if you have more time – and especially if you rent a car – we recommend you base yourself in the countryside or at the beach, where it is less expensive, more relaxed and more fun for kids, and travel into Florence for day trips. In each section below, where we describe the most famous hill towns of Tuscany and Umbria, we suggest alternative places to base yourself (such as **Viareggio** on the Tuscan coast, **Cortona** to the southeast or, **Orvieto** and **Perugia**) to explore what truly makes Tuscany and Umbria the soul of modern Italy.

FIESOLE

Fiesole is Florence's closest neighbor, located a mere five miles to the east and up, up, up the hill. In summer, Fiesole is a welcome relief from the unremitting heat of Florence. Breezes waft through the town, making summer days more pleasant. For families wanting a less hectic place to stay close to Florence, Fiesole is a great choice, combining the sites of Florence with country living. It's a 20-minute bus ride to Florence (bus number 7). For active families, you can try walking down to Florence from Fiesole. Follow the old lanes bedecked with gardens, lovely villas and great vistas.

No mere suburb, Fiesole has a history of its own. Around 2000 BC Fiesole ruled as the most important Etruscan city in the area, protected greatly by its hilltop location. When the Romans marched through the area, they found Fiesole too difficult to capture. Instead, they settled in what is now Florence, cut off supplies to Fiesole and eventually overtook the city. Florence took control of the city in 1125, with wealthy citizens using it as a summer retreat. It remains home to many of the most spectacular villas around Florence.

Fiesole has its own share of interesting sites. **Piazza Mino** marks the city's center. Cafés line the sidewalks where the bus will drop you off. The tourist office also is located here.

Getting Here

The easiest and least expensive way is to take bus number 7 from the Piazza della Stazione. Tickets can be purchased inside or at the ticket office cattycorner from the bus stop outside. A taxi ride should cost under $30.

CATHEDRAL SAN ROMULUS

Piazza Mino di Diesole. Open daily 7:30am-noon and 4pm-7pm.

The cathedral, built in 1125, contains the crypt of Saint Romulus. Works by Bicci and Mino de Fiesole are in the church. Listen to the ringing of the church bells. They chime every half-hour and hour.

ARCHAEOLOGICAL ZONE
Open winter 9am-6pm and summer 9am-7pm. Closed Tuesdays.
Behind the cathedral are the remains of Faesulae, the ancient Etruscan city. Kids will love the ruins, although they are relatively small. The **Roman Theater** dates back to the 1st century BC. Concerts and plays sometimes take place here in the summer. Check with your hotel's concierge for details.

CHURCH OF SAN FRANCESCO & CLOISTERS
Gardens and Basilica open 7am-7pm.
Kids need a strenuous hike? Try climbing the steep incline from the west end of the Piazza Mino up to the Church of San Francesco. Wonderful views greet you. Visit the cloisters and the small Etruscan museum. Below the church are the public gardens and the Basilica of San Alessandro, built on the site of the ancient Roman temple of Bacchus.

Tourist Information
Piazza Mino, 37. Open 8:30am-1:30pm. Tel.(39) (055)598-720. www.comune.fiesole.fi.it.

WHICH ONE IS MY ROOM?
VILLA SAN MICHELE ***** *Via Doccia, 4. Tel. (39)(055)59-451/ 598-734. Fax (39)(055)598-734. Web: www.villasanmichele.com.*

The reception area is an ancient chapel and the dining room bar is made from an ancient Etruscan sarcophagus. Welcome to the 29-room Villa San Michelle, a converted 14th-century monastery nestled into the woods. According to rumor, the building was designed by Michelangelo. Stunning views of the countryside and Florence can be seen from most rooms; several overlook the Italian garden. For the kids, a swimming pool beckons from a terrace above the hotel. You can eat under the stars on the veranda of the hotel's gourmet restaurant. It is ultra expensive, but well worth the investment.
VILLA BONELLI *** *Via Francesca Poeti 1. Tel. (055)59-513. Fax: (39) (055)598-942. Web: www.hotelvillabonelli.com.*

Breakfast included. Nineteen large rooms, fresh food, what more could you ask for? The Villa Bonelli is a good bet for the money.

VILLA FIESOLE *** *Via Beato Angelico, 35. Tel. (39)(055)597-252. Fax (055)599-133. Web: www.villafiesole.it/*
Does it have a pool? Yes. Situated in the middle of the Tuscan hills, its tranquil setting prepares you for a more hectic pace in the town below. Villa Fiesole once was a private home and, at another time, part of the San Michele convent.

PENSIONE BENCISTA *** *Via Benedetto da Maiano, 4. Tel. (39)(055)59-163. Fax (same). Web: www.bencista.com.*
A family-run hotel, the Pensione Bencista has been a favorite for travelers since its opening in 1925. The terrace offers enchanting vistas of the environs. It is a bit out of the way, so it's a better place to stay for those with a car. Two meals are included. Each room is different, offering a nice selection of style and accommodation.

VINCI

Hungry, starved and lost, we courageously biked on a trip before children through a light rain trying to make headway to our destination, Florence. Up and down the rain-slicked hills, through one not-in-the-guidebook town to another. Squinting through my rain-streaked glasses, I noticed the nondescript town's name – Vinci. Hmmm. Sounds familiar. Could it be? Leonardo? Sorry kids, its not DiCaprio's hometown, but another Leonardo, as in da Vinci. And that's how we found this treasure of a town with a museum that fifteen years later we couldn't pull our kids away from.

Vinci perches atop one of the hills of Montalbano, less than 40 kilometers west of Florence, and only a short detour off the highway to Pisa, Lucca and the coast. Gaze out over the Tuscan hills and understand where da Vinci and many others drew their inspiration. Green land awash in golden sunlight, growing more brilliant as the dawn moves into day. Dusk tempers the brightness until the hues of the Tuscan hills are deepened. A final burst of blazing orange sunset and the land finally bows to the blues and purples of a night sky. Agriculture continues to dominate in the heart of Tuscany, both the production of wine and olive oil. This is a place where you could sit for hours and admire the landscape.

Getting Here

By car from Florence (heading west), or from Pisa (heading east), take the SS67 to the city of Empoli (32 kilometers from Florence), then head north to the town of Cerreto Guidi, and follow signs another 5 kilometers north to Vinci.

By bus or train: take a COPIT bus from Empoli's Piazza Vittorio. You can get to Emploi from either Florence or Pisa, by train or on a LAZZI bus along SS67.

MUSEO LEONARDIANO
Open November-February, daily 9:30am-6pm; March–October open daily 9:30am-7pm. Tel. (39)(0571)560-55. Web: www.leonet.it/comuni/ vincimus/invinmus.html

Devoted to Leonardo's genius, the museum is housed within the **Guidi Castle**. Inside are amazing reproductions of Leonardo's machines and other inventions, painstakingly constructed based on the master's annotations and sketches from his *Codex Atlanticus* notebooks.

On the ground floor are Leonardo's machines – military, construction and scientific. Check out the tank. We could have left our son here for days – both when he was 6 and just recently at 14, as he tried to figure out how each of the machines might work in practice, or how they were flawed (many were).

The first floor centers on the theme of machines that move through air, water and earth. Each model on this floor is full-scale, including a bicycle and a diving suit, our daughter's favorite. Up an internal staircase is the video library that also contains models of solids designed by Leonardo for Luca Pacioli's *De Divini Proportione*.

Also in the complex at the Guidi Castle is the **Biblioteca Leonardiana**, which houses over 7,000 monographs in several languages.

Leonardo's birthplace, in the town of **Anchiano**, is located three kilometers from the museum (*photo at left*). Open 9:30-1pm and 3:30pm-6pm in summer; 2:30pm-5pm in winter; closed Wednesday. You can hike to it on the network of paths through these hills. Path number 14, with the first part called *Strada Verde*, is about a one-hour round trip to Casa Natale di Leonardo. A copy of the network is available at the tourist office, located near the museum.

Tourist Information

Via delle Torri 11. Tel. (39) (0571)568-012, Fax (39) (0571) 567-930. See also *www.leonet.it/ comuni/vinci.* a superb website with information about Leonardo, his museum, the town and the surrounding area.

WHICH ONE IS MY ROOM?

If you've fallen in love with Leonardo country, here are a couple of very special places to stay nearby.

HOTEL MONA LISA *** *Via Lamporecchiana, 27/29. Tel. (39) (571)56-266, Fax (39)(571)56. 7913. Web: www.hotelgina.it/.*

A plain and simple hotel close to Leonardo's museum. The backyard terrace is lovely and lush. A footpath takes you to the museum – you can walk or bike there.

SPAZZAVENTO

(agriturismo), Di Pasqualetti Dino, Localita Apparita N. 85. Vinci. Tel. 339.651-7704, Fax. 0571.585-712 Web: www.spazzavento.it.

Olive groves and vineyards embrace the small, family-run resort. Rooms are rustic and

> ### Fun Fact
>
> Read the heart-warming story, *Leonardo's Horse*, by popular children's author Jean Fritz and illustrated by Hudson Talbott. Fritz tells the tale of Leonardo's dream to make a bronze horse for the Duke of Milan. While he was able to construct a clay model, the Last Supper fresco and other projects captured all of his time and, upon his death bed, he was tormented by leaving the horse undone. But, in 1977, American airline pilot Charlie Dent was captivated by the story of Leonardo's horse and raised money to build the great master's dream. A clay model was ready to be cast in 1993, but by the following year, Dent stood at death's door, making his family promise that his and Leonardo's dream would be completed. It was. And, now, you can see a copy of the magnificent sculpture in the small piazza in Vinci. The original is in Milan. See *www.leonardoshorse.org* for more information.

wonderful. Spazzavento specializes in the production of Chianti wine and extra-virgin olive oil. Enjoy! To get here from Vinci, drive southwest towards Cerreto Guidi; after two kilometers, turn right towards S. Pantaleo; when you reach the town of Apparita, turn left and after about 40 kilometers you will see the resort on the right.

I'M HUNGRY!

RISTORANTE LA TORETTA $ *Via della Torre, 19 (just 50 yards from the Castella dei Conti Guida).*

LUCCA

A 16th-century wall protects precious Lucca, a gem of a hill town still not too overrun by tourists. Allegedly built to fortify the town, the extraordinarily wide stone walls are topped off with a charming tree-lined walkway that makes a 4 kilometer-long loop around Lucca. Gardens and playgrounds appear in the grassy areas on top of the walls, making for an enjoyable picnic and play spot for the family. Years before on our bicycle trip through Tuscany, we biked the pathway on the walls. People still do today, and many rollerblade as well. Be careful; although a large grassy area separates the path from the edge of the walls, there are no fences, and riding or running too close to the edge could end in a tragic fall over the steep wall.

The construction of the Luccan wall at the beginning of the Wars of Italy served as a prototype for other Italian cities. They remain one of the best preserved and certainly most functional walls in all of Italy.

Dramatically enter the city through the most elaborate gate – **St. Peter's Gate**. If you are driving, park your car at the gate's entrance or at your hotel (ask ahead: not all hotels have parking). You will want to walk this labyrinth of a city, and so will your kids.

Parent Tip: If you are overnighting in Lucca, ask the hotel which gate you should enter. While walking through the city with a light backpack is pleasant, you will arrive as cranky as a tired two-year-old if you are forced to march into unknown territory lugging those too-many, too-heavy suitcases.

The most fun we've had in Lucca is joining the Italians for their daily *passegiatta* (stroll) through the maze-like medieval streets or along the romantic breezy walkways on top of the walls that circumnavigate the old town. Lucca is a great place to relax and travel back in time.

Getting Here

You can take a train from Florence on the Florence-Viareggio train line; travel time is about 75 minutes or so. You can take a bus from Florence or Pisa, or you can drive by way of the A11 Autostrada.

PIAZZA DI SAN MARTINO

Enter St. Peter's Gate, and to the right along the Corso Garibaldi is Lucca's cathedral, an excellent example of Pisan architecture. St. Martin's is better known in our household as the candy-cane church because of its unique Pisan striped-marble design. In the same piazza as the church, Piazza di San Martino, an antique fair takes place every third Saturday and Sunday of the month.

SAN MICHELE IN FORO

Most tourists confuse San Martino, Lucca's cathedral, with San Michele in Foro, a church situated in Piazza San Michele. The churches  were built around the same time and both proudly display the Pisan style. Gaze up into the heavens and note the Archangel perched on the top of the church wearing a bracelet bedecked in real jewels. Puccini puts this church on the map. The great composer began as a choirboy in this church, where his father and grandfather were organists.

PUCCINI'S HOME & MUSEUM

Enter on Corte San Lorenzo, 9. Open Tuesday through Sunday, 10am-1pm and 3pm-6pm in summer, 11am-1pm and 2pm-4pm in winter. Closed Monday. Admission.

Across the street from San Michele, at Via di Poggio 30, stands the home in which Puccini spent his early years. Now it is a museum. The Steinway piano Puccini used to compose *Turandot* is on display here.

Parent Tip: Summertime is opera time in Lucca. Make sure you check with your hotel or with tourist information about the schedule. What a better way to introduce opera to children than in Italy. Here's a great web site to satisfy your operatic urges in Lucca: *www.puccinielasualucca.com.*

VIA FILLUNGO: SHOPPING, TORRE DELLE ORE
& CAFFE DI SIMO

To the east of San Michele is a lovely shopping district that runs up and down tiny medieval streets. The main avenue is Via Fillungo. Besides shops of all sorts, Via Fillungo is home to the 15th-century **Torre delle Ore**, or tower of hours. Take a break from shopping at the historic **Caffe di Simo** (number 58 on Via Fillungo).

ROMAN AMPHITHEATER
Follow Via Fillungo through to the 12th-century church, **San Frediano**. Near the church through narrow archways are the remains of the **Roman Amphitheater**. Bring a soccer ball and join the Italian children playing soccer where once gladiators locked horns.

OUTSIDE OF LUCCA
Chestnut groves blanket the green hills of the **Garfagnana** situated between the Apennines and the Apuan Alps. It's idyllic country, but also an area ripe for athletic endeavors.

If you have the time or need a break from cathedrals and museums, here are two exciting day trips outside of Lucca. Before you choose, however, consider that other very interesting towns (such as Collodi and its Pinocchio Park, desribed below) are not far from Lucca.

The Cave of Wind (Grotto del Vento). *Tel. (39) (0583) 722.024, Fax (39) (0583) 722.053. Web: www.grottadelvento.com.*

Children love this vast cavern dripping with stalactites and subterranean lakes and streams. Guided tours run regularly, with extensive tours for experienced cave climbers. Drive north to Braga and then on to the Grotto del Vento; be sure to get precise directions from your hotel.

Orecchiella Park in the Garfagnana Mountains. *Call the Visitor's Center for more information and directions: Tel. (39)(0583)65-169 or 955-525. You can also get maps for hiking and other relevant information.*

Eagles soar above this wild woodland and hiking paths zigzag up and around the rugged mountain. This is Tuscany? You bet, but one far removed from Etrucsia and Chianti, and Leaning Towers and Michelangelos. On one of our visits, the park offered an exhibition with a workshop for children on prehistoric objects.

Tourist Information
Piazza Santa Maria, 35. Tel. (0583)91-991. Web: lucca.turismo.toscana.it

Bicycle Rentals
Riding bicycles around the old wall is a fun time for the family. Rent bikes at:
• **Puntobici**, *Str. Del Crocefisso, 8, near Verdi Square. Tel. 347.922.6729. Web: www.puntobici.lucca.it/*
• **Poli Antonio**, *Piazza santa maria, 42. Tel. (0583)493.787*

WHICH ONE IS MY ROOM?

LA LUNA *** *Corte Compagni 12, off the Via Fillungo. Tel. (39)(0583)493-634, Fax (39)(0583)490-021; Web: www.hotellaluna.com.*
This is probably the best and most helpful hotel for families in Lucca. A charming, completely modern hotel located right off one of the main streets, Via Fillungo, and close to the amphitheater. It is located near a nice, quiet park at Corte Compagni. Every room has a private bath and TV. If you are driving, you can park in the hotel garage – a real plus in the (mostly) car-free old town. Book well in advance.

UNIVERSO *** *Piazza del Giglio 1 (next to the Piazza Napoleone); Tel. (39)(0583) 493-678, Fax(39)(0583)954-854. Web: www.universolucca. com.*
This hotel has history on its side. Established in the 11th century, long lists of famous  Europeans have stayed here over the centuries. It has a great location near the station and Duomo. The Luna is a better value, unless you prefer ancient ambience to modern comforts.

ILARIA **** *Via del Fosso, 26. Tel. (39)(0583)47-615. Web: www.hotelilaria.com.*
Upgraded to four stars since our last visit. The rooms are lovely and the small hotel is nestled on the banks of Lucca's baby canal.

HOTEL DIANA ** *Via del Molinetto, 11. Tel. (39)(0583)492-202. Fax (39)(0583)467-795. Web: www.albergodiana.com.*
Near the cathedral. Rooms are inexpensive, neat and clean. There are only nine of them, so reserve early. It's a good deal, but remember to ask for a room with a private bath, as only some of the rooms offer it.

PICCOLO HOTEL PUCCINI *** *Via di Poggio, 9. Tel. (39)(0583)55-421 or 53-487, Fax (39)(0583)53-487. Web: www.hotelpuccini.com.*
A well appointed three star located near the Piazza San Michelle. But double-check your reservation, emphasizing that you are traveling with kids.

We had booked a quadruple room several years ago, with credit card deposit and written confirmation (by fax). When we arrived about 9pm, we found our room had been given away and the only one remaining had just one bed about as big as the room. Management tried to shrug it off in a not-very Italian style. After much debate, they finally arranged for us to stay elsewhere (a rather down-and-out student hotel – the Moderno – above a noisy piazza), so the experience left us a bit grumpy. The Luna is a better bet for families.

I'M HUNGRY!

TRATTORIA DA LEO DEI FRATELLI BURALLI *$$ Via Tegrimi 1. Tel. (0583)492-236.*

Tired and hungry after biking from Pisa to Lucca 10 years ago, we stumbled on this restaurant and return every time we go back. Our favorite seat is beneath the portrait of a lion, tongue dripping from his mouth – probably in anticipation of the wonderful food to be served. The locals come here to eat. It's loud and boisterous – a perfect place for kids. Pizza, pasta, meat dishes, everything is fresh. This is not elegant dining. The service is brisk but friendly. Down-home Lucchese cooking at its best.

IL GIGLIO *$$, Piazza del Giglio 2. Closed Tuesday evenings and Wednesday. Tel. (0583)493-012.*

Located next to Hotel Universo, Il Giglio has some of the best seafood in Lucca – remember how close you are to the sea – or try a traditional Tuscan entrée, such as rabbit with polenta.

IL BUCA DI SANT'ANTONIO *$ Via della Cervia, 3. Closed Sunday evening and Monday. Tel. (0583)55-881.*

Try the freshly made ravioli. The kids loved it with ricotta, sage and butter. Il Buca di Sant' Antonio has been an inn since the late 1700s, and continues to serve traditional fare like smoked herring.

RISTORANTE PUCCINI *$$$ Corte San Lorenzo, 1. Tel. (0583) 316-116. Fax (0583)316-116.*

A lovely restaurant, slightly on the fancy side, that also features fish. The *penne agli scampi* (pasta with prawns) and the *grigliata mista* (mixed grilled meats) are highly recommended.

PIZZERIA ITALIA *$ Corto Compagni 2. Tel. (0583)493-012.*

Near the Luna Hotel and the Piazza dell'Antifeatro, this is the place to go for pizza in Lucca. An extensive menu of pizzas and calzones. Try the *pizza arrabiata* (with tomatoes, garlic and peperoncini). We loved sitting outside while the children played in a small and quiet piazza.

PIZZERIA K2 $$ *Via dell'Antifeatro, 107. Tel. (0583)47-170. Closed Wednesdays.*

Not as good a selection as Pizzeria Italia and more expensive. But it does have pizza and outdoor seating – so if the other one is filled to capacity, Pizzeria K2 is close by.

G. GIURLANI & C. *Via Fillungo 241. Tel. (0583)496-233.*

Not a restaurant, but a great picnic supplies store. Buy your cheeses, meats and treats here and take them to the wall for a grand family picnic.

COLLODI & PINOCCHIO PARK

Collodi, the birthplace of Pinocchio, seems to defy gravity. Even if you come only for Pinocchio Park and the gorgeous gardens of nearby **Villa Garzoni**, stop and take a good long look up at the town, which seems to spill down the hillside like a mountain river of rushing stone.

Only a few houses wide at most points, the town follows the curvature of the hill up and up. If you want some exercise and great views, take the steep hike through the old town. Collodi is so steep that in the days before automobiles, horses and mules wore a special type of horse shoe with built in hooks to help avoid slipping as they made their slow and dangerous trek down the cobblestone-covered hillside, pulling wagons loaded with silk made in Collodi's mills.

Getting Here

Collodi is located midway between Lucca (15 kilometers to the west) and Montecatini Terme (10 kilometers east). It is also an easy day trip from Florence (60 kilometers) and Pisa (32 kilometers). Viareggio, the major Tuscan beach town, is just a bit further than Pisa. It is easiest to come here by car, although buses run regularly. From Lucca, take road no. 435 toward Montecatini and Florence. LAZZI buses from the east (Montecatini, via Pescia) and from the west (Lucca) run several times daily. For more information, call the Parco di Pinocchio.

PARCO DI PINOCCHIO

Tel. (39)(0572)429-342. Web: www.pinocchio.it/park.htm.

Children's imaginations take wing in this delightful park that chronicles

Carlo Lorenzini's *The Adventures of Pinocchio*. Lorenzini took the pen name Collodi, ensuring forever the adoration of his adopted hometown, where he often stayed with his uncle at the local castle. The winding path that leads through exciting events in Pinocchio's wooden life is filled with splendid sculptures of beloved and evil characters – including the kind Geppetto, Jiminy Cricket and the Whale. This is based on Collodi's book, not the Disney version that excludes many of the characters and events.

Besides being a blast for kids, the park uniquely integrates nature and art. Plants indigenous to Tuscany serve as lovely backdrops for the literary scenes. Nothing is mechanical or high-tech here; Pinocchio Park is an elaborately whimsical sculpture garden and playground. Ask for the brochure that gives plant details in English.

The character sculptures are splendid. Not only will you take heart in your child's joy of play, but your soul will be touched by the way the aesthetic of art and nature unite in this park. While it was impossible to get our children to pick a favorite character, they both gave a big thumbs up to the Whale. If you stand among its teeth at the bottom of the exhibit, a strong spurt of water from upstairs will thoroughly drench you. The kids loved it. So did we, as it was an oven-hot summer day in Collodi.

Collodi residents are passionate about Pinocchio and have been for many years. Each year on May 25 the town has a festival to celebrate Pinocchio's birthday. In 1953, the town held a national competition for the Monument to Pinocchio and 84 artists threw their pallets into the ring. Two won equal merit: Emilio Greco with *Pinocchio and the Fairy* and Venturino Venturi with the *Mosaic Square*. Both are stunning and fanciful – to be enjoyed by all ages.

We can't sing the praises enough of Parco di Pinocchio. Return visits to Italy always are met with, "Are we going to Pinocchio Park?" It takes the virtual out of virtual reality, giving something to children that is more precious – imagination.

VILLA GARZONI & GARDENS
Tel. (0572)428-579. Open daily June-September; October-May, only Saturday, Sunday & public holidays. Garden open daily. Admission.

There are other things to see in Collodi. The Villa Garzoni, or Castle of the Hundred Windows, is the best of them. The 17th-century villa is surrounded by a fabulous Italian garden, complete with cascading waterfalls and spouting fountains. With its rigorous geometric layout, it is a magnificent example of the Italian Baroque style and one of the most charming gardens in all of Italy. Inside the villa is the old pine table where Carlo Lorenzini scripted his Pinocchio stories. The reception rooms are grand, with flowery frescoes and gleaming terracotta floors.

Nearby **Pescia**, five kilometers to the east, is another lovely old hill town that should prove irresistible for gardeners – it is the flower-growing capital of Italy.

PISA

The **Leaning Tower of Pisa** bedazzles all children, as it does their parents. "Look, mommy. It really does lean," blurted out our little girl – as if all those pictures were special effects and the stories were make-believe! Our children were equally amazed at the great efforts that were underway to save the tower on their first trip to Italy. This is a tourist trap, to be sure. If you get away from here without buying one or more tacky tower treasures, hats off to you. But it's fun to see, with lots of running room for little ones.

Pisa is about 56 miles west of Florence – a straight shot on the A11 *autostrada* or by train. Modern Pisa is not so much a place to stay (nearby Lucca is far more quaint and interesting, and even nearer Viareggio is a beautiful beach town) as it is a place to stop for a few hours. The main attractions are all located in the **Campo dei Miracoli** (Field of Miracles) located in the northwestern part of the city. One thing miraculous about the Campo is that it actually holds the thousands of tourists that beat on its door day in and day out. Be prepared to join the maddening crowd.

At one time Pisa reigned supreme in Tuscany. After it lost to Genoa in the Battle of Meloria in 1284 and the eventual silting of the Arno, Pisa lost its prestige as a ruling state, never to be regained again. Still, Pisa produced a top-notch university and forever made a mark in scientific history through two of its famous scholars: Galileo Galilei and nuclear physicist Enrico Fermi.

Getting Here

By Car: From Florence take the A11 straight to Pisa.

By Train: Trains from Florence arrive at the Stazione Centrale, about a 15-minute walk to the Leaning Tower. If that's too far for the kids, take bus number 1 from the station to the Campo dei Miracoli.

By Air: The international airport, Galileo Galilei, is located about 3 kilometers to the south. Take bus number 7 to the train station.

CAMPO DEI MIRACOLI

Like the field of dreams, the Pisans built a field of miracles and the tourists came – in droves – throughout the centuries. Not since the times of ancient Rome has so grand a complex been created. Pisa's glory days are ever present in the magnificent monuments on display in the square. The architects of the square introduced a new innovation known as Pisan Romanesque, inspired both by the Roman basilicas and Islamic architecture. The walls that surround the square were constructed in 1154, perhaps to protect the city's miracle forever.

THE LEANING TOWER

Web: www.opapisa.it/en/home-page.html. Open from April to September 8:30am to 8pm, except June and August, 8:30am to 11:00pm. October from 9:00a, to 7:00 pm, November through February from 9:30am to 5:30pm and December and January from 10am to 4:30pm. Admission. Limited to only 30 people for a 30 minute tour. Children under 8 not permitted. Book online at the website above.

This famously tilted *torre* stands as a perpetual symbol of Italy, both of the country's greatest achievements and of its dashed hopes. It is unique in the world because it, well, leans, quite a bit. But don't let its dramatic leaning (or the steel cables holding it up) keep you from ogling the beauty of the tower. Begun in 1174 by Bonanno Pisano and finished in 1350 by

Tomaso Pisano, the tower has nearly 200 marble and granite columns. The local and national government have spent millions of dollars since 1990 to stabilize the tower.

For quite some time, the tower wore a corset of steel, with sturdy steel cables securing it to a nearby structure. This was a safety measure put in place to protect engineers, who even today continue to inspect the soil in which the tower is planted. Thanks to their challenging and creative work, you can once again walk the nearly 300 stairs of the Leaning Tower.

Some historians claim the tower was built to lean, a silly and expensive trick played by its designers. But architects and engineers today believe it was meant to stand vertical, but started to incline during construction. Check out the Leaning Tower's official web site to see an incredible picture portfolio of this wonder of the world: *www.opapisa.it/en/home-page.html.*

THE DUOMO

Open 8am-12:30pm and 3pm-6:30pm.

The Pisan Romanesque style dominates the Duomo's facade. It was begun in 1063 by Buschetto and finally completed in 1118. Inside few of the original art works remain due to a raging fire in 1595. Look up at the lamp hanging in the center of the nave, called the Lamp of Galileo, named after the great scientist who discovered through observation and experiment the oscillation of pendulum motion.

Walk up to the exquisite Baptistery pulpit by Nicola Pisano (1259). His work is said to be the best and last of medieval classicists. The marble figures in each of the narrative religious scenes almost topple over one another, so dense are the panels. Three stalking lions support three of the different-colored marble columns. "They look more like a merry-go-round," declared our son. Nicola's son Giovanni designed and sculpted the marble pulpit for Pisa Cathedral around 1300. While some elements of style are similar, Giovanni's panels are not as densely populated as his father's work. Instead, glimpses of landscape appear about the figures.

Other works to view are Cimabue's mosaic of *Christ Pantocrator* in the apse and the ivory statuette of *Madonna and Child* also by Giovanni Pisano.

Tug-of-War Festival

Gioco del Ponte is held each year in June. This tug-of-war tournament was first mentioned in a 1568 manuscript. Two city factions played it on a bridge – one on either side of the Arno. Today, the wooden *targone* has been replaced by the *carrello*, a structure weighing several tons running on a 50-meter long track placed on the Ponte di Mezzo. The winning team is the one that forces the other to retreat more times. A colorful procession led by Pisans dressed in medieval garb kicks off the fun and games.

CAMPO SANTO

Open 8am-6:30pm. In January open only from 9am-4:30pm. Admission.
An eerie rectangle of a blinding-white marble corridor encloses this open-air cemetery. As the story goes, the cemetery began when Archbishop Lanfanchi and his battalion returned to Pisa from the Crusades with loads of soil from the Holy Land. Their intention was to bury their dead in this special sacred soil. Most of the frescoes on the walls are lost forever after a severe bombing raid during World War II.

MUSEO DELLE SINOPIE

Across from the Duomo. Open 9am-sunset, 8am-7:40pm in summer. Admission.
Sketches and plaster of the frescoes of Campo Santo lost in the bombings during World War II are on display in this museum.

MUSEO DEL DUOMO

Located near the Learning Tower in Piazza Arcivescovado. Open 9am-sunset. Summer 8am-7:40pm. Admission.
This museum contains a range of work, including interesting Etruscan and Roman artifacts. Find the odd griffin that used to roost at the top of the cathedral. It may have come from Egypt in the 11th century. Many of the works of the Pisano family are housed here, including Giovanni Pisano's *St. John the Baptist* and *Madonna del Colloquio.*

Tourist Information
Via Matteucci, Galleria Gerace, 14. Tel. (050)929.777. Email: info@pisaunicaterra.it. Web: www.pisaunicaterra.it.

WHICH ONE IS MY ROOM?

We love Pisa and once stayed over at a quaint hotel on a bike trip through Tuscany – BC (before children). But Pisa is no charming Tuscan hill town; it is a crowded, sprawling industrial city surrounding an island of gleaming antiquity. There are better places to stay in the area. We recommend visiting Pisa from Lucca, or – if you prefer the beach – from nearby Viareggio. Should you decide to spend the night, consider these:

GRAND HOTEL DUOMO **** *Via S. Maria, 94. Tel. (39)(050)561-894, Fax (39)(050)560-418. Web: www.venere.com/hotels/pisa/grand-hotel-duomo.*
Everything you would expect for a luxury hotel and located next to the Campo dei Miracoli in the center of Lungarno Pacinotti. The hotel has a roof garden and offers the use of a private garage.

HOTEL ROYAL-VICTORIA *** *Lungarno Pacinotti, 12. Tel. (39) (050)940-111, Fax (39)(050)940-180. Web: www.royalvictoriahotel.it.*

Modern decor with the best rooms looking out over the Arno. Drivers will delight in the parking garage. Pisa's a tough place to find parking.

HOTEL FRANCESCO *** *Via Santa Maria 129' Tel. (39)(050)554-109 Fax: (050)556-145; Web: www.hotelfrancesco.com.*

Small, family-run, charming hotel on the street that leads up to the Leaning Tower. Kind staff help you make yourself at home in Pisa.

VERDI *** *Piazza Republica, 5. Tel. (39)(050)598-947, Fax (39)(050)598-944. Web: www.pisaonline.it/HotelVerdi.*

Near the train station. Reasonable rates, clean and comfortable in a restored historic building.

I'M HUNGRY!

DA BRUNO $$ *Via Luigi Bianchi, 12. Tel. (39)(050)560-818. Outside the walls and several blocks east of the Campo. Closed Monday evening and Tuesday.*

One of the best near the Campo dei Miracoli. Traditional Pisan dishes, including satisfying dishes with *polenta*. A good selection of meat and fish dishes. It's touristy, but the food is good and the service friendly.

OSTERIA DEI CAVALIERI $ *Via San Frediano, 16. Tel. (39)(050)580-858. Closed Saturdays for lunch and Sundays.*

Our children enjoyed watching the Italian kids from the nearby local high school hang out around this restaurant. Pasta dishes are excellent, especially ones with porcini mushrooms. Located near the university, this is a solidly good restaurant with a local clientele.

DA GINO $$ *Piazza Vittorio Emanuele, 19. Tel. (39)(050)23-437.*

A good choice if you're stuck at the train station. Numerous pizza selections will keep the kids happy. Again, lots of fish and pasta.

KOSTAS $$$ *Via del Borghetto 39. Tel. (050)571-457.*

A Greek restaurant in Pisa? Not really. You get down-home Pisan cooking here. Try the *tagliolini al Nero* (pasta with squid's ink sauce) if you dare. It's good. Duck and rabbit dishes also good.

OSTERIA LA GROTTA $$$ *Via San Francesco 103. Tel. (050)578-105. Closed Sundays and in August.*

Faux grotto, folks. But it's fun and the traditional Pisan cuisine is delicious. One of our favorite dishes is the *risotto ai fiori di zucchini* (rice with zucchini flowers), although the restaurant is renowned locally for its meat dishes.

VIAREGGIO

Once a sleepy fishing village, Viareggio has blossomed into the quintessential Italian beach resort – Italy's largest in fact. Try not to be put off by the crowded and hyper-organized beach scene. Big Sur it's not – but Viareggio will grow on you. Where else could you wander out for an early morning run on the beach and find a nun, in full sister garb, veil floating in the breeze, vigorously keeping pace with you. A little heavenly intervention, perhaps!

Viareggio is a terrific place to base yourself – with a car – for sightseeing along the coast and throughout eastern Tuscany. Pisa, Lucca, Carrara, Cinque Terra and the so-called "Tuscan Riviera" are all an easy drive away for day trips. It is an hour's drive west from Florence and very close to Pisa. In July and August, enjoy the **Puccini opera festival** (*www.puccinifestival.it*) or the **Carnevale festival** in February and March (*www.welcometuscany.it/ tuscany/tuscany_beaches_coasts/versilia/carnevale_viareggio.htm*).

Each hotel has an assigned swatch of sand on the beach with chairs and umbrellas in the hotel colors all lined up in neat rows. A snack cafe, with just okay food, and showers for a fee, also are available. People-watching is a high sport here. There are few Americans and a high percentage of Italian families. During the week, many *mamas, bambini* and *nona* (grandmothers) are active in the beach life. The work-weary husbands show up on the weekends.

The waves are gentle and the water mild. There are lifeguards, but most are too busy girl-watching (and talking) to be counted on. In the evening, the long boardwalk offers a choice of dozens of restaurants, ice cream parlors and boutiques. We stayed at Viareggio at the end of a month-long visit to Italy – a great way to unwind after a whirlwind week or two of sightseeing.

Splashing in the gentle waves, taking an evening *passagiata* along the boardwalk, or a boat ride on the sea, Viareggio is a pleasant resort despite the crowds. Using the beach as home base, we explored the coast as far north as Cinque Terra (a must-see gem, described below) and Genoa, the capital of Liguria. The kids loved it because we always had the beach to come back to and, on some days, we didn't venture out at all.

*Web: www.comune.viareggio.lu.it/index.php?option=com_content&
view=article&id=313.*

WHICH ONE IS MY ROOM?

In 1917, a massive fire destroyed most of Viareggio. When it was rebuilt in the 1920s, Galileo Chini and Alfredo Belluomini were charged with design and construction. Chini is highly regarded as one of the inventors of Italian Art Noveau, or Liberty Style, and grandiose hotels from Italy's "Roaring '20s" line the boardwalk. These grand dames are the best for location, history and style – but there are also dozens of more modern (and less expensive) hotels up and down the beach. Most hotels are open only April through October.

GRAND HOTEL ROYAL *** *Viale Carducci, 44. Tel. (39)(0584)451-51, Fax (39)(0584)314-38. Web: www.hotelroyalviareggio.it/royalviareggio-HomePageen-121.html.*

A beautiful reminder of Belluomini's design talents, the 105-room Grand Hotel Royal is an impressive piece of architecture inside and out. The lobby lives up to its name – grand, with touches of neo-Renaissance decor. Oh, and the breakfast room is huge and elegant. You would never guess it is part of the American Best Western

chain. From our seaside room, a lullaby of waves lapping at the shore put us to sleep each night of our stay, while stars twinkled into our room from above. The hotel also has a swimming pool and pretty grounds. Tennis and golf are available nearby.

GRAND HOTEL EXCELSIOR *** *Viale Carducci, 88. Tel. (39)(0584)507-26. Fax (39) (0584) 507-29. Web: www.excelsiorviareggio.it/*

A Chini-Belluomini hotel, the Excelsior is another exquisite example of the 1920's style. The original decor from its 1923 opening is still evident in much of the hotel's common areas.

HOTEL PRESIDENT **** *Viale Carducci, 5. Tel. (39)(0584)962-712, Fax (39)(0584)963-658. Web: www.hotelpresident.it.*

The white and gold building elegantly takes its place near the end of beach row. Hotel President is a luxury hotel, with all the amenities you would expect, including suites with Jacuzzi tubs. In some rooms, the beds are placed in an alcove guarded by two Roman-style columns. Lovely views over the sea. The dining room reflects cool elegance, with crisp white linens and dark wood trimmings. An outdoor café in a loggia on a top floor gives you a wonderful panoramic view of the sea.

I'M HUNGRY!

Viareggio has scores of very similar outdoor cafes, most specializing in seafood and pasta, up and down the boardwalk and within a couple blocks of the beach in town. There's no particular reason to travel far for a meal here, but the following are a few tried and true favorites for lunch or dinner:

L'OCA BIANCA $$$ *Via Coppino 409. Tel. (0584)388-477. Closed Tuesday. Near the port in the south of the city.*
Seafood at its best, including *aragosta* (Mediterranean lobster).

GIORGIO $$ *Via IV Novembre. Tel. (0584)444-93. Closed Wednesday.*
Less formal than L'Oca Bianca, but the seafood is equally succulent. Take a look at the artwork on display, all from local artists.

PASTICCERIA FAPPANI $ *Viale Maconi 1. Tel. (0584)962-582.*
Delicious pastries, *panini* (little sandwiches) and great cappuccino.

CARRARA

"Waterfalls of marble" is how our little girl described the white-capped mountains. Approaching Carrara, we at first thought the mountaintops were blanketed with snow. Not until we journeyed up one of the mountains to the *cave di marmo* (quarries), did we realize the snow was actually cascading white marble. This is the source of marble that prompted Michelangelo and many other great sculptors over the centuries to travel here and spend days exploring for just the right block.

Since the beginning, Carrara was mined for marble. The Romans around 80 BC carted marble off to decorate their forums with enormous monuments. Documentation of the Roman quarries can be found in the **Civic Marble Museum**, where a large collection of marble specimens from ancient times is exhibited.

Getting Here

Carrara, along with nearby Massa, Montignoso and the Lunigiana area form the province of Massa e Carrara.

By Train: On the Genova/Roma line, take the train to the Carrara/Avenza station.

By Bus: Check the CAT and CLAP bus lines for a schedule.

By Car: From Viareggio, take the A12 highway north along the coast about 30 kilometers and exit at Marina di Carrara. To visit the city center and ascend to the quarries, follow Via Aurelia and Viale XX Septembre for about 7 kilometers. With a family, we recommend driving to visit the quarries. A car will give you maximum flexibility to visit the quarries of interest and see the sights along the way.

THE QUARRIES—CAVE DI MARMO

Marble is a hard, homogeneous and compact stone with a crystalline structure. It is composed mainly of calcite (calcium carbonate). One of its characteristics is durability; it wears well in any climate.

Michelangelo, fussy about his marble, frequented Carrara in search of the perfect stone. Quarry 46 – **Polvaccio** – is named the Michelangelo quarry since this was the master's favorite spot. This area is known for producing highly valued marbles such as Statuario or Stauario Venato. Quarry 60, called **Cave Mandria**, possesses significant traces of ancient excavations. Quarry 48 – **Galleria Ravaccione** – is a particularly beautiful underground quarry with incredible views over the mountains. **Cave Fantiscritti** has been producing marble since ancient Roman times.

Follow signs from the town center to visit the quarries, or stop first at one of the two tourist offices (listed below) for information about tours and private guides.

MARBLE MUSEUMS

Visit the **Museo Del Cavatore** (*Via Colonnata 2/ter, Tel. (0585)703-28 or 730-48 or 758-005*) located near both **Cave Fantiscritti** and **Cave Colonnata** (which was founded originally as a penal colony for Roman slaves). Kids love this place. On display are ancient tools, two life-size marble oxen (unbelievable!) and other sculpture and quarry paraphernalia. A small shop offers knick-knacks and more expensive pieces made from the mountain's marble.

Parent Tip: We highly recommend this excursion. Our children loved the quarry and the museum. The mountains are a glorious backdrop for the excavation of marble. And the trip is the perfect indoor-outdoor activity to keep even high-energy kids engaged for a long time.

The larger, more formal **Museo Civico del Marmo** is also worth a look if you really want to learn more about the geology and geography of this area. It's chock full of marble history, marble art and marble memorabilia as well. It is located on Viale XX Settembre, the main road between the town, train station and beach (*Web: urano.isti.cnr.it:8880/museo/*

home.en.php; open 10am-8pm, closed Sundays, admission). Look into their guided marble tours.

Tourist Information
> *Web: www.comune.carrara.ms.it/Home.aspx (in Italian) or www.aptmassacarrara.it.*
> In central Carrara: **APT**, *Piazza 2 Giugno. Tel. (39)(0585)706-68.* They can provide a list of private guides to take you on a tour of the quarries.
> In Marina di Carrara: *Via Genova, Angolo Viale XX Settembre, Tel. (39)(0585)632-218.*

Fun Fact

How is the marble excavated? Ancient Romans exploited the natural cracks in the rock by inserting wooden wedges that were first soaked so that they would expand and widen the cracks. Or, after making a V-shape cut between two parallel cracks, iron wedges were inserted and then hammered. Believe it or not, these methods were used until the beginning of the 1700s, when explosives became the chosen means of excavating the marble. Explosives were delicately placed in a hollowed out underground passage and ignited. This process was called a "launch." Safety and environmental issues limited the life of such a procedure.

In the 1800s, a hellicoid wire was first used to excavate the marble. The wire was filled with particles of siliceous sand that cut through the rock through abrasion. With these wires attached to pulleys and

eventually driven by clutch motors, massive cuts could be made without wasting much of the natural resource. Today a "sprocket chain cutting machine" and the "diamond wire cutting machine," more flexible than the helicoid wire, are used to extract marble. You can learn all this – and climb on antique equipment used over the centuries – by stopping at the little roadside Museo del Cavatore on the road up to Fantiscritti and Colonnata quarries.

WHICH ONE IS MY ROOM?

While Carrara is an easy day trip from Viareggio and even Pisa and Lucca, if you decide to stay overnight we recommend the following hotel:

HOTEL MICHELANGELO *** *Corso Rosselli 3. Tel. (39)(0585) 777-161, Fax (39) (0585)745-45. Web: www.michelangelocarrara.it.*

A very quiet, charming hotel with modern (if smallish) rooms. The owners are an American and her Italian husband; they offer excellent advice for visiting the quarries. The hotel is informally reputed to be the best in the area. They have connecting doubles as well as three- and four-bed rooms to accommodate families.

I'M HUNGRY!

CAPINERA $ *Via Ulivi, 8. Tel. (39)(0585)742-94.*

Good food, plain and simple.

ROMA $$ *Piazza C. Battisti 1. Tel. (39) (0585) 706-32. Closed Saturday and during August and September.*

In the center of town, this is a great place for traditional Tuscan cooking.

SOLDAINI $$ *Via Maazzini, 11. Tel. (39) (0585) 714-59. Closed Sunday evening, Monday and during August.*

Popular with the locals.

CINQUE TERRE

Cinque Terre (five lands) is the name given to a mountainous stretch along the eastern coast of Liguria – just north of La Spezia and south of Genoa – upon which the five small towns of **Monterosso**, **Vernazza**, **Corniglia**, **Manarola**, and **Riomaggiore** are so precariously perched. Few spots in the world are as romantic and naturally beautiful as are the Cinque Terre. Carved into the mountainside, these towns tumble down into the azure blue water, where pirates once prowled the sea and shore for treasures. Differences in landscape, soil, height, and agriculture have meant that there is a tremendous variety of flora in the area, and some species of plants grow here and nowhere else.

Today the villagers are mostly farmers and fishermen, though some are testing the waters as hoteliers. The towns are hard to reach, being hemmed in between the sea and the mountains, and this has greatly helped to delay the devastating impact of mass tourism. Even today, the only way to get from one town to the other is along footpaths that wind along the cliffs – or by train or boat. It takes about five hours to walk from the first to the last of the five towns, but, as they are also linked by rail, the journey can easily be broken into stages.

If you're visiting the area in late May, you will be treated to the **Lemon Feast** in Monterosso (Saturday preceding Ascension Sunday). In August, Monterosso hosts a fireworks display over the sea. Check *www.cinqueterre.it* for exact dates.

So, let's go for a walk! The walks on narrow footpaths that weave their way around the mountain from town to town are gorgeous. Flowers and vines drape the footpath, the views of the sea are stunning. These walks run from about an hour to as long as five hours. A great adventure for older children, perhaps not such a good idea for younger ones. To walk from Riomaggiore, the southernmost village, to Monterosso, the most northern, takes the longest – five hours – with some tough walking along the way.

One night, while the last few tourists tossed back their wine, ready to head home by train, a group of children from Riomaggiore charged down the hill toward the piazza with soccer balls, squirt guns, skate boards and lots of laughter. There they played, practiced soccer moves and perfected the fine art of Italian socializing. Soon our children, shyly at first, approached the Italian kids aged about 4 to 14, hoping to be able to play. In no time, everyone was playing tag and sharing treats and having a good time under sparkling stars dancing in the late-evening sky.

Tourist Information

Tourist Association Cinque Terre, *Piazza Garibaldi, 29. Monterosso al Mare. Tel. (39)(0187)817-838. Fax (39)(0187)778-335. E-mail: informazioni@cinqueterre.it.*

WHICH ONE IS MY ROOM?
Monterosso

PALME **** *Via IV Novembere, 18. Tel. (39)(0187)817.541. 50 rooms. Web: www.hotelpalme.it/uk/home.htm.*

A small hotel located near the beach. We hear the owners are planning to put in air-conditioning, but check before you go. It gets awfully hot here in August.

ALBERGO VILLA ADRIANA ** *Via IV Novembre, 5. Tel. (39)(0187)818.109. Fax (39)(0187)818-128.* Situated 100 meters from the sea, Villa Adriana is a lovely two-star. The hotel has a private beach and a lush garden. PENSIONE RISTORANTE LA PINETA * *Via Padre Semeria, 3. Tel. (39)(187)829-101. Fax (39)(0187)829-029.* Clean and cheap, with a private beach.

Santa Margherita

VILLA GNOCCHI ** *Via Romana, 53. Tel./Fax (39)(0184)283-431.*
Amy, a neighborhood friend, encouraged us to include this charming stone farmhouse as a relaxing haven for families enjoying Cinque Terre. Her family of five enjoyed the location, nestled in cliffs high above Santa Margherita and the port of Portofino. Two small stone farmhouses are tenderly cared for by Roberto Gnocchi, which have been in his family for years. There are nine, double rooms divided between the two farmhouses – each with spectacular views of olive orchards that tumble seaward. Roberto and his wife Simona were the perfect hosts, according to Amy, making her family's stay even more delightful.

I'M HUNGRY!
Cooking is high art in Liguria, Cinque Terre being a fine example of this honored tradition. Most restaurants will serve some of the world's best pesto and grilled fish. Also, try the soup of the season.

Monterosso

RISTORANTE PIZZERIA MIKY $ *Via Fegina, 104. (0187)817-608.*
Specializes in pizza and traditional Ligurian cuisine. Good place for fish.
RISTORANTE VELVEDERE $$ *Via Garibaldi, 38. (0187)817-033.*
Sit outside under the umbrellas and enjoy the soft sea breeze. The food is okay, given that everything else was so marvelous, but the location is grand
RISTORANTE L'ALTA MAREA $$ *Via Roma, 54. (0187)817-170.*
A warm and pleasant atmosphere, with outdoor seating. Expect and savor the traditional fare. Service is extremely friendly.

Vernazza
TATTORIA GIANNI FRANZI $ *Piazza Marconi, 5. (0187)821-1003.* Known for the pesto, this restaurant also serves up great down-home Ligurian recipes.
TRATTORIA DEL CAPITANO $ *Tel. (0187)812-224.* The view is as heavenly as the food. Pesto and grilled fish are our recommendations.

THE HILL TOWNS OF CHIANTI

Silvery olive trees cling to golden brown hills, while vineyards tumble up and down the rolling soil. This glorious patchwork of color and texture is Tuscany. Bicycling or driving through the heart of Tuscany are the best ways to discover the region, to meet her people, taste the fruits of her labor and enjoy living. So many towns tucked in the hills of Tuscany are worth getting to know. Here are a few we've stumbled on during our journeys.

GREVE

Located on scenic Route 222, about 25 kilometers south of Florence, on the way to Siena, Greve is the wine capital of Chianti country. It hits its stride in September during the wine fair. While the main piazza is tiny, it is charming.

Wine is abundant in Greve. Stop in several *enoteca* (wineshops) located under the porticos around the piazza. We liked **Enoteca del Chianti Classico** (*www.chianticlassico.it*). A lovely shop for art is the **Galleria Civetta** (*www.galleriacivetta.it*). The kids loved the Saturday market of clothes, handbags and cheap toys. A playground and field are located right outside of town and there are several castles to visit in the area. Pick up the local paper, *Chianti News,* in several languages including English, for ideas on other itineraries.

MONTEFIORALLE

Montefiorale is 1 km straight up from Greve. When battles ensued in the valley, locals hiked up to Montefioralle to escape the ravages of war. The old octagonal walls, tower house and two Romanesque churches are still intact. Children love the castle and are especially thrilled with the little playground sitting amidst the vineyard. Roosters, cats and dogs make their way around the grounds of this charming old but still working village.

VIGNAMAGGIO

About 1 kilometer east of Greve, this small, walled hill town is about 28 kilometers from Florence and 12 kilometers from Siena. Famous for its place in history as the birthplace of the world-renowned Mona Lisa.

PANZANO

About 6 kilometers south of Greve. Stay at the **Villa Barone** (see details in *Which One is My Room?*) for a great local experience.

CASTELLINI IN CHIANTI

Just off SS 222, this hilltop village, a former Etruscan settlement, is one of the most charming of the hill towns. The old circle of fortified walls remains virtually intact, with houses peeking out from various parts of the wall. In spring and summer, baskets overflowing with colorful geraniums dangle from homes and establishments. The browns and grays of the wall, castle and towers are framed by olive trees, lemon bushes and the deep blue Tuscan sky.

Of course, the children love the Rocco, a huge fortress signaling power and a "you-better-not-mess-with-me" attitude to all Tuscan warlords of the past. But most enchanting is the underground walkway, **Via della Volte**, built in the 15th century to help defend the city. Openings in the sidewalls give quick glimpses of the magnificent countryside. Our son ran through the walkway, dropping to the ground to peer out of the openings at imaginary attackers – in his case unwanted vagabonds from his own version of Star Wars.

RADA IN CHIANTI

Yet another well-preserved medieval town, 32 kilometers to Siena, 49 kilometers to Florence, off of SS429. The narrow streets zigzag around the fortified city, past the walls now supporting homes, past the sleepy Palazza Comunale to the still strong fortified walkway. Rada provides a maze of delights and wonder for children and adults who enjoy discovering the secrets of an ancient city.

Stop in at one of the many *enotecas* in the village, where you can buy wine, olive oil or vinegar.

WHICH ONE IS MY ROOM?
Greve
ALBERGO DEL CHIANTI *** *Piazza Matteotti 86, Tel. (39)(055)853-763. Web: www.albergodelchianti.it.*

A lovely place to stay, with a pool set in a lovely garden of lemon bushes and old stone walls. Only 16 rooms. Enjoy the wine and olive oils produced by the owners. They also run La Castellana, a restaurant situated in the Castle of Montefioralle about 1 kilometer away.

HOTEL CASPRINI *** *Via Giovanni Falcone, 68/70 in Passo dei Pecorai. Tel. (39)(055)850-715 or 850-716. Fax (39)(055)850-495. Web: www.cdaomero.com.*

Located a few kilometers outside of Greve, this is an inexpensive roadside hotel, with great family rooms. The owner, Luca Casprini, his wife and father, take great care of you during your stay – Luca's dad enjoyed our rambunctious little ones. Watch Italian bicyclists zoom by early on weekend mornings. Ask Luca to show you his family's wine cellar.

Vignamaggio

VILLA VIGNAMAGGIO, *Via Petriolo, 5. Tel. (39)(055)854-6653, Fax (39)(055)854-6676. Web: www.vignamaggio.com.*

This exquisite villa is cradled in the hillside outside of Greve. Lisa Gherardini, better known as Mona Lisa, was born here in 1479 (now we know why she was smiling).

Look out among the silvery olive trees, pointed cypresses and rows of vineyards. The villa is awash in soft pink plaster with hints of gold. The gardens are stunning. There is a playground and a pool. For a sneak peak at this resort's beauty, watch Kenneth Branagh's *Much Ado About Nothing*. The movie was filmed here.

Panzano

VILLA LE BARONE *** *Tel. (39)(055)852-621. Fax (39)(055)852-277. Web: www.villalebarone.com.*

This villa allows you to live like a Tuscan lord. A tranquil spot, just a half-hour away from Florence and Siena. The resort has a gorgeous pool overlooking a panorama of the Tuscan countryside. Enjoy tennis at the hotel and golf nearby.  Antique-filled common rooms and two connecting double-rooms for families. Twenty-eight rooms in all.

Castellini in Chianti

LA CASTELLINA *** *Via Ferruccio, 22, Tel. (39)(0577)741-867. Fax (39)(0577)740-386. Web: www.lacastellina.it/english/index.html.*

Located in the Palazzo Squarcialupi, near the underground walkway, complete with a wine cellar, frescoed common areas and a charming terrace from which to sip the local wine.

Rada in Chianti

RELAIS VIGNALE **** *Via Pianigiani, 8. (39)(0577)738-300, Fax (39)(0577)738-592. Web: www.vignale.it. Open: April through October.*

Enjoy the life of a "podesta" (mayor or big-shot) here. The 27 rooms, three of which are suites and another nine annexed to the restaurant, are well-appointed with antique furnishings. Common areas are cozy, one with a fine stone fireplace, and they overlook the countryside. The pool and courtyard come with a view. And the *enoteca* and restaurant offer the best of Tuscany. The local products, including wine, grappa, olive oil and vinegar can be purchased at the *enoteca.*

I'M HUNGRY!

Greve

Lunch at **Café Lepanto** on the piazza is a good bet.

Castellini in Chianti

The risotto was exceptional at the **Trattoria "La Torre**, *Piazza del Comune, 15, Tel. (39)(0577)740-236.* For pizza, try **Pizzeria il Fondaccio**, *Via Ferruccio, 27. Tel. (39)(0577)741-084.*

SIENA

Sibling rivalry pales in comparison to the internecine squabbling between Florence and Siena. Florence, with its big-sister flair for the intellectual, and Siena's I-can-do-anything-better-than-you attitude, battled furiously over the years for the right to rule the roost in Tuscany. Their rivalry was so fierce that during the Middle Ages, Siena at first sided with the Guelphs, but quickly switched to the Ghibelline banner so as not to be on the same side as Florence. While Siena surprised even her leaders by trouncing the Florentines at the Battle of Montaperti in 1260, Siena never again came close to being the dominant Tuscan town.

Little of note happened in Siena after the Renaissance – either artistically or in enterprise – until it became a hot spot for the literati in the 1830s, particularly Elizabeth Barrett Browning, Robert Browning and Henry James. Since then, Siena has rebuilt itself as a cultural city. And what a delightful, lively, even riotous town it is.

Palio

Siena's true colors show during Palio season, the more than 800-year-old medieval horse race held twice a year in the summer – on July 2 and August 16. Being here for Palio is the equivalent of being in Washington, D.C., for the Fourth of July. Boys from the 'hoods" – in Siena the all-important neighborhoods, or parishes, are called *contrade* – don their medieval garb to flaunt neighborhood pride in a parade and horse race to beat all horse races.

Whether or not you see the race, don't miss the elaborate procession through the streets of Siena that precedes it. Hundreds of Sienese don medieval attire and march as bishops, wealthy businessmen and soldiers. The children especially enjoyed watching the knights parade, some on horseback, others on foot sweating it out in full armor.

Seating for the race is by ticket with "I-can't-believe-these-are-so-small" stadium seats set up around the perimeter of the *Campo*; there also is luxury seating in boxes high above. If you have connections, use them. Part of the enjoyment of this event is watching slightly larger middle-age men squeeze into the tiny spaces allotted for one person on the temporary benches. Most Sienese, however, prefer to stand in the middle of the track, where it is crowded, rowdy and difficult to see the pageantry and race in progress.

We recommend spending the money to reserve seats in the bleachers. Order tickets through your hotel when you reserve your room, or contact Tourist Information – in either case, at least a month in advance. While there are 17 *contrade*, only 10 horses get to race because of limited space. Hence, it is held twice a

> **Fun Fact**
>
> There are 17 contrades, all with an animal as its symbol. Look for sculptures, banners and other signs of the animal that mark each neighborhood: Aquila (eagle), Bruco (caterpillar), Chiocciola (snail); Civetta (owl), Drago (dragon), Giraffa (giraffe), Istrie (porcupine), Leocorno (unicorn) Lupa (wolf), Nicchio (mussel shell), Oca (goose), Onda (dolphin), Pantera (panther), Selva (rhinoceros), Tartaruga (turtle), Torre (elephant), Valdimontone (ram).

year so that all *contrades* get at least one chance to win the coveted palio. Il Palio is not for the faint of heart, nor is it for some young children. It is a wild race, with horses and riders thundering around hairpin turns in the *Campo*. Jockeys are flung from their horses, sometimes stomped on by the oncoming horse traffic. At the race we attended, several elated (and no doubt inebriated) men from the winning *contrade* enthusiastically

dashed onto the track to greet the victorious jockey. The next group of horses, which did their best to dodge the humans, trampled them. Luckily, everyone was able to limp off the track, but it was a hair-raising experience for those of us new to the ways of the Palio. Both of our children had dreams of horses chasing them that night, and we do have regrets for taking young children to this occasionally violent event.

Parent Tip: Pick your favorite **contrade** before the race and spend time in their neighborhood. In the morning of the race, each horse is marched into the contrade's parish church and led up to the altar for a special blessing! All the neighbors come out for this event. And, if the horse leaves a little something on the altar, all the better – it's a sign of good luck! After the blessing, march out to one of the piazzas and watch the procession of contrades (ideally, watch it from the Piazza del Duomo, where it begins). Before the parade ends, dash inside the Campo to find your seats so that you can watch the parade march onto the field. Cheer for your contrade's *alfieri*, the famous flag-throwers. What is the palio? It's a gorgeous banner that is drawn into the stadium by oxen cart and hangs until the next race in the winner's *contrade*.

Besides the Palio, there are other more genteel sights to see in Siena. Ground zero for your walks around the old walled town is the brick-paved **Campo**. The site of an old Roman forum, this fan-shaped bowl of a piazza is perhaps the most picturesque in Tuscany.

Getting Here

By Car: From Florence and points north you can choose the superfast *Superstrada*, which will take about one hour. Or, you can select a more scenic route: from Florence, we recommend the SS222 through Chianti country, approximately a two-hour drive. From the south, take SS326 through Sinalunga, or the more scenic SS73 via Monte Sansovino.

Parking is almost impossible inside the walls of Siena, unless your hotel is near a gate and provides a garage. Follow the signs for parking near the *Stadio* (signs have a soccer ball on them). You will find paid parking inside the *Fortezza* (look for the big "P" sign).

By Train: Trains run frequently between Florence (one hour), Rome (two hours) and other nearby cities. The station is located about 1 1/2 kilometers from the center of Siena. You can either take a bus up to the city, or hire a taxi (there is a taxi stand outside the station at either end).

By Bus: Bus service connects Siena with most towns in southern Tuscany. The station is at Piazza San Domenico, on the west side of Siena near San Domenico church. The station has a tourist and hotel information booth.

PALAZZO COMMUNALE & CIVIC MUSEUM

Il Campo. Museum open daily 9am-6pm in summer. 9:30am-1:30pm in winter.

A glorious paean to the past, the brick and stone palace that rises imperiously over *Il Campo* continues to house the city administrative offices as well as the must-see **Museo Civico**, which occupies the top floors. Above the palazzo and Campo soars the **Torre di Mangia**, symbol of Siena. Be sure to look for the **Sala dei Nove**, the meeting room for the Council of Nine, who ruled the Republic of Siena from 1287 to about 1350. There is also a splendid collection of Sienese paintings, including pre-Renaissance masterpieces by Simone Martini and Guido da Siena.

Do you see the she-wolf on the facade? No, this is not the nurturer of Rome's founders, Romulus and Remus. Instead, this wolf is the nanny to **Senius** and **Ascius**, the sons of Remus. Tradition holds that the two boys founded Siena, one riding a black horse, the other a white one. Not surprisingly the city's shield is black and white.

Don't pass up climbing the **Torre di Mangia** (*open daily 10am-3:30pm, in summer sometimes until 7pm*). It is a harrowing climb, but well worth it. Imagine looking over the *Campo* encircled by the magnificent Tuscan landscape.

THE CATHEDRAL

Open 9am-7:30pm in summer, 7:30am-1:30pm and 2:30pm-5pm in winter.

Sienese for centuries rejoiced at one of Europe's most splendid facades, overflowing with saints, prophets and philosophers. Siena's Duomo was among the first Gothic cathedrals in central Italy. Construction began in 1200 and was not substantially completed until the 1400s. The sparkling mosaics, completed in the 1800s by Venetian artisans, are divine. The inside is as delightfully decorative as the intensely striped marble of the facade. Nicola Pisano completed the Carrara marble pulpit around 1280. Also take a close look at the stained glass – always interesting because they served as educational comic books about religion for the congregation, since only the most privileged could read in those days.

Near the Piccolomini Altar, off the left aisle, is the **Piccolomini Library** (*open daily 10am-1pm, 2:00pm-5:00pm and 9:00am-7:30pm. Admission.*) The library, with frescoes by Pinturicchio, was built for Aeneas Silvius, a member of Siena's version of the Medicis who eventually became Pope Pius II.

MUSEO DELL'OPERA – CATHEDRAL MUSEUM
Piazza Duomo, 8. Open 9am-7:30pm March 16 through October; 9am-1:30pm Nov through March 15. Admision. Web: www.operaduomo.siena.it.

The entrance to the Museo dell'Opera Metrolpolitana is around the right side of the museum, in what would be the cathedral's right transept. This is the place to come to see the original statuary from the facade, long ago taken in from the weather, carved by famous sculptors including Pisano, Urbano da Cortona and Jacopo della Quercia. There are also famous altarpieces that once hung inside the museum, including the *Maesta* by Duccio di Buoninsegna. From the top floor be sure to take the stairway up to the nave, where you can enjoy a splendid view over the city.

OSPEDALE DI SANTA MARIA DELLA SCALA
Open daily, usually between 10:30am-4m.

In the 9th century this was one of the world's greatest hospitals. Now it is home to one of Siena's art museums. Throughout are remnants of the old hospital – in the lobby area, **Sala dei Pellegrini**, are huge frescoes that depict events associated with the hospital. Care of abandoned children, or *getatelli* which means little ones thrown away, are featured in the wall painting.

The legend of the hospital's founding is pictured in another part of the fresco. Tradition has it that a cobbler named Sorore opened a hostel and infirmary for travelers making a pilgrimage to Rome. His mother had a vision on the spot of babies ascending a ladder into heaven and being greeted by Mary. A hospital was soon added to Sorore's hostel.

PINACOTECA NAZIONALE
Palazzo Buonsignori. Via S. Pietro, 29. Open daily 9am-7pm, Monday 8:30am-1:30pm, Sunday 8am-1pm. Admission.

This museum houses the largest collection of Sienese paintings, including the city-state's greatest masters from the 12th century through the first half of the 17th century. This peerless collection of Sienese art is arranged chronologically to help museumgoers acquaint themselves with the development of art trends in the city.

Tourist Information
APT, *Piazza del Campo, 56. Tel. (39)(0577)280-551. Email: infoaptsiena@terresiena.it. Web: www.terresiena.it/index.php?option=com_ contact&view=contact&id=1%3Aapt-siena&catid=12%3Aapt-siena&Itemid=18&lang=en.*

WHICH ONE IS MY ROOM?
If you arrive without a reservation, try the **Hotel Information Center** at the central bus terminus, Piazza San Domenico, open Monday-Saturday 9am-8pm; *Tel. (0579)288.084.*

Expensive
PALAZZO RAVIZZA *** *Pian dei Mantellini 34, near Porta Laterina. Tel. (39)(0577)280-462. Fax (39)(0577)271-597. Web: www.palazzo ravizza.it.*

This old town house on Pian dei Mantellini is a gorgeous 30-room hotel located right on the city wall. The common areas are stone and wood, cool and calm. Ask for room 6, if you don't mind staying in one large room. Marble columns and an archway separate the outer room from the bedroom – the children slept on rollouts that were quite comfortable. Open the tall shutters to reveal a lovely view of the Tuscan countryside. Down below is a cozy terrace for dining, complete with a small garden that is home to several large tortoises and some rather spry lizards. Our kids were kept busy turtle spying, while we enjoyed a romantic meal. The food – *molto bene*. This is the place parents will consider returning to for a second honeymoon.

VILLA SCACCIAPENSIERI **** *str.di Scacciapensieri 10. Tel. (39) (0577) 414-41. Fax (39) (0577) 270-854. Web:www.villascacciapensieri.it/ en/home.html.*

Swimming pool, tennis courts and a stunning garden – all this in the

heart of Tuscany, in a more relaxed rural setting away from the narrow stone alleyways of Siena. Don't forget, though, *La Dolce Vita* comes with a hefty price tag. There are 28 rooms and all modern amenities. A regular bus service brings you to Siena's gates in fifteen minutes.

Moderate
ALBERGO MINERVA *** *Giuseppe Garibaldi 72, Tel. (39)(0577)284-474, Fax (39)(0577)43-343, Web: www.albergominerva.it.*
Plain and simple, with a view of old Siena and the historic center. There are 59 rooms, decorated in a modern style. Quite comfortable.

Inexpensive
IL GIARDINO ** *Via Baldassare Peruzzi 35. Tel. (39)(0577)285-290. Fax (39)(0577)221-197. Web: www.venere.com/hotels/siena/hotel-il-giardino.*
A good deal, since it includes a swimming pool. Located near Porta Pispini with a nice view.
PICCOLO HOTEL ETRURIA ** *Via delle Donzelle 3. Tel. (39) (0577)288-088. Fax (39)(0577)288-461. Web: www.hoteletruria.com/index_eng.html.*
Near the Campo, off Via Banchi di Sotto. You can't beat the price. Newly remodeled and friendly, efficient service. Book well ahead during high season. Highly recommended by fellow travelers.

I'M HUNGRY!
RISTORANTE PIZZERIA SPADA FORTE $$ *on the Campo.*
Can't beat the location. Great people-watching spot and lots of room for the kids to play. A wide selection of pizza and, if you're daring, wild boar (*cinghiale alle senese*).
DA ENZO $$-$$$ *Via Camollia 49. Tel. (0577)281-277. Closed Monday.*
A standout for traditional fare, including fish, fowl and wild boar. Good homemade pasta selection. Truffles, when in season, are a special treat here.

TULLIO AI TRE CRISTI $$$ *Vicolo Provenzano. Tel. (0577)280-608. Closed Tuesday.*

Not surprising for a restaurant open since 1830, this one serves some of the most traditional and authentic Tuscan cuisine in Siena. Try (if you dare) the tripe with sausages, the wonderful stuffed guinea fowl (*faraona*), and the roast boar.

OSTERIA LE LOGGE $$-$$$ *Via del Porrione, 33. Tel. (0577)48-013. Closed Sunday.*

Rustic dining at its best. Owner Gianni Brunelli's cookbook is available in English. The fare is traditional Tuscan, so look for hearty soups, grilled meat and fresh pasta.

DA VASCO $ *Via del Capitano, 6/8. Tel. (0577)288-094.*

Steps from the Duomo, the restaurant is plain, simple and good for the price. We always enjoy the *penne all'arrabbiata* (tomato, garlic and pepper sauce – too hot for our kids).

SAN GIMIGNANO

San Gimignano is one of the best-preserved medieval hill towns in Tuscany, and every tour bus company knows it. This little village is swarming with visitors during the high season (and most weekends anytime). The walkway up to the center is lined with very upscale gift shops, wine stores and boutiques – making San Gimignano a little bit like an American shopping mall with a medieval theme. Nevertheless, despite the onslaught of tourists, San Gimignano maintains its charm. However, if you prefer a less commercialized hill town, Lucca or Cortona are better bets.

The children loved checking out the town's famous towers – 15, if you're counting. At one point, during the 1300s, the tiny town boasted 70 towers, which were built by wealthy families competing to stay a head taller than the Joneses.

To enter the city, walk through Porta San Giovanni and follow the street with the same name up the hill to the Piazza della Cisterna, which holds the town's well. Next to Piazza della Cisterna is the Piazza del Duomo. On one side is the Palazzo del Podesta and, on the other side, the Palazzo del Popolo, with the taller tower.

Parent Tip: Our kids loved finding each hill town's **well**, some quite beautiful and well preserved. We took pictures at each well and made cute collages when we got home. The children also had fun making wishes at each well.

Getting Here

By Car: From the north, take AI South and exit at Firenzie/Certosa. Follow the signs to Siena for about 30 kilometers. Exit at Poggibonsi Nord and follow signs to San Gimignano (about 11 kilometers). From the south, take A1 North and exit at Valdichiana. Drive toward Betolle-Sinalunga. Exit at Poggibonsi-Siena and follow the signs for San Gimignano (about 11 kilometers). There is a carport outside the main gate, Porta San Giovanni.

By Train: The train station is 11 kilometers away. Sometimes it is difficult to make a bus connection. We recommend either driving or taking the bus directly from Siena or Florence to San Gimignano.

By Bus: Buses are more frequent from Siena than Florence, although the Florence buses do run several times daily. The Siena bus line is the TRA-IN and the trip is about 38 kilometers. Expect to change buses in Poggibonsi. From Florence to San Gimignano it's about an hour and a half trip. All buses will leave you at the main entrance to the town, Porta San Giovanni. San Gimignano is a car-free town.

CIVIC MUSEUM

Go through the archway at the Palazzo del Popolo, and cross a quaint courtyard to the Museo Civico (open November-February 9:30am-12:50pm and 2:30pm-4:50pm and March-October 9:30am-7:30pm. Closed Monday). The Civic Museum contains wonderful works from Siena and Florence. Lovers of Dante should note the Sala del Consiglio or Sala di Dante, where the poet addressed the crowds in 1299 as ambassador of Florence. His job: convince the people to join the Guelph League. Take the kids up the Torre Grosso to see an amazing view of San Gimignano and the countryside.

Also in the Piazza del Duomo is the church, or **Collegiata**. To the left, is a small courtyard where musicians sometimes play in the summer. On one of our visits, a stage was built in this piazza and we enjoyed an outdoor snack while watching rehearsals for an upcoming opera.

Need to burn off some energy after spending too much time in the car? Hike up to the **Rocca**, the town's old fortress, which enjoys one of the best panoramic views of the neighboring countryside.

Tourist Information
Piazza del Lduomo, 1. Tel. (39)(0577)940-008. Web: www.sangimign ano.com.

WHICH ONE IS MY ROOM?
LA CISTERNA HOTEL *** *Piazza della Cisterna. Tel. (39)(0577)940-328, Fax (39) (0577)942-080. Web: www.hotelcisterna.it.*
Cool stone columns and archways remind you that La Cisterna is a 14th-century building turned into a hotel. The 50 rooms, furnished in a Florentine style, all include air-conditioning phone and TV. It is located across from the old well in the town square. Splendid views of the countryside and a great restaurant (see below) make La Cisterna a great Tuscan retreat.
HOTEL LEON BIANCO *** *Piazza della Cisterna. Tel. (39)(0577)941-294 Fax: (39)(0577)942-123 Web: www.leonbianco.com.*
Hotel Leon Bianco captures the medieval spirit and sprinkles it with all modern conveniences. The view over the Piazza, especially at night, is stunning. Countryside views are equally magnificent from most of the 25 rooms. Dining outside on the enclosed terrace is an added plus.
LA COLLEGIATA *** *Localita Strada 27. Tel. (39)(0577)943-201 Fax (39) 0577)940-566. Web: www.lacollegiata.it.*
Located just outside of San Gimignano, La Collegiata is situated amidst a beautiful garden. Originally it was a stone convent, transforming over the past 400 years into a welcoming hotel. All rooms have a splendid view. The common areas – a library, sitting rooms and dining area – are situated around a stone courtyard with its own stone well. And, it has a swimming pool.

I'M HUNGRY!
LE TERRAZZE IN THE HOTEL CISTERNA $$$ *Piazza della Cisterna. Closed Tuesday and Wednesday for dinner. Tel. (39)(0577)940-328.*

Book ahead for a window seat – it's well worth it. While you savor some of the best food in Tuscany, your eye spans the brilliant Elsa Valley – from Monteriggioni to Siena. The restaurant has a wood-beamed ceiling and wonderful window arches. The food is *soooo* good and the children were treated like a prince and princess. We will come back to San Gimignano simply for the treat of eating in this restaurant.

OSTERIA DELLE CATENE $$ *Via Mainardi 18. Tel. (39)(0577)941-966. Closed Wednesday.*

Saffron soup and a casserole with Chianti wine are two specials at this moderately priced restaurant specializing in regional cuisine.

IL PINO $$ *Via San Matteo 102. Tel. (39)(0577)940-415. Closed Thursday.*

Great traditional cuisine (especially the truffles!) and scandalous homemade dessert. Very good value; relaxed atmosphere.

LA GRIGLIA $$$ *Via San Matteo 34. Tel. (39)(0577)940-005. Closed Thursday.*

Truffles and game are the specialty here. Maybe a bit formal for young children.

MONTEPULCIANO & MONTALCINO

Leaving the Lake Trasimeno region, we decided to take the long way to Rome by driving through some of the world's finest and most beautiful wine country. Just across the Umbrian border in Tuscany sits **Montepulciano** (*www.montepulciano.com*), best known for its Vino Nobile di Montepulciano – an excellent wine. Stop by for lunch, or simply to shop at any of the wonderful enoteche around town.

Driving west and slightly south lies **Montalcino** (*www.montalcino.net*), another world famous wine region. Taste the dark Brunello and you'll understand why it is so highly regarded. Rather than champagne, we enjoyed a good Brunello upon the birth of each of our children!

This region of Italy is a magical place: rolling hills, with medieval towns jutting up from the rock. Low clouds encircling cities. Our teens found the scenery interesting, serene, and either dozed or read during our drive in the Tuscan countryside. We plan to come back soon.

CORTONA

Since antiquity the clouds have paid homage to Cortona, wrapping it in a soft, airy crown. From below, the city vanishes in the white puffs. From above, everything is awash in thick mist. Cortona has managed, during an age of globalism and encroaching tourism, to remain blanketed in the mystery of its past. And there is beginning to be a market in that for the Cortonese.

One shopkeeper told us that life has changed for Cortona since the publication of *Under the Tuscan Sun,* a best-selling, thoroughly enjoyable book by Frances Mayes. For a while the book became the tourist's bible. One tucked the book under the arm while touring the city and searching for Bramasole, the author's farmhouse and subject of the book. It's there, just outside the city walls, with the old Roman road nearby to lead you into the city. So far, Cortona has maintained the balance between being a working town and a tourist attraction. It's a lively city, filled with old women hobbling up and down the steep hills, young schoolchildren enjoying an afternoon break in the square, friendly shopkeepers and American university students from a University of Georgia program.

Most interesting to the visitor, however, is Cortona's Etruscan heritage. A vast Etruscan system had been established in this area – from Arezzo to Chiusa and from Cortona to Perugia – called the *dodecapoli*, the twelve-city federation. Eventually they joined forces with the Romans. Like the rest of Italy, numerous factions rose to the top to control Cortona during the Middle Ages and beyond, just to be defeated by another group. Even the Medicis had a hold on Cortona for a while, after King Ladislas of Naples captured the city and sold it to Florence.

Getting Here

By Train: Take the train from Florence (or Rome) to Camucia, then take the frequent LFI bus for the remaining 5 kilometers east to Cortona.

By Car: From Florence, take the *Autostrada* toward Perugia, then turn north on SS71 to Cortona; keep following the "bullseye" signs for *centro*, since the old walled city center is halfway up the mountain

from the highway turnoff. Expect to park along the outer wall, near one of the gates, since only local traffic with garage parking is allowed inside the walls.

PIAZZA DELLA REPUBLICA & THE PALAZZO COMUNALE

This is the lively heart of Cortona and a great place to begin your strenuous walking excursions around this hilly town. Students come to sit on the steps, watching and talking and eating lunch. Inside the palazzo is the **city hall** and **council chamber**. When we went inside the doors to the council chambers were ajar. It is a stately old chamber, with dark-wood paneling and ornate decorations. We stepped cautiously inside. Apparently, there was a meeting of the city council the night before. Papers were strewn across the floor. And at the main table, where people testify, were a dozen empty bottles of water and Chianti.

PALAZZO CASALI & MUSEO DELL'ACCADEMIA ETRUSCA

Open April-September 10am-1pm and 4pm-7pm. In winter, 10am-1pm and 3pm-5pm. Closed Monday. Tel. (39)(0575)637-248. E-mail: www.accademia-etrusca@libero.it. Admission, except children under 8 are free.

Legend has it that the **Palazzo Casali** was built on the ruins of ancient Etruscan and Roman buildings. Initially it served as the headquarters for the Terziere di Santa Maria, or council of the medieval neighborhood called Saint Mary. It later was bought by the powerful Casali family, finally being turned over to Florentine administrators.

To the right of the palazzo is the **Museo dell'Accademia Etrusca**. Ascend the steep, old stone steps to enter the museum. The collection is divided into three sections: the archeological collection, the Egyptian collection and the Medieval and Modern collection. One of the most interesting pieces in the archeological section is the Etruscan bronze lamp on display in an elaborate structure. It was found in a field near Cortona in 1840 and has been dated to the second half of the 4th century BC. Our kids enjoyed this room, both the lamp and the statuettes in the glass case next to the lamp. But, beware, sensors around the lamp are sensitive. We accidentally set it off once just gazing up at the lamp from its post in the ceiling.

On the main floor is a small room devoted to Cortona's own Gino Severini (1883-1966). Several paintings, including *Maternity* (1916) plus numerous drawings in Cubist and Futurist allusions, are on display.

An English guide to the museum is available for free at the entrance.

PIAZZO DEL DUOMO & THE CATHEDRAL

A more-or-less nondescript church originally built in the 11th century and restored in 1560. Inside there is a mosaic by Severini. The Piazzo also is nothing spectacular, but has a great view and leads to the charming Via del Gesu/Jannelli.

MUSEO DIOCESANO

Across from the Duomo; open daily except Mon, April-September 10am-1pm and 4pm-7pm; October-March, open 9am-1pm and 3pm-5pm.

The museum snakes through nine exhibit halls and holds works of art dating from 200 AD to modern times. The artwork is mainly from the churches of Cortona. **Sala 3** is the former church of Gesu, which was deconsecrated in order to maintain the museum. Gaze up at the beautiful ceiling created by Michelangelo Leggi in 1536.

UP TO (& DOWN FROM) THE MEDICI FORTRESS

Walking tours in Cortona go in two directions – up, way up and down, down, down. The kids just loved the steep inclines, although they needed extra encouragement to reach the top. But the payoff is excellent – the Medici Fortress, which is great fun for kids and offers views over all of Cortona and surrounding countryside. For adults and art- or religious-inspired children, there are Severini's Stations of the Cross. See a bit below for more details on the fortress.

Parent Tip: Bring some water and plan to stay awhile. Our kids delighted in this fortress, running around and playing imaginary games for quite some time. This is the ultimate playground for medieval make-believe. Lots of "secret" paths, bordered by grasses so thick and deep, it pulls children in to enjoy the coolness of its depths. Great photo-ops here.

It wouldn't be a fortress unless it was perched atop the highest hill. Here, on the northeast corner of the rectangular city walls, at the top of a steep incline, rests the fortress commissioned by Cosimo I in 1556. Built on top of old Etruscan and Roman ruins, the fortress is a grand illustration of military architecture. In its old age, it enjoys a more pleasant life as host to art exhibitions and a research center dedicated to the study of peasant history of the Valdichiana and Lake Trasimeno areas. Enjoy the view and make sure to investigate the huge stones with Etruscan inscription outside the Fortress.

Now descend, by a different route. From S. Margherita, to the left down Via Crucis to see Severini's evocative *Stations of the Cross*.

DOORS OF THE DEAD

Down from the Piazza del Duomo is the **Via del Gesu/Jannelli**, a cobblestone medieval avenue where some homes boast the *porte del morto* (doors of the dead). Travel back to medieval times on this most picturesque jaunt and enjoy a lovely view of the valley.

SAN FRANCESCO

A relatively short walk up from Piazza della Republica it is to this charming, little church built by Brother Elias, a member of St. Francis' troop. Brother Elias and Luca Signorelli are buried here. Look for a piece of the Holy Cross retrieved from Constantinople by Brother Elias that is encased in an ivory reliquary on the high altar. From here, follow the wonderful Via Berrettini up to Piazza Pozzo and Piazza Pescaia to the neighborhood near San Nicolo. Follow the sign to Chiesa di S. Nicole, walking up Vicolo S. Nicolo – the church is 100 yards on the right in its own courtyard.

CHIESA DI SAN NICCOLO TO SANTUARIO DI SANTA MARGHERITA

St. Nicholas's church was built in the beginning of the 15th century in Romanesque style. Luca Signorelli's fresco and paintings remain on display in the little church. Further up is the magnificent Church of Saint Margaret. In 1288 Saint Margaret along with St. Basil reconstructed an older church on this spot. In 1297, Margaret died in a small room at the back of the church. The Cortonese constructed a larger church designed by Giovanni Pisano in 1330, and they transferred the remains of Margaret to the larger church. Cortonese architect Domenico Mirri (1856-1939) designed the elegant facade and the saint's remains are located in a beautiful urn by Pietro Berrettini.

Bring water for the long, steep climb. A tiny café alongside the church has a wide variety of drinks and snacks, including ice cream, for your overheated family. Just a bit further up is the Medici Fortress. Come on, you've come this far.

SEVERINI'S STATIONS OF THE CROSS

The *Stations of the Cross* are stunning mosaics telling the story of Jesus's crucifixion. They are positioned at intervals up one of Cortona's steepest inclines, the **Via Crucis**, which is an alternative path up to the Medici Fortress. The mosaics were commissioned in 1947 by the city to give thanks for not having been struck during the war. We all made it up (we didn't realize that you could descend by this route from Santa Margherita), with a little coaxing for our six-year-old.

Our youngest discovered her own way to get up the hill. She took one of the many little balls she was collecting (for a coin, you could get these little balls in gumball-like machines in stores throughout Cortona). She would throw the ball up the hill and race up to get it before it started on its descent. The rest of us provided back up; big brother had a couple extra balls, just in case. It kept her mind off the hill!

PASSEGGIATA PUBLICA & THE PARTERRE (PUBLIC GARDENS)

At the very bottom of the descent from the Medici Fortress, below Severini's *Stations*, is the lovely, shaded public garden. From the center, at the end of Via Nazionale, near the Gothic church of San Domenico is the *Passeggiata Publica* and gardens. Best of all, there is a fun playground at the end of the public gardens, with slide, turn-around and swings. Our kids played there with newfound Italian friends, while we lazed under the trees on a bench, writing and dreaming of our next trip to Cortona. A pizza and ice cream parlor is open during summer months as well.

OLD ROMAN ROAD

Walk through the public garden, past the playground, to the chain across the road. Make a sharp left and an immediate sharp right. Follow the lane to the top, beneath the Medici fortress. A panoramic view greets you. Bring snacks, crayons and sketchpads for the kids. You'll have a grand and tranquil time. If you cannot resist taking a peak at Bramasole – the restored Cortona farmhouse and home of Francis Mayes, author of the best-selling *Under the Tuscan Sun* – it is located on the paved road at the bottom of the Old Roman Road (about 500 yards and on the left). Do not, of course, plan on paying a visit. There also are terrific views over Umbrian forest and farmland from this ridge behind the town.

THE MAZE

Katerina Ring, a young aspiring artist from the US, clued us in on "the maze." About two-thirds of the way back down from the Old Roman Road, as you walk toward the center, turn right up a short flight of steps. You are on a back road to the center of town. Kids love walking between the high walls, darting ahead and around corners. Katerina enjoyed the walk for more meditative reasons. You now can see her work in Lucca.

THE WALLS & THE GATEWAYS

The Etruscans around the end of the 5th century BC constructed the ring of walls outside the gates. The best preserved are on the west side. Four major gateways to the old city were created during the city's Roman era: Porta Santa Maria, Porta San Domenico, Porta Sant/Agostino and Porta Colonia (look for the Etruscan sewer spout in the area of Porta Colonia). During the Middle Ages, the double opening Etruscan gateway – Porta Bacarelli – was closed, but recently restored. Porta Montanina, Porta Berarda and Porta San Giorgio were opened during the Middle Ages; the last two were closed up probably during the 17th century. Finally, the Porta Santa Margherita was opened towards the end of the nineteenth century to give access to the nearby sanctuary of Santa Margherita.

Tourist Information
Via Nationale ,42. Tel. (39)(0575)630-353. Fax (39)(0575)630-181. Web: www.cortonaweb.net/eng/index.php.

WHICH ONE IS MY ROOM?
PORTOLE *** *Via Umbro Cortonese. 36. Tel. (39)(0575) 691.008/ 691-074. Fax (39)(0575)691-035. Web: www.portole.it.*

Located a few kilometers north of Cortona, along the mountain road

that helps to divide Tuscany and Umbria, is a modest but comfortable 20-room hotel in a garden setting. The family-run hotel is one of the friendliest we have visited during our tours of Italy – and one of the children's favorite places to stay. The morning fog was enchanting, making the small playground in the back a more exciting place to play. But the kids were on cloud nine climbing around on the old airplane, engine and other innards missing, which is the hotel's most obvious landmark. The owner, who served in the Italian air force, purchased the World War II aircraft and turned it into a charming curiosity for kids.

SAN MICHELE **** *Via Guelfa, 15. (39)(0575)604-348. Fax (39)(0575)630-147. Web: www.hotel sanmichele.net.*

An 18th-century building nestled inside the Etruscan walls. The two-level room in the tower has beautiful views. The rooms are beautiful and the hotel boasts a swimming pool as well. Ask for a cot for children.

HOTEL SAN LUCA *** *Piazza Garibaldi, 1. Tel. (39)(0575) 630-460/630-587. Fax (39)(0575) 630-105. Web: www.sanlucacortona.com/en/home.php.*

Plain and simple hotel, with one of the city's best restaurants, Tonino (see below). Seventy rooms, many with splendid views.

IL FALCONIERE **** *San Martino 370. Tel. (39)(0575) 617-679. Fax (39)(0575) 612-927. Web: english.ilfalconiere.it/mediacenter/FE/home.aspx.*

A luxury hotel four kilometers from town. A magnificent 16th-century villa, with a private chapel and well revered wine cellar. For the kids – a swimming pool. For us – wonderful antiques and canopy beds in the rooms.

I'M HUNGRY!

OSTERIA DEL TEATRO $$-$$ *Via Maffei, 5. Tel. (39)(0575)630-556. Closed Wednesday.*

Small, crowded tables give this *osteria* an intimate, family feeling. The walls are dotted with fun, theater pictures. Try the *risotto al carciofi* (artichoke risotta). Or, order the famous steaks of Chianina veal cooked in unique ways.

RISTORANTE TONINO $$$$ *Piazza Garibaldi. Tel. (39)(0575)630-500. Closed Monday evening and Tuesday.*

Elegant dining and excellent views over the valley. Come early for a window seat. Champagne and mint-green brocade tablecloths with Florentine dinnerware means dress the kids up a bit. The hot and  cold antipasto is mouthwatering. We recommend the *ravioli* with *pecorino* or the *ravioli* with *asparagi*. And the desserts are out of this world!

TRATTORIA PIZZERIA $ *Via Dardanno, 1. Tel. (39)(0575)629-32.*

Pizza per tutti! Your kids will have trouble deciding which pizza to order. An informal restaurant with pretty landscapes and ceramics dotting the walls.

LA GROTTO $$ *Piazetta Baldelli, 3. Tel. (39)(0575)630-271. Closed Tuesdays.*

Hidden off the main square, you'll have fun finding this restaurant, as you roam the narrow cobblestone streets. A wonderful selection of local cuisine.

PIZZA E FOCACCE $ *Via Benedetti, 6.*
In need of a quick slice of pizza? Best in town!

UMBRIA

Umbria is no longer a second sister to Tuscany. From the medieval splendor of **Assisi** to the chocolate heaven of **Perugia**, or from the sounds of jazz in **Orevieto** to the great outdoors at **Lago di Traesimano**, Umbrian towns hold their own as places to explore, learn and enjoy Italian life. Here are a few of the special places our family discovered during trips to Umbria. *Visit www.umbriaonline.com for more info.*

PERUGIA

The formidable hill town has a dastardly past, especially if you were a pope. One pontiff killed himself in Perugia, while two others were poisoned (hope it wasn't by chocolate!) Nevertheless, Perugia has emerged from the ashes as Italy's version of Hershey, Pennsylvania. If you love chocolate, you must stop here.

After an evening *passeggiata* down the lively Corso Vannucci, stop at the bar **Ferrari** (*Corso Vannucci, 43*) for a taste of Perugia's own Baci candy. Or try the beautiful **Sandri**, just down the street. Other pastry shops will tempt you as you stroll along the Vannucci. Be daring, try them all, you can't go wrong.

Or, visit the **Museo Storico Nestle Perugina** in nearby San Sisto (*Tel. (075)527-6796, Web: www.perugina.it/museo*) and arrange for a tour of the chocolate factory. And, yes, you get free samples at the end!! Your kids will owe you one. Just remember to call ahead to make reservations for the tour.

Getting Here
By Car: From Florence, take the *Autostrada* south until the junction for Siena and Perugia; exit and follow signs to Perugia.

By Train: By way of Florence (2 1/2 hours) and Arezzo (1 1/2 hours). To Siena requires a change in Chiusi (3 1/2 hours). Another line connects Assisi (25 minutes) and Rome (3 hours). The main station at Piazza Veneto, called the FS station, is about 3 kilometers from the center of Perugia, at the bottom of a long hill. Buses connect to the center. The other station, FCU, used for more local connections, is closer up the hill.

By Bus: The bus station is near the FUC, closer to the city center. Buses leave frequently for Assisi and other Umbrian cities. About five leave daily for Chiuso, a train stop for the Florence-Rome connection. One bus line, SULGA coaches (*Tel. 500-9641*), provide connections to Florence and Rome, including their airports. The SENA (*Tel. 572-1266*) goes to Siena.

NATIONAL GALLERY OF UMBRIA
Corso Vannucci, 19 (Palazzo dei Priori). Tel. (39)(075)572-1009 Email: direzionegnu@libero.it. Web: www.perugiaonline.com/ perugia_gallerianazionaledellumbria.html. Open: Monday to Sunday 8:30am-7:30pm. Closed New Year's day, Christmas day, first Monday of each Month. Admission.

The museum houses the most significant collection of 13th- to 19th-century art from Umbria.

NATIONAL ARCHAEOLOGY MUSEUM OF UMBRIA
Corso Cavour, Piazza Giordano Bruno, 10. Tel. (0755)727.141. Web: www.perugiaonline.com/museipgus.html. Open all year from 8:30am to 7:30pm.

If you are a lover of all things Etruscan, this is the place for you. The museum is housed in the former monastery and cloister of the church of San Domenico. In an underground room next to the cloister is the grave of the Cai Cutu family, from around the third century BC. Also of particular interest is the Cippo Perugino, or Perugia Memorial Stone, which is a travertine block engraved with one of the longest inscriptions in the ancient Etruscan language. We've found our children intrigued by the Etruscans, a rather mysterious and highly artistic people. But, if this is your umpteenth visit to an Etruscan museum, remember to bring books, crossword puzzles, sketch pads or ipods for older kids to keep them occupied. Or, roll the dice to see which parent takes younger ones for a jaunt throughout the historic center searching for the perfect candy.

ETRUSCAN WELL (POZZO SORBELLO)

Piazza Danit, 18. Tel (39)(075)573-3669. Open April to October, Monday to Sunday 10am-1:30pm and 2:30pm-6:30pm, November to March, Monday to Sunday 10:30am-1:30pm and 2:30pm-5pm.

Built circa the third century BC, this well demonstrates the sophistication of the Etruscan's understanding of hydraulic engineering. It is 35 meters deep and 5 meters wide, suggesting that it was used to supply water to the city in the event of a siege.

MEDIEVAL BOTANICAL GARDENS

Borgo XX Giugno, 74. Tel. (39)(075)585.6432. Web: www.unipg.it/comunica/guide/site6.html. Open: Monday to Friday 8am-5pm and Sat. 8am-1:30pm. Closed: Saturday, Sunday and holidays.

So Italian – a garden that combines art and history, myth and sacred stories. And, an outdoor space for little ones to enjoy on a bright, sunny day in Perugia.

LA CITTA DELLA DOMENICA

Spagnolia srl Col di Tenda, just 2 kilometer from the center of Perugia. Tel. (39)(075)505-4941. Email: citta.delladomenica@libero.it. Web: www.perugiaonline.com/citta_della_domenica.html. Open: every day from 23 march to 15 September from 10am-7pm. From 16 September to 3 November open on weekends only. Admission.

From Florence, take A1 highway, Valdichiana exit, then take the motorway (without toll) to Perugia, drive as far as "Ferro di Cavallo exit and follow signs from there. From Rome: Take A1 highway to Orte exit, take highway (without toll) to Perugia via Todi, in Ponte S. Giovanni, drive towards Florence as afar as Ferro di Cavallo exit and follow signs.

Sometimes called Spagnolia, this city is a town of fables and associated adventures. There are playgrounds and train rides and a "Far West" exhibit, complete with cowboys. Look for the King Kong statue. The park was created by the Spagnolia family and, though it began as a playground and park for children, under the direction of Mariella Spagnolia, the park is turning its attention to the preservation of animal species and environmental protection. A fun, aesthetic and educational experience right outside the gates of Perugia.

Tourist Information
Piazza IV Novembre. Tel. (39)(075)572-332. Fax (39)(075)573-6828. Web: www.perugiaonline.com.

WHICH ONE IS MY ROOM?

Fell for the chocolate and lingered too long at the Piazza IV Novembre? Here are a few places to overnight in Perugia:

LOCANDA DELLA POSTA **** *Corso Vannuci, 97. Tel. (39)(075)572-8925, Fax (39)(075)572-2413. Web: www.locandadellaposta.com/indexen.htm.*

One of the oldest hotels in town, evident by its ornate exterior. Parking garage makes it easier for drivers.

PRIORI ** *Via Vermiglioli, 3. Tel. (39)(075)57-3378. Fax (39)(075)583-3213.*

Great location in the historic center. Located in a recently renovated historic building.

LA ROSETTA **** *Piazza Italia, 19. Tel. (39)(075)572-0841. Fax (39)(075)572-0841. Web: www.umbriaonline.com/larosetta.*

Located in the heart of Perugia, a beautiful hotel decorated primarily in 1920s style, with a few rooms on the first floor resplendent in 18th-century furniture and paintings.

HOTEL IRIS ** *Via Marconi, 37. Tel. (39)(075)572-0259 Fax. (39)(075)573-6882. Web: www.perugiaonline.com/hoteliris.*

Also located in the center of historic Perugia near the Rocca Paolina fortress, the view from the Hotel Iris is the city and hills surrounding Perugia. It's a stunning 17th-century building, with comfortable rooms, each with lovely paintings.

The Scoop on Gelato

Try the Gelateria Veneta, *Corso Vannucci, 20*. Take your gelato to the Piazza IV Novembre and savor its sweetness as you and the kids people-watch.

I'M HUNGRY!

PAIOLO $ *Via Augusta, 11. Tel. (39)(075)572-5611. Closed Wednesday and part of August.*
Great pizza at good prices.
LA BOTTE $-$$ *Via Volte della Pace, 33. (39)(075)572-2679. E-mail: labotte@perugia online.com.*

Traditional Umbrian fare – from black truffles to grilled meat – is delicious. And, for fussy children, there is a good list of pizzas, all baked in a wood-fired oven. This restaurant is conveniently located in the city center.

DERUTA

Italian ceramics are known the world over for their fine quality, rich colors and ancient tradition. All this and more can be found in this tiny town situated southeast of Perugia. We learned about Deruta from our friends Suzie and Bill Menard, co-owners of Bella Italia, a great shop in Bethesda, Maryland, for ceramics, Italian food, travel books and more (www.bellaitaliaonline.com). Our last trip to Italy, over the Christmas and New Year holidays, we decided to base ourselves in charming Deruta to take day trips around Umbria. But, once we got to the town, we realized there are places to go in Deruta, as well.

Little is known of the origins of this town, except for the Etruscan and Roman artifacts found dating back to the 4th century BC. The small town faced numerous obstacles – from the devastation of the plague in the 14th century to several sacks in following centuries. However, by the end of the 15th century, peace settled over Deruta and the artistry of ceramics was

born. In modern times, Deruta took the lead in founding the Associazione Italiana Citta della Ceramica, a nonprofit group comprised of 33 Italian municipalities to promote the art and tradition of Italian pottery.

We certainly came to appreciate the talent

involved in ceramic production and were touched by a special heartwarming experience all travelers hope passes their way. Late one evening, we peeked into the window of one of the many ceramic shops and watched an elderly couple late at night hand-painting their beautiful ceramics. The lights were soft and their conversation soothing. Next morning, bright and early we stopped into town for a quick cappuccino and hot chocolate before driving to Perugia. In the shop window, back at work, were the same couple, lovingly painting their wares. Naturally, we stopped into the shop, chatted in a bit of Italian and a bit of English and walked off with several beautiful pieces (**Maioliche Artistiche,** *Lombrici F. Via Tiberina, 293. Tel. (39)(075)971-1272).* Up and down Via Tiberina, you will find store after store of authentic ceramics, many with their own factories just out the back door.

We also enjoyed the shop **Sberna** (*Via Tiberina, 146. Tel. (39)(075)971-0206. Fax (39)(075)971-0428. Email: sberna@sberna.com. Web: www.sberna.com*), where we bought a beautiful coffee set with the traditional Deruta dragon. Their factory is adjacent to the shop.

Parent Tip: There are so many ceramic shops and so little time. If you want to efficiently browse, leave the kids behind, or bring them with ipod or book. Our kids enjoy the museums, but dreaded the shopping tours. Remember, too, these shops showcase fragile items and your tab will run up if the kids run about! This is a good time for one parent to play soccer or watch the kids at the pool, while the other makes a purchase.

For us, Deruta is a convenient place to base ourselves as we scheduled day trips to Perugia, Assisi, Cortona and Orvieto. So, do stop by or stay overnight in a town that prides itself on continuing to produce museum quality ceramics for your home.

Getting Here

Buses go back and forth between Perugia (only a half-hour away) frequently each day, or you can easily drive if you have a car.

REGIONAL MUSEUM OF CERAMICS

Largo San Francesco. Tel. (39)(075)971-1000. Email: smuseo.deruta@libero.it. Web: www.museoceramicaderuta.it. Infoline for booking: Tel. 800.22.33.00. Open Monday to Sunday from April to June, 10:30am-1pm and 3pm-6pm; from July to September 10am-1pm and 3:30pm-7pm; from October to March 10:30am-1pm and 2:30pm-5pm. Closed Tuesdays October to March, New Year's day and Christmas day. Admission, children under 6 free.

Beautiful museum, filled with the history and technique of pottery making. The museum is divided into 14 rooms bursting with everything you wanted to know about the secrets behind this ancient art kept alive in Deruta. Teens groaning and younger ones near tears? Well, just slip out early for an hour and enjoy for yourself all this museum has to offer – from floor tiles to cakestands!

Tourist Information

Piazza dei Consoli. Tel. (39)(075)971-1559. Web: www.proderuta.it or www.comune.deruta.pg.it (both in Italian). Or, with an English option: *www.bellaumbria.net/home_eng.htm*, scroll down and click on Deruta.

WHICH ONE IS MY ROOM?

LE CASE COLONICHE *(agriturismo), Pontenuovo di Deruta, Strada SS 45, exit Deruta north. Tel. (39)(075)972-4121 Fax: (39)(075)972-9869. Web: www.lecasecoloniche.it.*

We've stayed in Deruta only once, at Le Case Coloniche, and we're ready to do it again! The country house sits in a quiet nook just off the highway, with working fields on one side and the Tevere (you know it as the Tiber) River meandering through nearby. Yes, there is a swimming pool AND a small soccer field. From here you can hike or fish or visit the town of Deruta just 2 kilometers away. Through management, you can book a cooking class or a course in ceramic painting. We stayed here over New Year's Eve on one trip. After coming home from a day trip to Perugia, we resigned ourselves to the most quiet New Year's Eve ever. Suddenly, at the stroke of midnight, a blaze of light and crackles of sound filled the night sky. Our son dashed outside in PJs under a coat, video cam in tow. Not only was the horizon exploding with fireworks from neighboring villages, but the inhabitants of our very own "quiet" country home were putting on one of the best fireworks shows outside of the 2006 Turino Olympics! With

cheers of joy and exhilaration, we joined in the mad hooting and hollering as we dodged firecrackers and Roman candles to heartily welcome in the new year. Count on the Italians to know how to throw a celebration party!

I'M HUNGRY!

Try either **Billo Odeon** (*$-$$ V. Str. S. Nicolo di Celle, Tel. (39)(075)974-169*); or **Fontanina** (*$$ V. Solitaria 14, Tel. (39)(075)972-4033*). For pizza: **Al Sasso** (*$ Via Tiberina 20, Tel. (39)(075)972-4119*).

ORVIETO

We stood, backs to the biting wind on a cold winter day in Orvieto, planning our itinerary. Etruscan underground? The Duomo? Etruscan museum? Suddenly, we stopped chatting, focusing on a familiar sound we heard faintly in the background. Impossible. New Orleans jazz? Out of the corner of our eyes, from one of the towns narrow streets marched a real, authentic, can't mistake it, New Orleans jazz band, led by the bandleader dressed in a canary yellow suit, twirling a fancy umbrella. We had stumbled onto the **Umbrian Winter Jazz Festival**. After we stomped and cheered, swaying to the music in the piazza, off we went to find out where and when more jazz would be played. After Hurricane Katrina, it was not such a small miracle that marched through Orvieto on that blustering winter day.

Orvieto, once called Urbs Vetus, like many towns in the area initially was settled by the Etruscans and their remains are plentiful in this town. From afar, you can see the outlines of the artistic Cathedral of Orvieto, perched on the top of a steep hill. This impenetrable hill, comprised of tufa rock, can be conquered by the modern tourist using either the funicular, cable car, or a clever system of escalators. It didn't surprise us to find out that Orvieto was created by an ancient volcano, the likes of which both carved out the 1,000 foot sheer cliff as well as enriched the soil with volcanic minerals. Umbria's wine country, dependent on the good soil of the region, rivals it's neighbor, Tuscany.

Parent Tip: Check to see package admission rates for museums that you can purchase when you buy your funicular ticket or at the tourist office in the Piazza Duomo. The ticket is called the *Carta Unica Citta di Orvieto* and grants admission to: San Brizio Chapel in the Duomo, the Torre del Moro, the Museo Claudio Faina and the Orvieto Underground.

Getting Here & Getting to the Top

From Rome, Orvieto is about an hour and 15 minutes by train. From Florence, the train trip will take about an hour and 45 minutes.

Leave your car behind. Orvieto is a car-free city, although a mini-bus service covers the entire town. Park at the railway station and take the Bracci funicular up to the top. Our kids loved this option. You also can use the system of lifts and escalators from Campo della Fiera, where there also is a large parking lot. **Funicular:** *Open weekdays from 7:20am to 8:30pm, running every 10 minutes. On Sundays and holidays from 8am to 8:30pm, every 15 minutes. Tel. (39)(076)330-1224.*

PIAZZA DEL DUOMO

A charming, little square at the top of the hill. On one side is the stunning 13[th-]century Duomo. Across from the cathedral are old rowhouses, including the tourist office, Museo Archeologico Claudio Faina e Museo Civico and an enoteche, to taste and purchase the hearty Umbrian wine. This is an excellent meeting place for families who may wander separately throughout the small hilltown.

ORVIETO CATHEDRAL

Piazza del Duomo. Tel. (39)(0763)341-167. Open: 7:30-12:45, Afternoon opening varies by season: 2:30-5:15 from November-February, 2:30-6:15, March-October, and 2:30-7:15, April-September. Free.

We've seen grander cathedrals, larger more robust. But, this Technicolor Cathedral, with its richly colored mosaics trimmed in gold, dazzling in the sunlight, offered us a unique and splendid view of the spiritual. The story behind the façade also is fascinating. According to lore, a Bohemian priest named Peter was asked to celebrate Mass in the nearby town of Bolsena. Peter was quite skeptical of the Church's claim of transubstantiation, which is the belief that at the time of communion, the host actually becomes the body of Christ. During Peter's Mass, the host

dripped blood on the linens draping the altar. Peter, taking this as a sign, rushed the linen's up the hill to Orvieto, where the pope was staying. Pope Urbano IV declared it a miracle, created the feast of Corpus Christi and promised the people of Orvieto a new cathedral to keep safe the relic of the miracle. In 1290, the cornerstone was laid to Orvieto's Cathedral, and the church was completed in 1617 by a series of architects, including Lorenzo Maitani of Siena, Andrea Pisano, and Sammicheli.

The Gothic facing is adorned with a polyptych decoration of mosaic pieces and Maitani's bas-reliefs, which tell the story of the creation to the last judgment based on the Christian faith. It is a masterpiece only outdone by the natural beauty of the Umbrian hills.

Inside are two chapels. The **Cappella della Madonna di San Brizio** contains an amazing set of frescoes begun in the late 1400s. On one side is Christ in Judgment, begun by Fra Angelica and completed by Signorelli. The other side of the chapel contains a chaotic scene: The Last Judgment complete with the teaching of the anti-Christ and the Resurrection of the Dead. Both the design and execution of this fresco are by Signorelli. Look to the left of the anti-Christ to find a self-portrait by Signorelli, who also painted Fra Angelico, as they both listened to the preaching of the anti-Christ.

The other chapel, **Cappella del Corporale** contains several frescoes, including the Miracle of Bolsena by Ugolino and Madonna dei Raccomandati by Lippo Memmi, both completed in the mid 1300s.

MUSEO ARCHEOLOGICO CLAUDIO FAINA

Piazza Duomo, 29. Tel. (39)(9763)341-511 Fax (39)(0763)341-250 Email: fainaorv@tin.it. Open: April to September 9:30am-6pm, guided tour at 11am and 4pm; October-March 10am-5pm, guided tour 11am and 3pm; and November-February, Closed Mondays. Admission (you get a discount with your funicular ticket).

This is one of our family's favorite museums. Similar to the Guggenheim in Venice, it is a small and quite accessible museum for young children and teens. Families also can get a children's guide to the exhibit, written in English and Italian. The guide asks questions at different points throughout the exhibit and provides the answers. For younger children, you will need to read the explanations, but our teens went through this museum on their own with the guide. Anyone doing a school project on the Etruscans? This guide is a good first-step.

The museum is the private archaeological collection of Mauro and Eugenio Faina, who began in 1864 to acquire Etruscan artifacts from the Orvieto area. A remarkable coin collection from antiquity interested our teens. We all marveled at the refined artistry of Etruscan vases, pottery and sarcophagi. Many of the attic black or red-figure pottery vases were found during an excavation of Orvieto's necropolis, Crocefisso del Tufo. Contemporary art, peppered throughout the museum, made for a stark contrast to the Etruscan works and gave us a lot to talk about as we made our way through the museum. A real find awaits you on the top floor: A long marble hallway with the best view in the house of the exquisite Duomo and serene countryside. We sat on benches facing the windows, just a few minutes to relax and organize ourselves for the rest of the day. Our teens sketched and wrote in journals until erupting in that perpetual groan of teenage hunger. Good thing, food was just a few strides away.

ETRUSCAN UNDERGROUND
Piazza Duomo, 24. Tel: (39)(0763)344-891. Fax (39)(0763)391-121. Email: speleotecnica@libero.it. Web: www.orvietounderground.it. Tours run at 11am, 12:15pm, 4pm and 5:15pm. Departure from Piazza Duomo, 24. Admission, children under 5 are free.

Beneath the earth of Orvieto lies a city originally constructed by the Etruscans. A fascinating network of passageways, wells, animal stables and coops for messenger pigeons are guaranteed to amaze children of all ages. The tufo walls and ground are now equipped with 21st-century lighting and comfortable enough walkways for even the youngest of children. We all walked away impressed with the ingenuity of an ancient civilization.

TORRE DEL MORO
Palazzo dei Sette, Corso Covour, 87. Web www.oveitoonline.com/orvieto_palazzo_dei_sette_orvieto. Open: 10am-1pm and 4pm-8pm. Admission, but the Torre is one of the sights included on the Carta Unica Citta di Orvieto, which you can purchase at the funicular.

The Palazzo dei Sette, first owned by the Della Terza family, eventually was passed on to the Church in the 1200s. At this point, it was used by the city's seven-member government, hence Sette, which is the Italian word for seven. Directly to the right of your entrance is the stairway that leads to the top of the tower. But, for those who disdain long climbs, you can take an elevator up part of the way and climb the rest. This is a very, very comfortable climb. And, your reward awaits you at the top: An unbeatable panoramic view of the Umbrian hills surrounding Orvieto. It was quite cold when we made our way to the top of Torre del Moro, but we all stayed for quite some time taking photos and just relishing the view.

PARCO DELLE GROTTE
On a hot, summer day, the Parco delle Grotte offers a shady area to rest weary feet and enjoy a snack or lunch. Pines and pergola trees are scattered about the park, which is just steps away from the Duomo and just above the Orvieto Underground.

Tourist Information
Piazza del Duomo, 20. Tel. (39)(0763)341-772. Email: info@iat. orvieto.tr.it. Web: www.orvietoonline.com.

WHICH ONE IS MY ROOM?

Either of these are good three-star choices:
HOTEL ITALIA *** *Via di Piazza del Popolo, 13. (39)(0763)390-028. Fax: (39)(0763)390-235 Web: www.grandhotelitalia.it.*
HOTEL PICCHIO *** *Via G. Salvatori, 17. Tel. (39)(0763)301-1144. Fax (39)(0763)301-144. Web: www.bellaumbria.net/hotel-Picchio.*

I'M HUNGRY!

TRATTORIA VINOSUS $$ *Piazza Duomo, 15 Tel (0763)341-907.*
We enjoyed a charming lunch in this relaxed little restaurant in a prime location just across from the Duomo. The frescoed ceiling contrasted

wonderfully with the modern art hung on all walls. The stone fireplace was burning, since this was a rather cold, winter day. But we also noticed a lovely outdoor patio for those traveling during more pleasant seasons, where you get a panoramic view of the Umbrian countryside. The food was excellent – from a cheese and salami platter to pasta and truffles. And the wine – out-of-this-world, as it should be when a restaurant has the motto: "Life is too short to drink bad wines!

Our children particularly enjoyed one family's delightful and huge dog who, after waking from a nap under the table, stood on hind legs, paws on the paternal head of the family's shoulders, waiting patiently for a bite of food. Dogs are allowed in restaurants in Italy, and this pet-owners' luxury always surprises and enchants our children.

CASTIGLIONE DEL LAGO

Years ago, biking through Italy (without children) we stumbled onto this town, too weary to make it closer to Assisi. What a delight! **Lake Trasimeno** is a sparkling jewel in the summer and an active resort year round for Italians who want to unwind. Trasimeno is the fourth largest lake in Italy, and not as well-known among non-Europeans as are Lake Como and Lake Guarda in the north. From the hills of Cortona, you can see

– on a clear day – Lake Trasimeno, a low-key beach town nestled between rows of olive trees and the rolling hills of vineyards.

What to do? There are sailing, windsurfing and water skiing schools in the summer. A golf course is nearby, as are stables for horse riding lessons and tours. Try any one of the eight public beaches, or three public swimming pools. Tennis and archery are available.

Go to the lake to windsurf, or bike, or walk, or just play in the sand. You also can take a boat to **Isola Maggiore**, one of the islands in Lake Traseimeno that is home to fishermen and lacemakers. Let your imagination soar while playing around the remains of an old medieval castle near the town center. Legend has it that in 1211, St. Francis of Assisi threw back to the lake a pike given to him by a local fisherman. The fish, ever so grateful, followed St. Francis around the lake until the saint bestowed on "Brother Fish" a special blessing. These events are documented in Isola Maggiore's church, San Michele.

Do your kids like kites? Well, make sure you are in Lake Traseimeno for the **Coloriamo I Cieli** – Colors in the Sky – Festival. Kites of all kinds and colors zoom and dive throughout the sky from the end of April to early May.

Tourist Information
Piazza Mazzini, 10 Tel (39)(075)965-2484 Web: www.comune. castiglione-del-lago.pg.it (in Italian).

WHICH ONE IS MY ROOM?
HOTEL MIRALAGO *** *Piazza Mazzini, 6. Tel. (39)(075)951-157 or 953-063. Fax (39)(075)951-924. Web: www.hotelmiralago.com.*

After so many years, we found again the hotel where we rested weary bike bones after another 75-mile ride. And, it remains as charming as we remember, with simple but lovely rooms quite comfortable for our family of four. Ask for a room with a view of the lake. There is a lovely sitting room right off of the lobby. Breakfast is available, and the very friendly staff make an excellent cappuccino to start your day!

I'M HUNGRY!
RISTORANTE LA CANTINA $ *Via V. Emanuele, 93. Tel. (075)596-2463.*

Get cozy in the garden while enjoying a beautiful view of the lake, with hills rising far off. A nice place for lunch and there's pizza – all kinds – for the kids.

RISTORANTE L'ACQUARIO $-$$ *Via V. Emanuele, 69. Tel./Fax (075)965-2432.*

Fish, fish, fish, and wonderful pasta, too.

ASSISI

Castle, piazza, torre, narrow, winding medieval streets. Oh yes, set up on a hill with some of the world's most picturesque landscape. Add lots of charm and friendly people and you have your quintessential Tuscan/Umbrian town. Then comes Assisi. You don't have to believe in saints or miracles or the stigmata to be touched by this magical of all cities. Biking or driving from the valley, Assisi ascends to the heavens. The walls lovingly preserve this city that has survived the plague, wars and earthquakes.

Assisi began as an Etruscan village and emerged as a vibrant community of the Roman Empire. Traces of this distant past are still apparent, such as the facade of the temple of Minerva, parts of the ancient walls, ruins of a Forum and bits of a theatre and amphitheater in the upper part of the town.

All was not peaceful in Assisi, whose people battled it out with the Perugian forces during the Middle Ages. But the real story of Assisi tells of the life, time and passions of **St. Francis**. Francis was born into the Bernardone family during the winter of 1181-1182. His birthplace in Assisi, **San Francesco Piccolino** in Piazza del Comune, is marked with an inscription: "This is the oratory at one time a stall for oxen and donkeys in which Francis, the mirror of the world, was born."

After living a relatively well-off life, Francis dedicated himself to peace and the poor. Taking a vow of poverty, he and his followers began the the Franciscan movement, which continues throughout the world and especially in Assisi.

Getting Here

Rent a car if you can. If not, it's about a two hour train trip from Rome, or 90 minutes by either train or bus from Perugia. If Perugia is your base, contact local tourist office there for schedules, but trains and buses are fairly frequent.

The **Basilica of St. Francis** (*open 7am-12pm and 2pm-sunset, April-October 7am-sunset, closed Sunday morning during services*), along with Siena's cathedral, are the first examples of Italian Gothic. Tradition says that Francis had chosen to be buried at the place where criminals had been put to death, arguing that he was the worst sinner. Simone di Pucciarello, in March 1228, donated the site to the Franciscan friars and soon after construction of the church began. Francis' remains were placed in a plain stone sarcophagus which was embedded in the solid rock beneath the main altar, today located in the lower church. Pope Innocent IV in 1253 consecrated the church, and the interior decorative work commenced. Brother Elias, one of the original members of St. Francis' troop designed the structure.

Today, the church possesses exceptional artwork by Maesro di S. Francesco, Simone Martini and the great Cimambue and his student Giotto. The upper church houses the remarkable Giotto frescoes depicting scenes from the life of St. Francis, including the beautiful *Sermon to the Birds.*

From the Basilica, take Via San Francesco to the Piazza del Comune. Walk past no. 14, the house of the Comacini Masters, **Casa dei Maestri Comacini**, or mason's guild. The building dates to 1474. Further along at no. 11 is the Oratory dei Pellegrini, which once was a 15th-century hospital, the Ospedale dei Pellegrini. Near the entrance to the Piazza del Commune

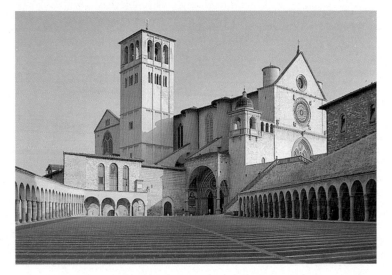

at Via Portica 1 is the **Collezione Archeologica** (*open daily 10am-1pm and 3pm-7pm and October-March 10am-1pm and 2pm-5pm, closed Monday; admission*). The museum is located where the church of San Nicolo once stood and includes some interesting Etruscan pieces. Children enjoy walking through the museum's passageway into the ancient Roman forum underneath the town square.

Once you've reached the Piazza del Comune, take a look at the Temple of Minerva (100 BC), now a church dedicated to the Madonna. The Corinthian columns and travertine steps stand out in this mostly medieval town square. Once in the piazza, you can visit the **Pinacoteca Civica** (same hours as the Collezioine Archeologica; purchase a joint ticket to see both). The museum contains paintings in the Umbrian tradition from the 12th to the 17th century. Also in the square is the **Chaise Nova**, a 17th century church said to be built on the site where stood the house of Peter Bernardino, father of Francis.

From the Piazza del Comune hike up Via di San Rufino to the **Cattedrale di San Rufino**, the church where both St. Francis and St. Claire, who followed in Francis'

Fun Fact

On September 26, 1997, Assisi began to shake and groan, as the rumbling of an earthquake raced through the town destroying homes. The upper basilica shuddered and portions of the Giotto and Cimabue frescoes collapsed in ruin. Interestingly, the rubble was different for each artist's work. Why? Cimabue used the old practice of plastering large areas before painting. Giotto introduced a new tactic. He plastered small areas and worked while the plaster was still wet. Giotto's paintings both endured better throughout the centuries with the colors showing more magnificently, and the earthquake caused his frescoes to break into pieces. Cimabue's work almost shattered. Scores of art restoration experts descended on Assisi to pick up the pieces of the destroyed basilica. On November 28, 1999, a little more than two years after the earthquake hit, the Basilica of St. Francis reopened to applause worldwide. The masterpieces were restored in extraordinary and expeditious fashion, leading some to herald the work as "the miracle of Assisi."

footsteps and founded the Second Order of St. Francis, the Poor Claires, were baptized. Muster up the energy and climb even further up Via Porta Perlici to the fortress, the **Rocca Maggiore**. It was first recorded as a fortress in 1174, with additions made here and there until 1538. It is majestic and the panoramic views spectacular.

Unwittingly, on our last trip here we decided to trek up to St. Francis' woodland retreat, high in the hills of Monte Subasio. The Benedictines gave **Carceri delle Eremo** (also known as **Le Carceri**) to St. Francis and his brothers as a place for meditation. We marched out of the town through Porta dei Cappuccini and began the allegedly four kilometer walk up the hill. Well, maybe it is four kilometers, but it certainly seemed much further and we are intrepid hikers.

Thankfully, there was a no-name restaurant about halfway up where we got water and rested with a group of German travelers. Exhausted, even on this cool Spring day, the kids tumbled into the gates of Le Carceri in a more contemplative, or maybe spaced-out, mood than when we started! The retreat: serene, sublime, other-worldly. Franciscan monks continue to live here and are quick to cry "silenzia" if the muffled whispers among travelers becomes too audible.

Our children thoroughly enjoyed Le Carceri. We were concerned that they would not be able to handle the "silenzia," but they did and admirably so. They were intrigued by the grotto where St. Francis dwelt during the end of his life. Through a series of tiny doors into tiny rooms (adults must duck their heads in this *Alice in Wonderland* retreat) you end up in St. Francis' room where you can see his bed carved from solid rock. Outside, the children appreciated the walk along the path bordered by woods to the outdoor altar, where St. Francis and his brothers prayed. Back to the hermitage the children flitted with immaculate white doves that continue to live in a room set aside for them. We recommend taking children here; just remember you can take a taxi to the top if you want. At the souvenir stand outside the gates, you can also call a taxi to bring you back down.

Parent Tip: In this hilly town, where cars jostle people for room to maneuver in the narrow, steep streets, the **Piazza del Comune** is a great place for parents to relax and kids to run or spend time playing around the main fountain. However, beware of tourist-trap restaurants. We spent a lot of time and money on what we expected to be a quick lunch here. Better to eat elsewhere, and grab a gelato or pastry treat and drink, and enjoy sitting on the steps around the fountain.

WHICH ONE IS MY ROOM?

HOTEL SOLE ** *Corso Mazzini 35. Tel. (39)(075)812-373 or 812-922. Fax (39)(075)81-706. Web: www.assisihotelsole.com.*

Recently renovated, this traditional hotel has 35 simple but comfortable rooms. Our family enjoyed meals at the hotel's medieval restaurant, the Ceppo della Catena (*see below*).

HOTEL GIOTTO *** *Via Fontebella, 41. Tel. (39)(075)812-732, or 812-744 or 812-209. Fax (39)(075)812-567. Web: www.hotelgiottoassisi.it/ home_engl/index.html.*

Ask for room 9 or adjacent rooms. Although the rooms have only two beds, the spacious patio gives children and adults space to play and view the valley from the garden terraces. At sunset, we enjoyed watching the swallows nose-dive in formation over our patio. Rooms are elegant with cathedral ceilings and antique furnishings; the suites are luxurious, Enjoy a pretty breakfast area, also with good views and top service.

HOTEL SUBASIO **** *Via Frate Elia, 2. Tel. (39)(075)812-206. Fax (39)(075)816-691. Web: www.hotelsubasio.com/homepage-en.php.*

An ancient hotel, just steps from and linked by a portico to the Basilica of St. Francis. The airy common areas are decorated with antiques, sparkling chandeliers and frescoes. Panoramic views from the balconies of Subasio are perhaps the most stunning of any Assisi hotel. Enjoy both indoor and outdoor dining areas. Rooms have television, refrigerator and telephone. For travelers using a car, there is a garage. The hotel restaurant, popular with locals and tourists alike, is marked by its medieval vaulted architecture.

HOTEL DEI PRIORI *** *Corso Mazzini, 15. Tel. (39)(075)816-804. Fax (39)(075)816-804. Web: www.assisi-hotel.com/home-en.htm.*

Situated in an historical building from the 18th century, Hotel Dei Priori is simply and tastefully furnished. Bedrooms are small, with dark wood beds and armoires. Each room has a private bath and telephone. The dining room is bright and airy. Located just off the main piazza.

HOTEL SAN FRANCESCO *** *Via San Francesco, 48. Tel. (39)(075)812-281 or 813-690 or 816-818. Fax (39)(075)816-237. Web: www.hotelsanfrancescoassisi.it/eng.*

San Francesco is the only hotel located adjacent to the Basilica, which means you can gaze directly on the grounds of the church. But remember, it also means you will see throngs of tourists who congregate outside the Basilica. The hotel is neatly decorated with modern furnishings. Each of its 44 rooms has air conditioning, TV, phone and mini bar.

Enjoy the roof garden, where you can gaze upon the Basilica of Saint Francis and enjoy the pastoral views of the valley below. The hotel

The Scoop on Gelato

Gran Caffe, Pasticceria Gelateria, *Corso Mazzini, 16a/16b. Tel. (39)(075)815-5144.* Our children picked the Gran Caffe's gelato as the best in Assisi. But the Gran Caffe is more than a gelateria. Scrumptious cookies and mouthwatering pastries tempt you. The café is light and airy, with a golden bar. Angel frescoes adorn the walls. A little bit of heaven in Assisi.

restaurant also overlooks the Basilica from its veranda.

I'M HUNGRY!

Beware of the cafes bordering the main piazza, Piazza Republica. The *coperto* (tax) is stiff and the food unpleasant, at best. Frequent the cafés only for a coffee and *dolce* (dessert), which are scrumptious. Or, bring a picnic of cheeses and bread and enjoy at the fountain.

RISTORANTE MEDIO EVO $$$ *Via Dell'Arco Dei Priori 4. Tel. (39)(076)13-068. Closed Wednesday and Sunday evenings.*

Bigger than it appears from the outside, Medio Evo is a pretty restaurant with frescoes adorning the walls. Many dishes are traditional Umbrian. Our children devoured the insalata caprese. Try the risotto with porcini and truffles. It is intense and perfectly done.

CEPPO DELLA CATENA $$$ *in the Hotel Sole, Corso Mazzini 35. Tel. (39)(075)812-373.*

What you expect from an Italian restaurant – good food, friendly service – you will find at the Ceppo della Catena. Our children, when they were little, were cooed over in a so-Italian way. They left their meal to watch a movie about St. Francis, and the owner set them up with little chairs and candy while we finished our dinner. The restaurant is situated in a 15th-century structure, with stone walls and archways (*see photo below*).

Pastas are fresh and good. Try their *faraona*, an Umbrian dish of roasted guinea-fowl. Also, order the hearty *Rubesco*, the local red wine of Assisi.

5. VENICE

Venice (Venezia) is fairyland. Gondolas whisking passengers along streets of water. Mazes for walkways and the fun of getting lost and finding your way. Tiny bridges to skip up and down. Delightful and sometimes scary masks peering at you from the windows of artists' shops. Cats (live) and lions (sculpted) sneaking up on you at every corner. Venice is for children!

The magic of Venice begins with the fact that there is any Venice at all. Venice exists three feet above sea level – most of the time. During rainy season, the waters flood St. Mark's Square and many streets. Wisps of mist encircle the slivers of land, as if some sea sprite lifts her head draped with a flowing white veil that unfurls over the city just so she, too, can get a glimpse of the city of light. Venice is truly enchanting.

SO MANY SIGHTS, SO LITTLE TIME!

Venice is an easy city to balance the interests of adults with the needs of children. Here are recommendations for how to get the most out of a short trip to Venice.

Day 1

Morning (3 hours): Begin your day early in the **Piazza San Marco**, sipping cappuccino at one of the cafés. While the kids entertain themselves by feeding the pigeons, wait in line to enter the **Basilica San Marco.** Gaze at the beautiful **Clock Tower** in the Piazza while in line. After a short visit to the church, walk the few steps to the **Bell Tower**, and wait in another line. Someone can take the kids to get a snack or to run around the enormous piazza.

Afternoon (3-4 hours): Take the *vaporetto* to the **Accademia** and, if possible, the nearby **Peggy Guggenheim Museum,** believe it or not, a top choice for lunch! Walk back to your hotel – giving kids time to burn energy and maybe even join a soccer game underway in one of the piazzas.

Evening: After dinner, take your evening *passegiatto* (stroll) down the boardwalk along the Grand Canal, passing the Public Gardens or perhaps the Arsenale – there's not much to see, so no need wasting daylight for this site. Or, hire a gondolier to gallantly take you home by way of the sea. Enjoy Venice at night, illuminated by moonlight and soft lamps.

Some time during the day, ask your concierge about arranging a boat trip over to Murano on your second day.

Day 2

Morning (3 hours): Again, begin your morning in San Mark's Square, this time prepared to tackle the **Doge's Palace.**

Lunch: Leave by foot or *vaporetto* to the **Rialto Bridge,** where there is a great outdoor market. Pick up treats for lunch or try one of the cafes along the canal.

Afternoon (3 or more hours): Take a trip to Murano.

Evening: Walking back to your hotel, from the vaporetto stop, count lion statues along the way.

Day 3

Morning (3 hours): Take a walking tour of Venice that takes you by a mask-making shop, a gondola factory and the fun Naval Museum.

Afternoon: After all the walking, give the kids time to romp and stomp in the Public Gardens. (Take a *vaporetto* to the **Public Gardens** if you are too far to walk.)

Evening: After dinner at an outdoor café in a lovely piazza (where you can watch the kids play while you finish eating), take a *seranate* gondola cruise; glimpse the moonlight shimmering on the dancing waves, while the docked gondolas rock to the rhythm of the sea.

Day 4

Morning (2 or more hours): Jump on a *vaporetto* to the **Island of the Dead** for a walk through Venice's past. Or, take the boat to Burano to see lacemaking.

Afternoon (2 or more hours): Walk to the Jewish Ghetto. If you have time visit the **Accademia** or **Peggy Guggenheim Museum** since you probably didn't have time to see both on the first day.

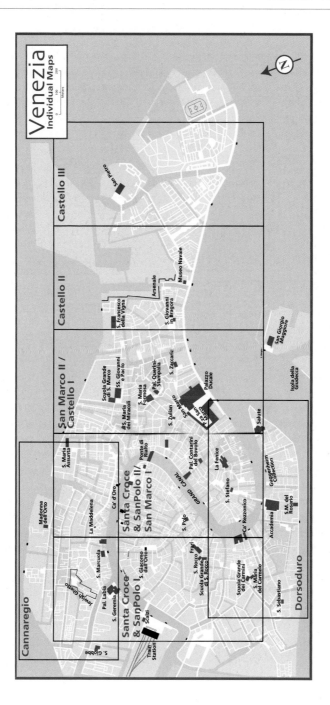

Venezia
Individual Maps

0   100   200
Meters

Cannaregio

Santa Croce & SanPolo I

Santa Croce & SanPolo II / San Marco I

San Marco II / Castello I

Castello II

Castello III

Dorsoduro

S. Giobbe

Train Station

Scalzi

Pal. Labia

S. Geremia

S. Marcuola

L'Ab/Pal. Gritti

S. Giacomo dall'Orio

La Maddelena

Madonna dell'Orto

Ca' d'Oro

S. Maria Assunta

Ponte di Rialto

GRAND CANAL

Frari

S. Rocco

Scuola Grande di S. Rocco

Scuola Grande del Carmini

S. Maria del Carmelo

S. Sebastiano

S. Polo

Ca' Rezzonico

Accademia

S.M. del Rosario

Guggenheim Collection

Salute

S. Stefano

La Fenice

Pal. Contarini del Bovolo

S. Maria del Miracoli

Scuola Grande di S. Marco

SS. Giovanni e Paolo

S. Maria Formosa

S. Zulian

San Marco

Piazza San Marco

Palazzo Ducale

Pal. Querini Stampalia

S. Zaccaria

Isola della Giudecca

San Giorgio Maggiore

S. Francesco della Vigna

S. Giovanni in Bragora

Arsenale

Museo Navale

San Pietro

Day 5

Spend your last day at the **Lido** – Venice's nearby beach resort. A great way to unwind and prepare to leave Venice. You can either book a room – in advance, of course – at the Lido, or return on the *vaporetto*.

GETTING AROUND TOWN

By Vaporetto

Tickets for these public waterbuses can be purchased at the *tabacchi* shops, at the main ACTV office in Piazzale Roma or at the main vaporetto stops. There are options for families and groups. Ask at the ticket counter. It is rather ambiguous who rides free – under six, perhaps? When in doubt, ask. They may give you a break. Here are some of the most-traveled routes:

- **No. 1**: Stops are made at every landing on the Grand Canal. This is the slowest route, but a great way to view the palazzi and other fantastic architecture along the length of the canal.
- **No. 82**: Take this from the Stazione di Santa Lucia (train station) or Piazzale Roma (bus station) to the Rialto, Accademia and San Marco stops.
- **No. 52**: A wonderful ride to islands of San Michele and Murano.
- **No. 12**: This *vaporetto* stops at Murano, Burano and Torcello.
- **No. 6**: Off to the Lido and back!

Single tickets (valid for one hour: €6.50, half-price for children age 6 through age 12 and free for children under age 6; 12-hour travel card is €16, 24-hour card, €18; Also, for the Rolling VENICECard for young people – age 14 to 29. See *www.hellovenezia.com/jsp/en/venicecardrolling/index.jspp*. Savings is significant and the cards can be purchased in any tourist office.) For more information go to: *www.hellovenice.com*.

By Water Taxi

Significantly faster and more expensive than the *vaporetto*, but if you don't like crowds, a private motorboat is the way to go. Expect a ride from one end of the Grand Canal to the other to cost over €50 per person, extra for baggage. Be aware of unlicensed taxis that could gouge you for more. Ask the price before taking off.

By Gondola

Who can resist at least one ride on these romantic boats? Shiny black and sleek gondolas, gently rocking in the waves, ferrying you off to a

Venetian adventure. Once upon a time, they were the preferred mode of transport for citizens of Venice. Now, their ranks having dropped from 100,000 to 400, gondolas are preserved as a tourist attraction. And a delightful, though expensive, one they are. Expect to pay over €50 per half-hour, but remember to bargain.

We recommend using them to transport you to a single destination – an elegant way to arrive for dinner. Since the Grand Canal can be seen easily by riding *Vaporetto* No. 1, gondolas are best used to get a flavor for some of the small side canals. Gondolas also can be hired for a *seranate* (think serenade!) – a group ride joined by a singer or accordion player who will serenade throughout the canals of Venice. Best at night!

If hiring a gondola is a bit rich for your blood, you can cross the Grand Canal in a *gondola traghetti* for about €5. This is a public service to help people cross the Grand Canal between its three bridges. Ask your hotel for the closest pick-up point – but be prepared for a bit of a balancing act, since the custom is to stand for the short crossing.

Talkin' Venetian

Venice has its own dialect and definitions for words that may be useful as you make your way across town:

Calle: the street you walk along
Campo: town square or piazza
Campiello: a little campo
Canale: reserved for the Grand Canal (see rio)
Corte : a blind alley
Fondamenta: street that runs next to the canal
Piazza: reserved for St. Mark's Square (Piazza San Marco)
Piazzette: the two squares adjacent to St. Mark's Square
Piazzale: used only for Piazzale Roma
Rio: a canal, except for the Grand Canal
Riva: places where you can walk that run alongside the Grand Canal, or the lagoon.

Parent Tip: For families with babies, a backpack is best because of all the bridges to cross. However, we brought a baby jogger stroller – the smallest, most collapsible kind – and barely broke a sweat in the heat of August, strolling our youngest when her "skipping got lost," in her words. Jogger strollers are made light to be easily carried and maneuvered through the twists and turns of narrow streets and bridges. We used it as a luggage carrier from the train station to the vaporetto and from the canal to our hotel. Keep in mind your level of endurance and your child's when you make the decision of what stroller, if any, to bring.

By Foot

Our preferred mode of transportation in Venice has been by foot, even with young children. Much of the charm of Venice is navigating its labyrinth of narrow alleyways with no need to keep the kids safe from cars and the speeding scooters that infest other big Italian cities.

A word on using maps in Venice. Forget it if you're looking for precision. We've not met one map that has worked. There are so many side streets jutting off of main walkways, that as far as we can tell no one has gotten it just right. Where's Americo Vespucci when you need him? Take the risk! Ask directions, first at your hotel, and then along the way to your destination. A little of the fun and intrigue in Venice is getting lost and discovering your own secret attractions in the streets.

Finding Your Way Around Venice

Venice is divided into six neighborhoods called *siestieri*. Street numbering is, shall we say, unique in Venice. Here's the secret: Numbering is not done by street. It is done by the entire *siestieri*. For example, each *sesiteri* has a number 1. If that's not confusing enough, the numbers spiral out from each *siestieri's* center in random fashion. Couple the numbering system with the fact that some street names are spelled three or more different ways and some streets share the same name, and you have confusion, Venetian-style.

Here are the 'hoods of Venice (*see map on page 184*):

- **Cannaregio.** The largest of Venice's *siestieri*, Cannaregio is home to the Jewish Ghetto. This is where you can see a Venice not overcome by tourists. Take your children and let them play with the kids of Venice in this neighborhood.
- **Santa Croce.** Not much here other than freight yards and the prison.
- **San Polo.** Adjacent to Santa Croce, but more lively. Here you will find the Rialto markets, the Natural History Museum and Goldoni's House.
- **San Marco.** The heart of tourist land, San Marco reigns as Venice's cultural center.
- **Dorsoduro.** A great place to watch the sunset is at the Zattere, located in the Dorsoduro. The Accademia and Peggy Guggenheim museums also are here.
- **Castello.** This *siestieri* stretches from San Marco east. The Arsenale and Giardini Pubblici reside here. In the far eastern corner are many of the city's boatyards and few tourists.

Parent Tip: We gave our kids walkie-talkies and let them blaze new trails zigzagging through Venice's narrow streets. We always knew where they were – usually not far in front of us – but they enjoyed the fun of exploration and a bit of independence!

WHERE ARE WE GOING NOW?

Piazza San Marco

The first glance at the enormity and magnificence of the Piazza San Marco left our children speechless – and that takes a lot. Standing on the side farthest from **St. Mark's Basilica**, looking down the long, ornate porticos and past the **Campanile** to the lavishly decorated church and soft pink **Doge's Palace**, you can see why Napoleon called the Piazza San Marco "the most beautiful drawing room in Europe."

The changing seasons deepen the magic of San Marco. Autumn's high water perpetually threatens the survival of this lowest lying section of Venice, but the artist's eye sees only a reflecting pool of beauty. In winter, most of the square is lost in a mist of eerie gray. Come summer, the sun sparkles on the basilica's golden mosaics as children gleefully feed the birds amidst throngs of tourists.

Two tiny squares buttress the basilica on either side. The **Piazzetta San Marco** on the right also borders the Canal and the **Piazzetta dei Leoncini** to the left, with regal lion statues.

Along the periphery, under the loggia, are famous cafes – one of them hundreds of years old – where in good weather you hear a "battle of the bands" between orchestras playing classical standards and occasional jazz. Lightening-fast charcoal artists both peddle impressions of local scenes and become part of the night's entertainment, attracting small crowds who watch them adroitly complete a detailed sketch in minutes.

The only thing more numerous than tourists on a

Fun Fact

Venice consists of 118 islands boasting 200 canals, all joined together by 400 bridges. How appropriate, then, that from the air Venice looks like a fish!

Tourist Offices

You can find tourist offices at the following locations:

- Venice Pavilion, *San Marco - Giardinetti Reali, Open: 10am - 5.30pm. Tel. (041)2424*
- Marco Polo airport, *Hellovenezia Office, Open 8.10am - 10pm, Tel. (041)2424*
- Isola nova del Tronchetto, *Hellovenezia Office, Open 7am - 6.30pm. Tel. (041)2424*
- Santa Chiara, *Piazzale Roma , Open 7am - 9pm , Tel: (041)2424*
- Train station, *Open 7am - 9pm, Tel. (041)242*

The main tourist website is: *www.turismovenezia.it.*

summer day is the pigeons. Hundreds and sometimes thousands of them waddle, ascend, scatter, beg, flutter and peck at the children – who for a few coins purchase kernels of dry corn and seeds loved by the birds.

When you exit the Piazza San Marco facing the Grand Canal, notice the two huge stone columns pillaged from Constantinople. Perched atop the first column is the winged lion (or "lion angel", as our daughter called them), the companion of St. Mark. On the other is St. Theodore, Venice's first patron saint, with a dragon. Venetians consider it unlucky to walk between the two columns because that was the place of execution in days of yore.

Parent Tip: Once your kids see others feeding the pigeons, it's hard to get them away. Men with street carts sell the pigeon food in little bags for about a few Euro. Although we haven't heard of any problems, be a bit cautious because the pigeons are fearless – they will perch on a child's arm, shoulder or head if that's what it takes to nip a treat. It's a great photo-op, but can also be a bit scary for little ones.

SAINT MARK'S BASILICA

Monday-Saturday 10am-5:30pm and Sunday and holidays 3pm-5:30pm. Tel. (041)275-0462.

DressCode: Dress conservatively. Like St. Peter's in Rome, men must wear a shirt and long pants. Women must cover their shoulders. No shorts or short skirts (except for young children – but not teens). Church officials have no problem banning entry to the church for inappropriate attire.

Begun in 1063, St. Mark's is a shining example of the Second Golden Age. Its gaudy and gilded exterior fits perfectly with the carnival-like culture of Venice. St. Mark's was designed in Byzantine style, with a cross plan inscribed within a square. Each arm of the cross is emboldened with a dome made by bulbous wooden helmets covered by gilt copper sheeting and topped with lanterns. The effect is to make the domes more prominent.

The facade includes the brightly hued mosaics, one replacement completed by Paolo Uccello. Only one original has survived – the 13th-century lunette above the far-left door, which tells the story of Saint Mark's arrival – in relic form – at the church.

Children love to look up at the horses of the upper loggia. They also enjoy searching for the signs of the Zodiac located a little lower in the middle arch. Old Testament scenes are depicted on the facade at the Piazzetta dei Leoncini to the north.

Sanctuary & Pala d'Oro
Open 9:45am-5pm. Admission.

Located near the ceremonial pulpit of the high altar is the Sanctuary and Pala d'Oro, one of the most important works housed in the basilica. This altar screen is enormous (10 feet by 4 feet) and is made of gold with a splattering of precious gems – sapphires, emeralds, garnet, amethysts, pearls, rubies and topazes. Sitting on top, of course, is Saint Mark, with a handful of saints and panels representing the New Testament around him.

Museo Marciano & Loggia dei Cavalli
Open 9:45am-5pm. Admission.

Near the Portal of San Clemente is the door leading to a steep stone staircase up to the gallery. Climb to the loggia for a

Fun Fact
Just who was **Saint Mark**? Mark was the secretary to Peter, one of Jesus' chief apostles. Mark wrote down many of Peter's preachings of Christianity and the writings became Mark's own chapter in the Bible. Legend has it that Peter sent Mark to Alexandria in Egypt to preach the gospel. He did and eventually was killed by enemies in the church where he preached. His friends buried him in Alexandria. About 800 years later, two Venetian merchants stole St. Mark's body from his tomb, brought it back to Venice and hid it in St. Mark's Church. The Venetians were honored to have the relics of such a high-ranking saint in their church, so they tossed out their former saint, Theodore, a Greek, and anointed Mark as patron saint of Venice.

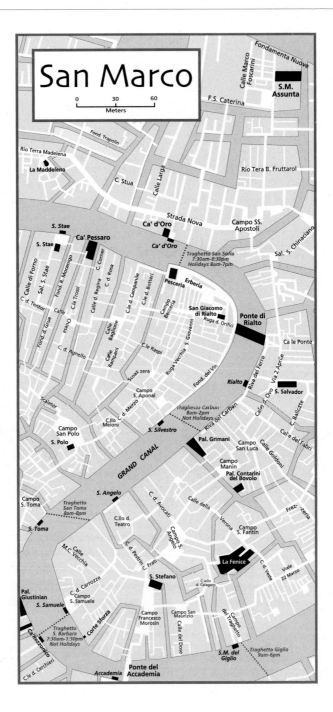

San Marco

0   30   60
Meters

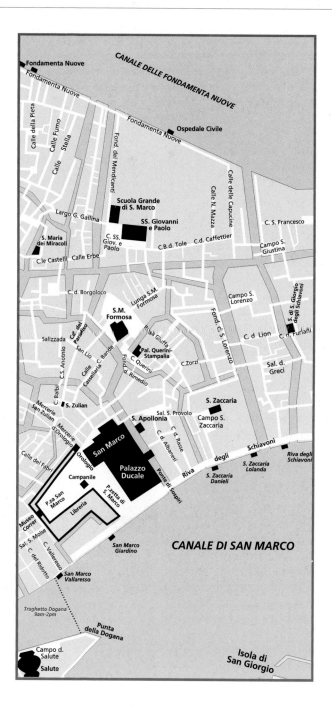

Fondamenta Nuove

CANALE DELLE FONDAMENTA NUOVE

Fondamenta Nuove

Fondamenta Nuove

Calle della Pieta

Calle Fumo

Calle Stella

Calle

Fond. dei Mendicanti

Ospedale Civile

Calle N. Mazza

Calle delle Capucine

Scuola Grande
di S. Marco

Largo G. Gallina

SS. Giovanni
e Paolo

C. S. Francesco

S. Maria
dei Miracoli

C. SS.
Giov. e
Paolo

C.B.d. Tole

C.d. Caffettier

Campo S.
Giustina

C.le Castelli

Calle Erbe

C. d. Borgoloco

Campo S.
Lorenzo

S. di S. Giorgio
degli Schiavoni

Lunga S.M.
Formosa

S.M.
Formosa

Riva Giuffa

Fond. C. S. Lorenzo

C. d Lion

C. d. Furlani

Salizzada

Cal. del
Paradiso

Pal. Querini-
Stampalia

C. Querini

C.Zorzi

Sal. d.
Greci

San Lio

C.S. Anotnio

Calle

Casselaria

C. Bande

Fond. d. Rimedio

C. Balbi

S. Zulian

Mercerie
San Zulian

Mercerie
d'Orologio

S. Zaccaria

Sal. S. Provolo

S. Apollonia

Campo S.
Zaccaria

Calle del Fabri

San Marco

Orologio

C. d. Rasse

C. d. Albanesi

Schiavoni

Riva degli
Schiavoni

Palazzo
Ducale

degli

Riva

S. Zaccaria
Lolanda

Campanile

P.za San
Marco

Libreria

P. zetta di
S. Marco

Ponte di Sospiri

S. Zaccaria
Danieli

Museo
Correr

Sal. S. Moise

C. Valleresso

C. del Ridotto

San Marco
Giardino

CANALE DI SAN MARCO

San Marco
Vallaresso

Traghetto Dogana
9am-2pm

Punta
della Dogana

Campo d.
Salute

Salute

Isola di
San Giorgio

birds-eye view of the piazza. Enjoy the horses at close-up range, but remember they are only copies; the originals are now stabled inside the basilica. No one is sure when the originals were sculpted, although they are estimated to have been created somewhere from the 3rd century BC to the 2nd century AD.

St. Mark's Treasury
Open 9:45am-5pm. Admission.
Near the altar of St. James is St. Mark's Treasury, which holds treasures stolen from Constantinople, primarily 12th-century Byzantine gold and silver objects.

CAMPANILE
In front of St. Mark's. Open 9:30am-4:15 in winter. 9am-7pm summer. Tel. (39)(041)522-4064. Admission.
Imagine the hubbub in town when Galileo demonstrated his telescope to Venetian leaders from this bell tower. The line often is long, so come early. A quick ride up the elevator lands you high above the piazza. The view is dazzling: the rooftops of Venice, St. Mark's Square, the network of canals, the surrounding islands and the bobbing sea.

But this is not the original Bell Tower, which emerged in 912 as a lighthouse and went through

Fun Facts

• For entertainment years ago, a rope was strung from the Campanile to the Canal and daredevils would walk along the tightrope tempting fate.

• Teenage girls in your travel party? Have them check out the 20-inch high platform shoes called zoccoli in the Museo Correr, the cool thing to wear in the Renaissance. We thought it might be to allow them to walk the streets of Venice during floods. But, no, that's too practical (and certainly gives away our age). The purpose, in true Venice style, was for the women to be able to wear fancier dresses.

many restorations up to 1515. On July 14, 1902, the Bell Tower collapsed, killing only the guard's beloved cat, and a new, more sturdy one was built in its place. Just look out when the bells ring. If you're on top, they ring loud and clear, inches from your ear.

TORRE DELL'OROLOGIO
Piazza San Marco. Tel. (39)(041)423-1879. Admission.
One way for kids to pass the time waiting in line at St.Mark's or the Campanile is to examine all the Torre Dell'Orologio has to offer. A stunning clock, gilded and blue, with Saint Mark's winged lion proudly pawing the Bible. High above, ringing the bell to tell the time are two male statutes said to be Moors. Mauro Codussi built it in 1499 with works by Paolo and Carlo Rainieri. Below the lion is a statue of the Virgin and Child said to be completed by Alessandro Leopardi in the early 1500s. Kids especially enjoy noticing how the clock indicates the changing seasons, movements of the sun and phases of the moon.

MUSEO CORRER
Procuratie Nuove and Ala Napoleonica. 9am-7pm, last tickets sold at 9pm. Admission includes entry to Palazzo Ducale.
Parents will probably like this museun better than kids. The two porticos that border St. Mark's square are called Procuratie Vecchie, which adjoins the Clock Tower, and Procuratie Nuove, across the square. Procuratie Vecchie was begun by Mauro Codussi in 1500 and completed in 1530 by Sansovino. Scamozzi and Longhena designed Nuove between 1582 and 1640. Today Venice leases the elegant space to shops, but has retained the Procuratie Nuove and Ala Napoleonica, the arcade that links the two procuratie, for the Museo Correr. This museum offers a hodge-podge of items. Upstairs is a picture gallery of wonderful Venetian art.

PALAZZO DUCALE – DOGE'S PALACE
Piazzetta San Marco. Tel. (39)(041)522-4951. 9:00am-5:00pm Admission. Vaporetto: San Marco.
"I don't want to go there." Don't let them get away with that plea when it comes to visit the Palazzo Ducale. This is not just any museum. It easily could have been the set for a Star Wars episode – the nerve center of the Empire – Venetian, that is. The palace is dazzling, inside and out – uniquely combining Islamic, Gothic and Romanesque styles. The white Istrian stone and red Verona marble adds drama to this enchanting building that housed intrigues, plots, power struggles, victories and defeats.

Wanna Know a Secret?

Take your kids on a Secret Itineraries Tour of the Doges Palace. The visit must be pre-booked. A guide will lead the way and explain all the intrigues of each special room. Price: €16 or Reduced Price €10 for children age 6 to age 14 and students age 15 to 25. Families with two adults and at least one child age 6 to 18 pay one full price and the rest reduced. Tours are offered in English at 9:55am, 10:45am and 11:35am. *Visit www.vivaticket.it/ evento.php?id_evento=409912&idt= 566&op=museiCivici to purchase tickets.*

Begun in the 9th century by the Doges Angelo and Giustiniano Partecipazio, it was completed in the 1400s. Fires ravaged the building in 1574 and 1577, only to see it rebuilt in the later part of the 16th century.

Stride into the palace through the Porta Della Carta (Paper Door), perhaps named so because the clerks' desk once rested in this entranceway. The Bon family created the doorway in the 1400s, in soaring Gothic style. The statue is of Doge Frascari who is kneeling before the ever-present winged lion. From the Porta Della Carta you enter the grand courtyard. Scan the interior and taste the riches of Venetian architecture – the archways, sculptures and most impressive staircases.

The courtyard contains two gorgeous wellheads and the ticket office. Float up the grand **Scala d'Oro**, a staircase crafted in the 1580s by Sansovino, to the first floor. Here are the private apartments of the Doge, now used for special exhibits. Continue up the golden staircase to the second floor where affairs of state were conducted. The frescoes are by Veronese and Tintoretto. In the **Sala delle Quattro Porte**, ambassadors waited to be seen by the Doge. Some of the best art is in the next room, **Anticollegio**. Here you can view paintings by Tintoretto, Veronese and Jacopo Bassano.

Critical meetings were held in the next room, **Sala del Senato**, as Venetian ambassadors, the Doge and the Senate often met here to discuss business. But the next room was the true hot seat. In the **Sala del Consiglio dei Dieci**, the dreaded Council of Ten exerted their full power, embarked on secret missions or determined the life or death of a citizen.

Parent Tip: The courtyard is a great meeting place if children cannot take any more of the palace. One parent can take them here to play, while family members hot on the trail of a cunning Doge plot can fulfill their mission of completing the tour.

Kids bored? Take them directly to the **Sale d'Armi** where an overabundance of medieval and renaissance armor is showcased. Now, try to get them out of this room! The secret word? You're getting closer to the **Bridge of Sighs**. If there's something kids might like better than weaponry, it's the secrets hiding in prison cells of old.

Fun Fact

Warring siblings take note: Maybe you will want to hang a **Bocche dei Leoni** (lion's mouth) in your house (located in the Sala della Bussola, the Ten's waiting room). This is where citizens could tattle on their neighbors who, for one reason or another, were annoying them. But woe to anyone who lied about their neighbor's evil ways. The liars were allotted the same punishment that would have been given to their neighbors had they been found guilty.

Take the tiny staircase down to the equally small **Sala del Guariento**, where Guariento's huge fresco of the *Coronation of the Virgin* (1365-1367) is on display. Peek into the **Sala del Maggior Consiglio** where the Great Council met. Follow the **Sala dello Srutinio** where votes were counted. The portraits are of the last 44 Doges.

Here you are. At the **Ponte dei Sospiri**, the **Bridge of Sighs**. Tradition has it that as prisoners were led to their jail, they had one last chance to set their eyes on splendid Venice, and their sighs of despair echoed throughout the land. Our young children marched through the Bridge of Sighs, sighing loudly, to the **Palazzo delle Prigioni**, or prison. Both kids were appalled at the darkness and smallness of the cells.

Castello

ARSENALE
Campo dell'Arsenale. Vaporetto 52.

We weren't impressed with the Arsenale. There is not much to see except the magnificent gate, an impressive structure built by Antonio Gambello in 1460. It must have been something in its day, as Dante praised the structure in Canto XXI of the *Inferno*. Thousands of men in the 16th century dedicated their lives to the shipbuilding and sailing of the many boats docked inside the gates. Our kids did enjoy the lions resting out front,

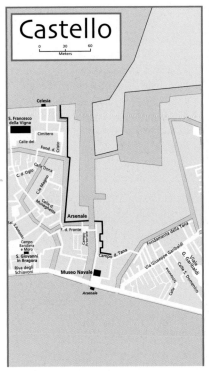

adding them to their lion count. Walk into the tiny pavilion and peek through black bars at the deserted shipyards. Hmmm. Best to quickly move on to the Naval Museum.

NAVAL HISTORY MUSEUM

A 15-minute walk from St. Mark's down the Riva degli Schiavoni just steps from the Arsenale, or ride the Vaporetto no. 1. Open: Monday-Friday 8:45am-1:30pm; Saturday 8:45am-1pm. Admission.

Cool for kids! Ships and boats and things nautical are aplenty in the museum. For kids not so into battle, steer them to the remarkable shell collection donated by Roberta di Camerino, a Venetian designer.

GIARDINI PUBBLICI

Just beyond the Naval History Museum along the Canale di San Marco. Vaporetto no. 1. Open daily until dark.

A wee bit of the green in watery Venice. And THE place to take kids who've had more than enough art and culture for the day. This is no Central Park. The playground equipment has seen better days. But our kids played endlessly in this Venetian garden, while we kicked our feet up on a park bench mesmerized by the sun's last glittering dance on the waters before sinking beneath its waves.

For refreshment and one of the best views in Italy, sit on the upper terraces of the **Caffe Paradiso**, located a bit farther out the Viale Dei Giardini Pubblico in the section where the Biennale art festival is held from June through August in even-numbered years.

Dorsoduro

GALLERIA DELL'ACCADEMIA

Campo della Carita. Tel. (39)(041)522-2247. Web: www.gallerieaccademia.org. Open Monday 8:15am-2am, Tuesday to Sunday 8:15am-7:15pm. Admission. Vaporetto, Accademia.

The best of Venetian art is on exhibit at this picturesque museum. The museum had its origins in 1750, when the Republic of St. Mark's provided a venue for local artists to display their creations. Napoleon, in 1807, ordered the art to be moved from its first establishment, now the Port Authority, to a religious complex. Since then, the collection has expanded and is considered one of the major exhibits in the world, which means it's a heavy dose of art for the youngins'. Here are highlights you don't want to miss, especially if you must keep your visit short. Remember the museum is organized chronologically.

Rooms of interest include:

Room 1: Nicolo di Pietro's *Madonna, Child and Donor* (1304); Michele Giambono's *Coronation of the Virgin* (15th century)

Room 2: This room features several large altarpieces

Room 3: Cima's *Pieta*

Room 4 : Montegna's *St. George;* Bellini's *Madonnas;* Piero della Francesca's *St. Jerome and Devotee*

Room 5: Giorgione's *The Tempest*

Room 10: Jacopo Tintoretto's *The Miracle of the Slave* and *Translation of the Body of St. Mark*; Veronese's *Christ in the House of Levi;* Titian's *La Pieta*, which he worked on in his 90s and is his last painting

Room 11: More large-scale paintings by Tintoretto

Room 13: Titian's *Madonna and Child* and portraits by Tintoretto.

Room 17: Venitian art of the 18th century

Room 20: Paintings of various scenes of Venice in the 1490s, including Bellini's *Procession in the Piazzo San Marco.*

Room 21: Devoted to Carpaccio's *Legend of St. Ursula*

Room 24: Titian's *Presentation of the Virgin*

PONTE DELLA ACCADEMIA

Vaporetto: Accademia.

One of the three bridges that cross the Grand Canal, and the most modern. Made of metal and wood, with wide steps, kids clamor to jump up these big steps.

PEGGY GUGGENHEIM COLLECTION

Palazzo Venier dei Leoni, 701. Tel. (39)(041)240-5411. Fax (39)(041)520-6885. Web: www.guggenheim-venice.it. Open 11am-6pm. Closed Tuesday. Admission, with children under 8 free. Vaporetto: Accademia.

A great art museum to take children. It's small, beautiful and unhurried. The paintings – all modern art – are big with bright colors. It has a café, which serves excellent pastas, salads and sandwiches. It has an outside sculpture garden. It also has a porch where you can go out and look up and down the Grand Canal. Amenities aside, the museum showcases art representative of some of the major movements of the 20th century. The permanent collection is organized to highlight the progression of early 20th-centry art from cubism and constructivism, to abstract expressionism and surrealism.

Peggy Guggenheim, the American copper heiress, filled her life with modern art, including those works by her second husband, Max Ernst. Look for his *Robing of the Bride*, which is possibly a tribute to Guggenheim (ask the kids whether they think she was flattered!).

Other works include Picasso's 1937 *La Baignade*, Salvadore Dali's *Birth of Liquid Desires*, Kandinsky's *Landscape with Church*, and several works by Alexander Calder. Although it's not classic Italian art, this is an important museum, befitting Venice's role as host of the Biennale art festival – possibly the most important in the world. Our kids enjoy this museum every time we visit. Stop by the gift shop.

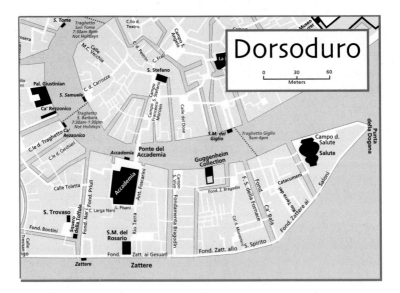

San Polo & Santa Croce

RIALTO BRIDGE & MARKETS
Vaporetto: Rialto.

Ponte Rialto is another of the three bridges that cross the Grand Canal, and perhaps the most historically famous. Certainly it is the most charming, with shops clinging to its sides bursting with delights. Originally built on boats in 1181 by Nicolo Barattieri, it was called the Ponte della Moneta. In 1250, it was replaced by a wooden bridge and during the early 1400s shops sprouted up, perhaps leading to the name change. After two collapses, a stone bridge built by Antonio da Ponte in 1591, replaced the wooden one. Today, the bridge continues to lead to the Rialto markets, where lively commerce has endured for centuries. Small boats ease into the canal moorings heaping with fresh produce. There are fruit, fish and vegetable stalls. Visit the market every morning, except Sunday.

Fun Fact
Venetians flocked to the Rialto Bridge in 1444 to honor the marquis of Ferrara who was passing by in his boat. Much to the shock of those on the bridge, the Rialto collapsed, landing many in the Canal's waters. Eventually, the wooden bridge was replaced with a stone one that kept many of the same features of the original. And, it hasn't collapsed since!

Cannaregio

JEWISH GHETTO
Guided tours of the synagogues available every hour on the hour from 10am-4pm and Sunday 10am-noon. Vaporetto: San Marcuola.

Venice coined the word "ghetto" for this area, the first Jewish ghetto in Europe. The section originally was a cannon foundry, called a getto in Italian. Once Jews were forced to reside in this area around 1516, the name getto stuck. Today the area preserves Jewish tradition with several synagogues, a nursing home, preschool, library and kosher restaurant. The **Museo Communita Israelitica/Ebraica** also is located here. Visit **Gam**

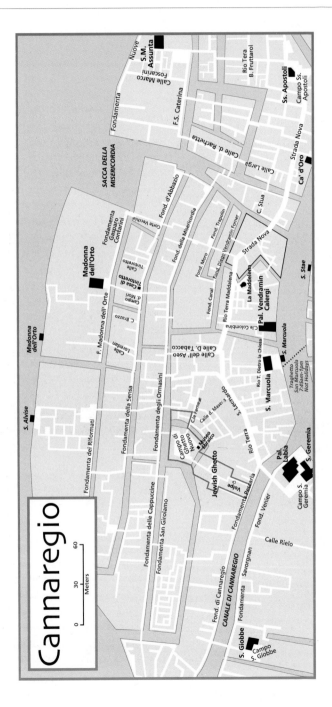

Cannaregio

Gam Kosher Restaurant, *Sotoportego Ghetto Vecchio, Tel. (39)(041)715.284*, for traditional Jewish and Italian cuisine. **Locanda del Ghetto**, *Piazza Ghetto Nuovo, Tel. (39)(041)275.9292*, includes a kosher breakfast.

MUSEO EBRAICA
Campo del Nuovo Ghetto. Tel. (39)(041)715-359. Web: www.museoebraico.it Open June 1 to September 30 from 10am-7pm and from October 1 to May 31 from 10am-6pm. Admission.

Opened in 1953, the museum displays numerous Jewish religious pieces, including prayer shawls and old marriage contracts. A tour can include three *scuolas* (schools) and the synagogues.

PONTE MUTI
Site of another boatyard. The Ponte Muti is located near Campo dell'Abbazia and the Scuola Vecchia della Misericordia, a Gothic church. The Sottoportico dell'Abbazia under the church leads to the Ponte Muti. If you don't cross the bridge and instead turn right on Corte Vecchia to Fondamenta Gasparo Contarini, you will be able to view the island of San Michele, Venice's floating cemetary.

CAMPO & CHURCH OF MADONNA DELL 'ORTO
Monday-Saturday 10am-5:30pm, Sunday and holidays 3pm-5:30pm.

Come here to see soccer park, where the local kids often play the game. From the Fondamenta Gasparo Contarini (see Ponte Muti) pass the Palazzo Mastelli. The campo is west of the fondamenta. The Church of Madonna dell'Orto was Tintoretto's parish and he and his children are buried inside.

Elsewhere in the Venetian Lagoon

MASK MAKING

Venice is known for its mask making. During the plague, a doctor invented the mask with a long beak. Inside the beak, the doctor placed garlic to cover the smell of the sick. You can see variations of this "plague mask" in shop windows. There are many mask shops in Venice. Look for ones where the artists make the masks in the shop. Here are some we enjoyed visiting:

"**Papier Mache,**" *Calle Lunga S. Maria Formosa, 5175 (Corner Shop). Tel. (39)(041)522-9995.* In Castello. This artist's' workshop and store invites you to watch the creation of masks – from sketch to clay model to delicate painting. Floor to ceiling windows allow a full view of artists at work. Feel free to come in to watch and browse. Stefano, a mask maker for over 20 years, gladly shares the history of this Venetian tradition and will answer any questions about the process and art of mask making. While many shops display masks, "Papier Mache" is as much an artist's workshop as a place to purchase masks. Our children loved this shop, and enjoyed petting and cuddling Stefano's two lovely dogs.

MondoNovo, *Rio Terra Canal, 3063, Campo Santa Margherita. Tel. (39)(041)528-7344. Open 10am-1pm and 2pm-6pm. Monday-Saturday. In Dorsoduro. Eyes Wide Shut* director Stanley Kubrick purchased masks here for his movie. So can you – buy masks that is.

Ca'Macana, *Calle delle Botteghe, Dorsoduro. Tel. (39)(041)277-6142. Fax (39)(041)520-3229. Web: www.camacana.com. Open 10am-7:30pm daily. In Dorsoduro.* All types of masks are available in this fanciful shop. Most fun is the lecture on mask making the artist is more than willing to give to anyone interested in listening.

GONDOLA FACTORY

In the 1500s, ten thousand gondoliers made their living in Venice. Today only four hundred continue the tradition passed from father to son (no daughters among the ranks of gondoliers, yet). Gondolas are tricky to make. They are 11 meters long, 1.4 meters wide and weigh about 500 kilos. They also tilt to the right so they do not travel in circles. The gondolier stands on the "poop" and sculls on the right with one oar. Gondolas require about six or seven coats of black paint and are made out of several types of wood. Only about four are made each year.

On one trip to Venice we stumbled onto a gondola factory tucked away in a tiny, remote piazza in the Castello. And, during a subsequent trip

with our young teens, we rediscovered this boatmaking piazza. You can easily miss this unique shop, so keep alert and ask for directions, if you must. It is found at building number 4725 on calletta Rota (remember street numbering is erratic in Venice, so don't expect order!).

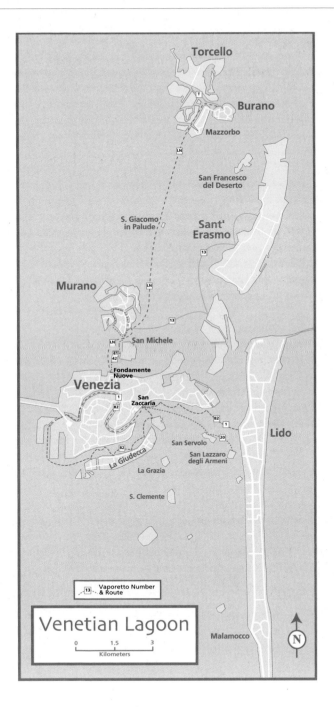

Here are our new and improved directions for finding this Venetian treasure: From the Accademia, as you face the entrance to the Accademia, follow the first passageway to the right (Calle Gaunbara) for two blocks to a small canal. Turn left and proceed to the second foot bridge (Porte S. Traviso), which is just in front of the popular enotecca (marked by a sign: Vini al Bottegon.) If you walk 100 yards further on, you can view the boatyard from across the small canal. To visit, cross the Ponte S. Traviso, turn immediately left on the fondamonte Toffetti, pass the church, then go out to the street and turn left. The factory is just on the left, number 4725. Whew! You made it. Knock on the door and ask, preferably in Italian although hand signs, finger pointing and gracious smiles work pretty well, too, if your family can admire the work underway in the factory. Whiff the odors of walnut and beech blended with the smell of varnishes and glue. The proprietor, a man of few words in any language, allowed us to examine one gondola that remained semi-built and another that was being painted glossy black. It is an ancient craft, diminished over time, but still retaining its wonder. Our children thoroughly enjoyed this visit.

MURANO

From San Zaccaria, take vaporetti numbers 52 or 23. From Fondamente Nuove, take numbers 12 and 13. Or, arrange for private (and often free) transport from your hotel.

Glassmaking is serious business in Murano, with family secrets passed down through generations. By the end of the 13th century Venice's glassmaking furnaces were centralized on the island of Murano. The craft peaked in the 16th century, and though still going strong, has not been able to retain the elegance of its past. Nowadays, amidst the light-catching chandeliers and delicate champagne glasses are more tacky glass oddities, for which strangely enough there is a market.

There are six significant factories remaining in Murano. One of the oldest in continuous production, is the **Vetrerie Riunite Colleoni Murano** (*Fondamenta dei Battuti, 12, Tel. (39)(041)739-169; Fax (39)(041)736-329; E-mail: colleoni@tin.it.*). The factory is over 600 years old and resides in an old church. After leaving the boat, you are ushered into the factory where you get to see first-hand the blazing furnaces and feel, even at a distance, the incredible heat.

After the factory visit, you are paraded into the display room, where all types of glassworks are for sale – artistic glass sculptures, formal stemware, jewelry. Surprisingly, there was no pressure to buy. But, since we were in the market, the Colleoni brothers took turns keeping the children occupied by encouraging them to draw designs for future glass projects! Everyone had a marvelous time and we splurged on a belated anniversary gift.

Another factory is **Civam** (*Viale Garibaldi, 24. Tel/ Fax (39)(041)739-323; located near the docks*). Also visit the **Glass Museum** (*Museo dell'Arte Vetraria. Fondamenta Giustiniano and Fondamenta Manin. Tel. (39)(041)739-586. Open Monday, Tuesday, Thursday, Saturday 10am-4pm and Sunday 9am-12:30pm. Closed Wednesday*).

We purchased a beautiful Venetian chandelier at **Vetreria Nuova Bisanzio** (*Tel. (39)(041)739-222 Email: bisanzioglass@hotmail.com*). Just remember to purchase light bulbs there; the standard is different from the U.S.

Obssessed with glassmaking? Here's a good site to answer all your questions: www.venetian-glass.info.

Parent Tip: Glassblowing was a highlight of our kids' trip. You watch the process from start to finish. At **Colleoni**, the owners were genuinely enamored with the children, answering their every question. They even let them blow a little glass and gave them cute candies – made of glass, of course.

BURANO

From Fondamente Nuove, take vaporetto 12.

A lovely island dressed in gum-drop bright colors and draped in lace. Italian lacework, an art nearing extinction, is everywhere in Burano. Take your sketch pads and crayons here! Visit the **Scuoloa dei Merletti** in Piazza Galuppi (*Tel. (39)(041)730-034. Monday through Saturday, 9am-6pm, Sunday 9am-4pm. Admission*) to see a handful of women engage in the intricate work of stitching lace. We also visited the **dalla Lidia Merletti D'Arte** (*Via Galuppi, 215. Tel. (041)730-052. Web: www.dallalidia.com*). Beautiful table linens, dresses, doilies and so much more. Most exciting, however, was a small tour of their private collection of lace items – from Louis XIV fans to full-length wedding gowns.

A curiosity is the **Church of San Martino** with its own leaning tower (Piazza Galuppi).

Fun Fact

Why are the houses painted so brightly? Legend, and the good word of several Burano residents, has it that women painted their houses so colorful so that their husbands, who fished the deep sea, would recognize their home immediately upon turning into the harbor.

If your kids are crying for green space, Burano is a great place to come. There is plenty of grass to run, play and picnic. Enjoy a snack or lunch in one of the many cafes and *trattoria* on the island.

There are many restaurants on the island. We enjoyed **Trattoria Da Romano**, *Via Galuppi, 221. Tel. (39)(041)730-030. Fax (39)(041)735-217. Email: info@ daromano.it. Web: www.daromano. it (in Italian). Closed on Wednesday.* Fish is a good bet here. But, we also enjoyed the spaghetti al pomodoro and angelini with lemon and basil. The pretty rose leather benches and pink tablecloths added to the island's relaxing aura. In good weather, you can sit in a walled

garden with terra cotta walls, yellow table and chairs, topped with deep blue umbrellas. Euphoric!

SAN MICHELE: THE ISLAND OF THE DEAD

From Fondamenta Nuove or Piazza Roma, take Vaporetto 52.

Our children loved the story tape, *Vivaldi: Ring of Mystery*, that mentions the spooky Island of the Dead, and they wanted it see if for themselves. As with all of Venice, the cemetery is unique because no one can be buried underground since there is only the sea beneath the grass. To compensate, the Venetians stack everyone up in long rows. The tranquil island is actually beautiful, with tall cypress trees reaching to the heavens. Few tourists take this trip – a Venetian's last boatride.

THE LIDO

Vaporetto 6 or 11.

The place to go to the beach, sort of. You dream of long walks on the beach or glorious views of pale sand, with blue-green waves lapping at the shore. Forget it. You're in the Lido and that means beach cabana central. Cabanas are everywhere and those oh-so-big hotels privately own the beach, except for a sliver of land, across the street. Even from our hotel window, we could barely get a glimpse of sand because of all those cabanas. The Lido is expensive and overcrowded. But it is a beach and the kids usually don't care about crowds or money. It is also just a short *vaporetta* ride from San Marco, so it's quite possible to stay here in the summer and take day trips into Venice for sightseeing. To get to the public beach, **Spiaggia Comunale**, take a 15-minute walk from the *vaporetto* stop at San Nicolo (proceed down the Gran Viale and make a left on Lungomare d'Annunzio to rent a, yuk, cabana). Remember, cars and buses are allowed on the Lido.

The Lido is also the best sports outlet available in Venice:
• **Barbieri**. *Via Zara, 5*. Rents bikes and tricycles.
• **Circolo Golf Venezia**. *Via del Forte, 30011. Tel. (39)(041)731-015. Fax (39)(041)731-339*
• **Lido Tennis Club**. *Via San Gallo, 15. Tel. (39)(041)760-954*

WHICH ONE IS MY ROOM?
Note: If you are driving and parked at the Tronchetto Park, ask your hotel if they offer a discount parking coupon.

Castello
HOTEL LONDRA PALACE **** *Riva degli Schiavoni 4171. Tel. (39)(041)520-0533. Fax (39)(041)522-5032. Web: www.londrapalace.com.*

Located on the waterfront just steps from the Piazza San Marco, the Hotel Londra Palace is an elegant hotel, quite comfortable for families. We enjoyed its location, nestled between the hubbub of the Piazza San Marco and the more serene Giardini Pubblici. Originally built in 1860, the hotel was recreated by an eminent Italian architect, Rocco Magnoli, who also designs Versace boutiques around the world. Most rooms overlook the Grand Canal, and those that do not offer a splendid view of the terra-cotta rooftops, spires and bell towers of Venice. The hotel's restaurant, Do Leoni, is one of the best in Venice, serving traditional Venetian fare.

Hotel Prices

Very Expensive – over €400/night
Expensive — €250-400/night
Moderate – €150-250/night
Inexpensive – under €150/night

HOTEL DANIELI ***** *Riva degli Schiavoni, 4196. Tel. (39)(041)522-6480. Fax (39)(041) 520-0208. Web: www.danielihotel enice.com.*

Luxury seekers will be pleased with accommodations at the Hotel Danieli. Marble, Murano chandeliers, a golden staircase – need we say more? The largest hotel in Venice, this Gothic palace was turned into a hotel in 1822. Babysitting services are prominently advertised.

SANTA MARIA DELLA PIETA ** *Castello 3701, Calle della Pieta, Tel. (39)(041)5222.171) or 523.7395, Web: www.pietavenezia.org.*

Built in the 14th century by the Franciscans as a home for abandoned children, this sunny hotel offers 15 spacious rooms with shared baths. It's noted for its cleanliness and wonderful staff. Enjoy breakfast and delight in the laughter of children playing in the garden. Or, climb up to the rooftop and take in the views of the city. A very convenient location, too!

San Marco

HOTEL CONCORDIA **** *Calle Larga San Marco, 367. Tel. (39)(041)520-6866. Fax (39)(041)520-6775. Web: www.hotelconcordia. com.*

Uniquely situated on the Piazzetta dei Leoncini, a charming corner of St. Mark's Square, is the family-run Hotel Concordia. With 57 wonderful

rooms, this historic hotel, established in 1667, offers a unique combination of tradition and comfort. Walk up a marble staircase to the contemporary reception area, then whisk off to your room, decorated in more traditional Venetian fare. The service is tops at Hotel Concordia. Ask them to set up a trip to the island of Murano for your family. This is the only hotel in the city overlooking Piazza San Marco and its central air conditioning will be refreshing for the kids on those hot, steamy days.

HOTEL GRITTI
PALACE ***** *Campo Santa
Maria del Giglio. Tel.
(39)(041)794-611. Fax
(39)(041)520-0942. Web:
gritti.hotelinvenice.com.*

Bathe yourself in head-
to-toe luxury in this 15th-
century Grand Canal palace.
The Gritti once belonged to
Doge Andrea Gritti and he certainly would not be disappointed in the place
today. Murano chandeliers dangle and sparkle in almost every room. The
Burano lace table linens are exquisite. Surprisingly, the staff is more than
cordial and quite pleasant with the little ones. There are 214 rooms and
three suites.

HOTEL FLORA *** *Calle Bergamaschi, 2283A. Tel. (39)(041)520-
5844. Fax (39)(041)522-8217. Web: www.hotelflora.it/en.*

The 1920s staircase and tranquil garden help make Hotel Flora a
delightful place to stay. Some of the 44 rooms are small, others have a
delightful view of the garden and its patio. Enjoy the children's tea served
daily at no extra charge. Fill out their Little Needs Form to help them help
you when you travel with babies and tots.

HOTEL KETTE **** *Piscine San Moise, 2053. Tel. (39)(041)520-
7766. Fax (390(041)522-8964. Web: www.hotelkette.com.*

A pleasant, family-run hotel a bit off the beaten track. Each of the 70
rooms is well appointed and the common areas quite comfortable. If you

like a more quiet, less hectic
place to stay, still just a
short walk from all Venice
has to offer, you will enjoy
your stay at the 16th-
century Hotel Kette. Some
of the rooms feature
splendid marble baths.
Triple rooms also are
available for larger families.
Note that there is no hotel restaurant or bar.

ALBERGO SAN MARCO *** *Piazza San Marco. Ponte dei Dai, 877.
Tel. (39)(041)520-4277. Fax (39)(041)523-8447. Web:
www.hotelsanmarcovenice.com.*

Plain and simple in a great location just off St. Mark's Square. Affiliated with the Best Western chain, which operates many hotels throughout Italy.

San Polo

HOTEL MARCONI *** *Riva del Vin, S. Polo, 729. Tel. (39)(041)522-2068. Fax (39)(041)522-9700. Web: www.hotelmarconi.it.*

Catch a glimpse of the elegant Rialto Bridge, just a few feet away from this 16th- century palace, the Hotel Marconi. The hotel has been located in this bustling, commercial center of Venice since the 11th century. The 26 rooms exude Old World charm, with splendid Murano glass chandeliers, and are quite comfortable for families. Wonderful restaurants nearby, including Madonna. Though you will be treated to a feast at the hotel's breakfast. Ask the conceirage about special arrangements at the Lido, Venice's beach, or for private water taxis to Murano. Staff are warm and gracious. And, do ask head conceirage how his son's music lessons are going! The next Vivaldi, perhaps?

LOCANDA STURION *** *Calle del Sturion, San Polo 679. Tel. (39)(041)523-6243. Fax (39)(041)522-8378. Web: www.locandasturion. com.*

Another lovely hotel next to the Rialto Bridge that beautifully balances Old World splendors with modern-day conveniences. The mosaic floors of the eleven rooms are marvelous. Ask for a family room (Rooms 1 and 2 offer a stunning view of the Canal and the Rialto Bridge. We also enjoyed Rooms 9 and 10 on the top floor, where we left the doors open and shuttled back and forth making last minute plans and goading our teenage son to get his "the-jeans-I-got-last-month-don't-fit-me-anymore body out of bed!). The breakfast and reading room, rich wood tables and leather seats and a lovely Venetian chandelier, overlooks the Grand Canal, where we

watched the comings and goings of traveller and Venetian alike. While you must walk up three flights to the reception desk, we find the Locanda one of the friendliest, coziest hotels in Florence. Do book music, theater or museum tickets with the front desk. And, visit the Gallerie dell'Accademia to see *Il Miracolo della Croce*, a 1494 painting by Vittore Carpaccio that shows the facade of this hotel with its signpost.

San Croce

SANTA CHIARA HOTEL *** *Santa Croce, 548. Tel. (041)520-6955. Fax (041)522-8799. Web: www.hotelsantachiara.it.*
Situated in Piazzale Roma, Santa Chiara is the crossroads between highway and waterway. On one side, is the road leading to mainland Venice, while steps away lies the Grand Canal that will take you to the heart of Venice. Piazzale Roma is far from the most beautiful spot in Venice, but, for some, it is a convenient way to spend a few short days in Venice, allowing for a quick escape to other destinations in the Veneto. The hotel is fine, boasting beautiful Venetian chandeliers and most with views on the Grand Canal. There is a parking garage (think long lines, though) at Piazzale Roma.

Dorsoduro

ACCADEMIA VILLA MARAVEGE *** *Fondamenta Bollani 1058. Tel. (39)(041)521-0188. Fax (39)(041)523-9152. Web: www.pensioneaccademia.it.*
Steps from the Grand Canal, this recently renovated villa still possesses 17th-century charm. Only 17 rooms, this hotel once was the home of the

Russian Embassy. Call ahead. This charming hotel may be more difficult to book than many 5 stars!
ALLA SALUTE DA CICI ** *Fondamenta Ca'Bala, 222. Tel. (39)(041)523-5404. www.hotelsalute.com/Home.aspx?language=en.*
A family-run 50-room hotel, part of an old palazzo, situated in a cozy and quiet corner of a quiet square.
MESSNER ** *Dorsoduro, 216. Tel. (39)(041)522-7443. Web: www.hotelmessner.it/index.php?lang=en.*
Neat, clean, modern. Several rooms well suited for families.

The Lido

QUATTRO FONTANE **** *Via delle Quattro Fontane, 16. Tel. (39)(041)526-0227. Fax (39)(041)526-0726. Closed November through March. Web: www.quattrofontane.com/en.*

Charm abounds at this quaint country inn. The common rooms are resplendent with antiques, including several Oriental puppets that delighted our children. Rooms are large and comfortable, some with a balcony that runs the length of the room. But don't expect great views – most hotels at the Lido sit a block or more back from the beach.

The Quattro Fontane offers two connected double rooms for families, with a king-size bed in one room and two singles and a sink in the other. The hotel has access to a private beach. Be prepared. Beach access does not come cheap: about $50 for a cabana that houses beach furniture, parasol, tables and storage space for beach supplies. A public beach is about a kilometer further away. The hotel also has a tennis court, small outside terrace and restaurant. Most important, the hotel has a wonderful staff that enjoys and delights in their youngest guests.

EXCELSIOR PALACE ***** *Lungomare Marconi, 41. Tel. (39)(041)526-0201. Fax (39)(041)526-7276 Closed mid-November through mid-March. Web: www.ho10.net/excelsior. Children under 12 free.*

The stars come out at the Excelsior Palace during the Venice film festival. And no wonder. This hotel puts the extra chi in chi-chi. Built in 1907, the Moorish archways and design make it a visual treat. Besides unbelievably lush digs, the hotel offers tennis courts, three restaurants, a nightclub, private boat service to Venice and beach cabanas along its private beach that your family could live in for the rest of your stay. Of course, the pampering comes with a price. If you can afford it, enjoy *La Dolce Vita!*

VILLA PARCO *** *Via Rodi, 1. Tel. (39)(041)526-0015. Fax (39)(041)526-7620. Email: Web: www.hotelvillaparco.com.*

A family-friendly villa about one block from the water. Enjoy the tiny garden and great service.

DES BAINS **** *Lungomare Marconi, 17. Tel. (39)(041)526-5921. Fax (39)(041)526-0113. Web: desbains.hotelinvenice.com.*

Another magnificent hotel, now part of the Sheraton chain. Enjoy a saltwater pool, two tennis courts, and private boat service to Venice. The Liberty style permeates the 190-room hotel, giving it that old grand-hotel feeling. The hotel has a wonderful veranda dining room for intimate and romantic dinners.

I'M HUNGRY!
San Marco
DO FORNI $$ *Calle dei Specchieri, 468. Tel. (39)(041)523-2148. www.doforni.it. doforni@infinito.it. Closed Thursdays in winter.*
Small, crowded, elegant but quite child-friendly, the two-dining room Do Forni is a good choice for a great Venetian meal. We started with strawberry champagne. Seafood is abundant. Try the fried scampi and baby squid. Or, you can create a mild spectacle by ordering the sea bass, which comes stuffed in a puffed pillow of wax paper where it is baked in its own juices and served with a variety of vegetables. Our children enjoyed the vermicelli and *insalta caprese.*

AL TEATRO $$$ *Campo S. Fantin, 1916. Tel. (39)(041)522-1052. Closed Monday.*
In a tucked away corner of Venice nestled up against La Fenice is Al Teatro, a restaurant for more than the theater crowd. White linen under white umbrellas set against the old stone wall of the theater makes for a warm and intimate setting. Choose a corner seat, if you're sitting outside, near Albergo Ateneo, and let your kids play in the square. One young artist passing by handed our children chalk. They drew spaceships and the universe and played games while we got to chat and plan for the next day. While the pasta is competent, the fish is superb. Try the fried calamari and scampi.

VINO, VINO $$ *Campo S. Fantin, 1983. Tel. (39)(041)522-4121. Closed Tuesday.*
Here's a little secret. The same chefs that cook outrageously expensive meals served at the upscale Antico Martino prepare meals for the connecting, reasonably priced Vino, Vino. Basically a storefront with a few scattered tables, the restaurant is known for its buffet of meats, vegetables and pastas.

AL BACARETO $$ *Calle Crosera, 3447. Tel. (39)(041)528-9336. Closed Saturdays for dinner and all day Sunday.*
Sit outside and watch the comings and goings of Venice while you dine on some of the best cuisine in the city. This is a neighborhood *trattoria*

serving tasty Venetian dishes, which means fish, fish, fish. Kids who just say no to fish will enjoy plain pasta dishes. Ask the waiter to just add butter to the plain pasta, if necessary.

CAFÉ QUADRI, FLORIAN, *and* **GRAN CAFÉ CHIOGGIA** $$$ *Piazza San Marco. Closed Monday.*

These three grand cafes are situated in the historic Piazza San Marco (*photo below of Florian*). Are they expensive? Yes. Is the food the best ever? No. Is it a cool place to hang out? Absolutely. To sit at a café in Santo Marco is to savor the present while daydreaming of the past, when travelers from

equally exotic places rested weary bones to gaze on the grandeur of Santo Marco.

This is a great place to unwind at day's end or for one parent to relax while the kids play as the other, unlucky one, waits in one of the long lines to get into the church, tower or doge's palace. For a few pennies, the kids can feed the birds – hundreds of pigeons who call the piazza home. Or, they can simply cavort in the old piazza while you tune into the dueling bands. Each café has a band featuring classical, jazz or big-band sound. They take turns playing so you can enjoy them all.

McDONALDS $ *Across from the Concordia Hotel on Calle Larga San Marco. No credit cards.*

Yes, there's a McDonald's in Venice for anyone having a Mac-attack.

Castello

ACIUGHETA $$ *Campo S. Filipo e Giacomo. Tel. (39)(041)522-4292 or 520-8222. Closed Tuesday.*

This is a quick service *trattoria* with good food. The *insalata caprese* is fresh, just a bit of oil smothering the cheese and tomatoes. The lasagna is hearty. There are numerous pizza selections for the kids and, although our pizza was watery, it tasted great. Ask for the house Chianti, an excellent choice. The kids were thrilled when the serenading accordion player belted out a few tunes at our table.

DO LEONI $$$$ *Riva degli Schiavoni, 4171, at the Hotel Londra Palace. Tel. (39)(041)520-0533.*

Some of the best dining in Venice. The food, many traditional Venetian dishes, is perfectly prepared and presented. The dining room is opulent. A piano bar is open until about 1am. This is elegant dining, but somehow our kids made it through (sketch pads and crayons did it) and we enjoyed one of our best meals eating out.

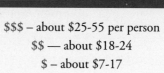

Restaurant Prices

$$$ – about $25-55 per person
$$ — about $18-24
$ – about $7-17

DA REMIGIO $$ *Salizzada dei Greci, 3416. Tel. (39)(041) 523-0089. Closed Monday and Tuesday evening.*

Popular with the Venetians and a perfectly wonderful traditional cuisine. Good pasta dishes for the kids at this neighborhood favorite.

OSTERIA AL MASCARON $$$ *Calle Santa Maria Formosa, 5525. Tel. (39)(041)522-5995. Closed Sunday.*

Considered by some Venetians to be the best *osteria* in Venice, Al Mascaron is certainly a fish-lovers paradise. Lobster, cuttlefish ink, octopus and tuna dominate the limited menu. But for non-fish eating youngsters, *pasta pomodoro* or simply with butter is available. Typical of almost every Venetian restaurant, Mascaron's decor consists of wood-beamed ceilings and copper pots. Also dotting the walls, however, are curious drawings of fish and their eaters by local artists. Our children were inspired by the humorous art and set out to draw their own fish stories on the crayon-friendly place mats. A big hit for families.

Santa Croce/San Polo

ANTICO CAPON $ *Piazza Santa Margherita, 3004. Tel. (390(041)528-525. Credit cards accepted.*

Situated in a large piazza, the Antico Capon is frequented primarily by students and locals. The service is gruff but helpful. The ambience is worn but comfortable. The food – most of it quite good. Try the *pasta primavera*. The swordfish is excellent. Skip the house wine, though, too watery. The kids loved the mixed salad that was sprinkled with fresh corn, walnuts and apples. Pizza also is *molto bene* here.

ACQUAPAZZA $$ *Campo S. Angelo, S. Marco, 3808/10. Tel. (39)(041)277-0688. Fax. (39)(041)277-5421. Closed Monday.*

Charming upscale pizza, fish and salad ristorante. The fish is fresh from the Amalfi coast.

ALLA MADONNA $$ *Calle della Madonna, 594. Tel. (39)(041)523-3824. Credit cards accepted. Dinner for four, L135.000 Closed Wednesdays and all of January.*

A boisterous mix of tourists and locals visit Alla Madonna, making it a child-friendly *trattoria* for lunch or dinner. Located just steps from the

Rialto Bridge, the restaurant specializes in fish. Try their *fritto misto di mare* (mixed fried seafood) or their *spaghetti alla vongole* (with clam sauce). The *pasta e fagioli* (pasta and beans) was a hit with the kids.

PIZZERIA AL GIARDINETTO $ *Rio della Frescada, 2910. Tel. (39)(041)522-4100. Credit cards accepted.*

A charming restaurant in a pretty garden framed by hanging vines. Pizza is the house favorite, and there are so many to choose from. Our children keep it simple and always order *Pizza Margherita* (cheese, tomato, basil). But you can be more daring.

DA SANDRO PIZZERIA $ *San Polo, 1473/1411/1412. Tel. (39)(041)523.4894. Closed Thursday.*

Near the Rialto Bridge, just off Piazza San Polo, this is a pleasant little trattoria with good, basic pizza.

TRATTORIA DA IGNAZIO $$ *Calle Saoneri, 2749. Tel. (39)(041)523-4852. Closed Sunday.*

Good prices, decent food.

Dorsoduro

CIPRIANI $$$$ *Fondamenta San Giovanni, 10. In the Cipriani Hotel. La Guidecca Venezia. Tel. (39)(041)707-744.*

Totally elegant. Extremely expensive. The dinner menu is extensive, with Venetian and international cuisine. Try the *blinis alla russa con salmone scozzese* (Russian blini with smoked Scottish salmon) for an appetizer. Lunch is served by the pool and includes generous antipastos.

TAVERNA SAN TROVASO $$ *Fondamenta Priuli, 1016. Tel. (39)(041)520-3703. Credit cards accepted. Closed Monday.*

Eat a meal with the locals. The talk is loud and passionate, the food is tops. Seafood reigns supreme – try the spaghetti Newburg (shrimp, tomatoes and a thick cream sauce). The gnocchi quatro formaggi is very cheesy and the vegetable soup tops. Ask for the house Chianti; it's superb. The Taverna recieves the best gelato in a restaurant award. We liked vanilla with cherry and vanilla with lemon. An excellent restaurant.

TRATTORIA AI CUGNAI $-$$ *Pisc. Del Forner, 857. Between the Academia and Guggenheim Museums. Tel. (39)(041)528-9238. Closed Monday.*

We love this place, and keep coming back. Is it the two old aunts who hustle-bustle you to your seats, each jousting the other for your attention and order? Or the chatter of Venetians enjoying one of the best, cheap meals in town? Could it be the fried calamari Michael lives for? Plain and simple cooking, with lots of meats and fish. "Even the noodles taste good," noted our daughter. Alas, the chirping canaries living in a cage set in an itsy-bitsy garden are "caput," but this joint is still hoppin'.

ENOTECA CANTINONE $ *Gia Schiavi, S. Trovaso, 992. Tel. (39)(041)523-0034. Email: cantinone@maac.com*

Very popular enoteca (wine bar) with a wide selction of *bruschetta*, little sandwich snacks called *cicchetti*, with toppings such as the uniquely Venetian *sarde in saor* (sardine in vinegar.)

Cannaregio

CASA MIA $ *Calle dell'Oca, 4430. Tel. (39)(041)528-5590. Closed Tuesday.*

A fun pizzeria near the Campo SS. Apostolli sought out by the Venetians. Sit in the 6-table courtyard and let your kids enjoy the outdoor space.

ANTICA MOLA $$ *Fondamenta degli Ormesini, 2800. Near the Jewish Ghetto. No phone. Closed Wednesday.*

Typical and well-prepared Venetian fare – fish, risotto, pasta. The good news is there are tables by the canal. The bad news for some families with rambunctious little ones: There are tables by the canal.

HONG KONG $$ *Strada Nova, 4386. Tel. (39)(041)523-6040.*

Located near the Ca' d'Oro. Not bad Chinese food for family members tired of Italian cuisine. Outside tables available on the Strada Nova.

6. VERONA

You are fated to fall head over heels in love with Verona, with its cobblestone streets, stoic Arena and majestic Castlevecchio. But, wait, is that you Juliet, standing at your balcony, beckoning the young Romeo to your side? Yes, her balcony is here, along with the Juliet statue of pure gold that Lord Montague said he would raise as a symbol of friendship, albeit a bit late, with the Capulets. Juliet's house is the destination that romantics (and fans of Leonardo DiCaprio and Clare Danes) will remember forever. For the rest – there's what must be the world's most dense display of graffiti (more on this later).

Verona forever will be famous for the burning desires and desperation of the two star-crossed lovers, **Romeo and Juliet.** But the city is so much more. Verona is said to be the "Gateway to Italy" for travelers approaching from the north. It graciously combines natural beauty with man-made architectural splendor and easy living. Verona rests up against the rollicking Adige River, which swirls in, out and around the city. The background of mountains provides the perfect frame for this picturesque town.

The first record of settlement dates to about the first century BC and shows how vital Augusta Verona was to the Roman Empire. Three major ancient Roman roads began here – the Augusta, the Gallica and the Postumia. Verona's location helped promote the city as a trade center, but its position also caused it to become the epicenter of many battles. Verona endured with grace and style, emerging as a cultural and art capital of Italy.

Dante, for example, resided in Verona during his exile from Florence. The city honored the great writer with his own piazza, affectionately nicknamed Piazza Dante.

Despite natural disasters, including the flood of 1882 and the devastation of numerous wars, Verona was one of

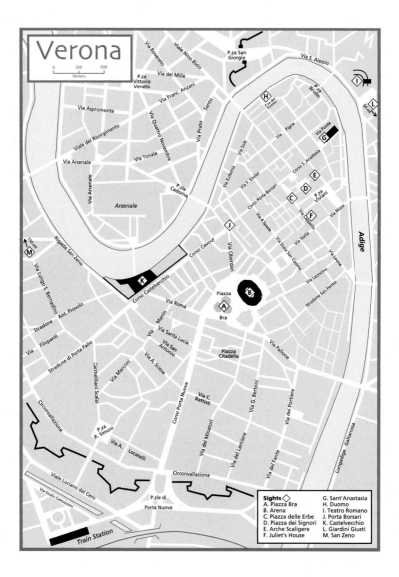

Verona

0 300 600
Meters

Sights ◇
A. Piazza Bra
B. Arena
C. Piazza delle Erbe
D. Piazza dei Signori
E. Arche Scaligere
F. Juliet's House
G. Sant'Anastasia
H. Duomo
I. Teatro Romano
J. Porta Borsari
K. Castelvecchio
L. Giardini Giusti
M. San Zeno

of the hardest hit cities during World War I. But like the phoenix, Verona continues to rise from ashes and regain its position as a player in the world of poetry, prose, art and architecture.

Parent Tip: Our family appreciated the traffic-free city center, the better to watch in-line skaters jag and jut around the Arena or window shop in the fashion district. For tourist info, go to *www.tourism.verona.it*.

WHERE ARE WE GOING NOW?
PIAZZA BRA

One of the most picturesque squares in all of Italy, Piazza Bra is a delightful spot for relaxing before or after a day of visiting the sites. The **Portoni della Bra**, an enormous double archway built by Gian Galeazzo Visconti at the end of the 14th century makes for a dramatic entrance to the Piazza Bra. Standing tall on one side of the gateway is the **Torre Pentagona**, also erected at the end of the 14th century.

A stretch of cafes greets visitors to Piazza Bra, tempting them with wonderful cappuccino, scrumptious dinners or gelato and treats. In the center of the piazza are the public gardens, complete with a sculpture honoring **Vittorio Emanuele II** (1883) and a more recent one dedicated to the **Partisans of World War II**. A splendid fountain spouts streams of water as Veronese children – our kids right behind them – run, bike and skate on the path circling the fountain.

Sitting at the cafés looking past the garden is the ancient Roman Arena, still in great shape and often used for concerts and theater. Two

other structures dominate the Piazza Bra – the **Palazzo della Gran Guardia**, built in 1610 by Domenico Curtoni and the **Neoclassical Palazzo Barbieri**, dubbed the Nuova Gran Guardia by the locals, which houses municipal offices.

The broad sweep of pavement around Piazza Bra is known as the **Listone** and it's where you will find many Veronese taking their evening stroll.

Parent Tip: The **Piazza Bra** is a top spot to give kids, and yourself, the chance to unwind and burn energy. We were comfortable sipping a cappuccino while keeping an eye on our children playing in the park.

ARENA/AMPHITHEATER

Piazza Bra. Tel. (39)(045)800-3204. Web: www.arena-verona.com. Tuesdays-Sunday 8am-6:30pm in the summer. 8am-3pm during opera season. Closed Monday. Admission.

The Arena is Verona's crowning glory. Erected possibly as early as the 1st century, the Arena continues to be used today for musical and theatrical productions. Its use has not always been for such lofty performances. For some time it was the place to witness the butchery of gladiator games and public execution. By the 16th and 17th centuries, the Arena was put to better use as a fairground for tournaments and theater.

Verona's Arena is dwarfed only by Rome's Colosseum. The Verona amphitheater is elliptical, measuring 456 feet by 360 feet, and the dimensions of the pit are 243 feet by 144 feet. Looking up from the pit, you become mesmerized by flight after flight of wide steps originally used for seating.

If you're lucky enough to be in Verona during opera season, but unlucky enough not to have a ticket, just hang out at the Arena when the performance is underway. We caught bits and pieces of the music. And the kids were especially tickled to see actors, in full Renaissance garb, waiting around on the outside of the Arena for their cue to come on stage!

PIAZZA DELLE ERBE

Open 8am-1:30pm.

A bustling market built over the Forum of ancient Roman days. Look for the Verona Madonna statue in the center perched on top of a marble basin taken from the Roman baths. This piazza was a big hit with the kids. They enjoyed darting in and out of the stands, searching for the best fruits and treats.

This is also a great place to purchase delicious snacks.

The architecture is stunning. Stand at the corner of Via Mazzini, the southwest corner, find the low building with battlements and porticos. This is the **Domus Mercatorum**, a Romanesque building designed in 1301 by Alberto I della Scala. At the far end of Piazza Erbe is **Palazzo Maffei**, constructed in 1681. The six statues are of the gods: Hercules, Jupiter, Venus, Mercury, Apollo and Minerva. Peek in at the beautiful spiral staircase in the courtyard. To the left of the Palazzo Maffei stand the **Torre del Gardello**, commissioned by Cansignorio della Scala in 1370, with the belfry finished in 1626.

Look to the northeast corner for the lovely **Casa Mazzanti** (16th century by Cavalli). Next door is the **Domus Nova**. Nearby is the **Palazzo del Commune** and its **Torre dei Lamberti**, the tallest in Verona and built between 1172 and 1464. Tel. (39)(045)803.2726. Open 9am-7pm. Closed Monday.

Our children loved the **Fountain of Madonna Verona**, commissioned by Cansignorio in 1368. The female figure stands on a column that emerges from a basin from which the water overflows into a wider basin below the smaller one. They also pointed out another "lion angel," the winged lion of St. Mark.

PIAZZA DEI SIGNORI

Lovingly called Piazza Dante by the locals, it is the next piazza over from Piazza Erbe. Where Piazza Erbe is lively and invigorating, Piazza Dante is the essence of tranquility. Even watching the mamas chatting while their little children played tag, running safely to mama's legs as a base, you feel relaxed in the cozy square, surrounded by beautiful buildings and dotted with several cafes.

Entering from Piazza Erbe, the **Palazzo del Commune** (14th century) is on your right. It has the distinctive alternating bands of brick and stonework, the leitmotiv of Verona. Next is the **Palazzo del Capitano**, with its dramatic entranceway created by Sanmicheli in the 16th century. The 17th century **Porta Bombardiera**, an archway of stone pillars, ushers the light of the next square into Dante's Piazza.

The courtyard holds many architectural charms – the **Renaissance well** where children congregate, the **Loggia del Consiglio**, built in the late 15th century and the 18th- century facade of the **Domus Nova**, which houses one of the square's two cafes, Caffe Dante. Surmising the square throughout the centuries is Dante himself, sculpted by Ugo Zannoni and completed in 1865.

CHIESA DI SANTA MARIA ANTICA & ARCHE SCALIGERE
Via Arche Scaligere.

Just outside the Piazza Signore is the church of the Scala family, which by now you have come to realize is Verona's version of the Medici. The family's church was founded around the 7th century, a grand illustration of Romanesque architecture decorated in the Veronese style of alternating bands of brick and stone. The **tomb of Cangradne I della Scala**, outside high on the left as you face the church, is a 14th-century masterpiece. It resides under a Gothic canopy, similar to, but less ornate than, the one protecting the tomb of Cansignorio. This one, a breathtaking piece of work, is by Bonino da Campione and Gaspare Broaspini. Our son, the budding artist at age seven, was so inspired by the detail of the work, he grabbed his pad and pencil and sketched the tomb and canopy, drawing a crowd of Veronese remarking on his fine choice of subject.

Parent Tip: This is a great church to take the kids to. It is exquisite, but small. If you want to take more time, one adult can accompany the kids back to Piazza Dante.

JULIET'S HOUSE
Via Capello, 23. Tel. (39)(045)803-4303. Open 8am-6:30pm. Closed Monday. Admission.

Even those who think a romantic evening is one spent hugging the armchair, chugging a warm beer while cheering for their favorite *American Idol,* will respond to Cupid's bow at the sight of Juliet's balcony. Well, maybe, though they may point out that no one is sure this is her house, or even if there was a Juliet.

All those up on romance or Shakespeare or graffiti art – more on that later – must amble over to the Capulet's house and relive those precious balcony scenes. Her house is close to Piazza Erb, down Via Capello. But it's hard to find. Just ask someone as you walk down the street. As you walk through the tunnel to the inner courtyard, the first thing that catches your eye is, naturally, the balcony. It is romantic, clinging to the stone wall with ivy hanging to one side and a wisp

Fun Fact
The story upon which Shakespeare based his **Romeo and Juliet** was first written about by Luigi da Porto, a Veronese writer. Dante, while living in Verona, also wrote about the bickering of the two families.

of a white curtain peeking through the arched window on the other. Picture postcard perfect – and you can buy one at the gift shop across the courtyard. Near the entranceway is the bronze statue of Juliet by N. Constantini, not quite the gold model promised by the don of the Montague family, but a pretty rendition nonetheless. Inside, the house has been maintained as it was during the 14th century.

Equally intriguing is the **graffiti** that smothers the walls as you enter through the tunnel to the courtyard. Naturally, we gave our kids a quick lecture on the evils of destroying someone else's property. We emerged from the tunnel and were shocked to see the graffiti all over the wall to the house close to the entranceway. Looking closer, we realized the graffiti was all about, that's right, LOVE. *Paolo amore Margherita*, Laura you're mine forever, John, etc., etc., in all languages. Hearts everywhere in red-hot reds and blushing pinks. Even more surprising, you can buy a postcard of the graffiti art form, obviously sanctioned by the authorities, in the gift shop.

ROMEO'S HOUSE
Via delle Arche Scaligere, 4.

Romeo's house just doesn't have the luster, or the graffiti, of Juliet's, but to complete the cross-struck lovers pilgrimage, you should visit the site. The medieval house is built of brick, with some traces of the original battlements. At this point in time, visitors are not allowed in the courtyard.

MUSEUM OF NATURAL HISTORY
Lungadige Porta Vittoria, 9. Tel. (39)(045)807-9400. Open Monday-Saturday 8am-7pm. Sunday 1:30pm-7pm. Closed Friday.

Twenty rooms of cool kid stuff – from minerals to fossils and mammals to bugs, the Museum of Natural History in the Palazzo Pompei is a good break for art weary kids. Architect Sanmicheli between about 1530 and 1550 built the lovely palazzo the museum is housed in.

Look for the enormous mammoth tusk.

DUOMO
Piazza del Duomo. Open 7am-noon and 3pm-7pm.

The cathedral, consecrated in 1187, uniquely blends Romanesque and Gothic styles. The highlight of the interior is Titian's *Assumption of the Virgin*, located in the first chapel on the left aisle. Surprisingly, the bell tower remains incomplete although Sanmicheli began it in the 16th century.

TEATRO ROMANO & ARCHAEOLOGICAL MUSEUM
Regaste Redentore, 2. Tel. (045)800-0360. Open 8am-1pm. Open Tuesday-Sunday 8am-6:30pm. Performance days 8am-1:30pm. Closed Monday. Admission.

Near the Duomo is the Roman Theater, situated on the banks of the Adige. It was built in the second half of the 1st century BC. The theater is impressive, set against the green tufa hills. Its semi-circular tiers of seats remain largely intact along with the stage, which was partly recovered, and the dramatic ruins of the wings. Unfortunately, not much is left of the facade.

PORTA BORSARI
Porta Borsari is the best preserved of the Roman gates. The others include the **Porta dei Leoni** and the **Porta Palio** (named after the *palio,* or horserace, that was run in the neighborhood). This archway dates from the second half of the 1st century and bears an inscription that gives Verona its Roman name: *Colonia Verona Augusta.* It is located at the end of Corso Porta Borsari.

CASTELVECCHIO
Corso Castelvecchio, 2. Tel. (39)(045)594-734. Open Tuesday-Sunday 8am-6:30pm. Closed Monday. Admission.

Your kids will love this castle, beginning with the **Medieval Ponte Scaligero**, a bridge named after the ever-popular Scala family. Built in 1355 by Cangrande II della Scala for military purposes, it is put to more gentle uses today. The views from the red brick arches and towers are lovely and the games our kids played of hide and seek and lookout were equally enjoyable.

The castle itself was erected in 1324-1355 by Cangrande II della Scala, with part of it an appendage to the city walls. Entering the "Old Castle," you come upon the interior courtyard, with its small fort built by Napoleon. Six roofed towers jut from the exterior walls; the one taller than the rest is called the **Mastio**. A moat surrounds the castle walls that in olden days was flooded by the Adigetto, the little Adige River. Recent excavations unearthed the **Morbio Postern Gate**, part of the inner ramparts and the remains of a tiny, ancient church called **San Martino**.

Although the museum housed in the castle is ready-made for kids, you may want to linger longer. The courtyard and the bridge make for a fun meeting spot where one adult can bring the kids to play while the other continues through the museum.

Castlevecchio's museum holds many surprises, especially for kids. Rooms 1-5 include various sculptures dating from the 12th to the 14th century. Walk through the Morbio Postern Gate to the Great Tower and to the other rooms, including Room 6 where the ancient bells of Verona are on exhibit. Here's what the kids have been waiting for – Room 7 houses the Da Prato Collection of ancient firearms, jousting spears, knives, helmets and armor. It's all here, grandly displayed. Through the weapons room and up a flight of zigzag steps is a long, empty portico to explore, where the views of Verona are lovely.

Continuing through the museum look for examples of the International Gothic School in Room 11. In Room 15 there are several Bellini paintings and in Room 16, examples of works by Veronese Renaissance painters, inkling Domenico and Francesco Morone. Works from the 16th century by Venetian artists Veronese and Tintoretto are in Room 23.

The rooms conclude with 16th and 17th century art by Jacopo, Aarinati and Bassetti in Rooms 24 and 25.

GIARDINI GIUSTI
Via Giardini Giusti, 2. Tel. (39)(045)803-4029. Open 9am-dusk in summer and 9am-8pm in winter. Admission.

The garden has been blooming since 1580 and is a fine example of a Renaissance Italian garden, complete with fountains, flowerbeds, and a great maze for kids to run in.

SPORTS & RECREATION
Bicycling
A gentleman rents bikes and sometimes rollerblades in front of the Gran Guardia building in Piazza Bra. *Open daily 9am-7pm (mostly).*

Shakespeare Festival
Held in July and August.

Jazz Festival
Held in August.

Water Fun & GardaLand
Web: www.gardaland.it/en/home.php.
It's a half-hour train ride to Lake Garda. Near Lake Garda, the kids will love **GardaLand**, an Italian version of Disneyland (*see section on Sirmione in Chapter 8 for more information*).

WHICH ONE IS MY ROOM?

Many of the hotels in Verona will provide babysitting services with one-week notice. Babysitters are either hotel staff or university students.

Very Expensive

HOTEL GABBIA D'ORO ***** *Corso Porta Bosari, 4/A. Tel. (39)(045)800-3060. Fax (39)(045)590-293. Web: www.hotelgabbiadoro.it.*
A warm and cordial staff welcome you at this understated, yet elegant, five-star hotel. Located in the heart of romantic Verona, you may for a few fleeting minutes forget you're traveling with children, as images of a second honeymoon titillate your being. Old stone walls warmed by Persian carpets and beamed ceilings grace the common rooms, adding a sense of coziness. Each guestroom is individually decorated, and beautifully so. Junior suites are available to give your family more space. The inner courtyard is a great place to begin or end each day.

HOTEL SAN LUCA **** *Vicolo Volto San Luca, 8. Tel. (39)(045)591-333. Fax (39)(045)800-2143. Web: www.sanlucahotel.com.*
Light and bright hotel lobby, with pastel chairs complemented by elegant Persian carpets. The breakfast area is similarly light and lovely, Individual rooms are modern and comfortable, with all conveniences. This is a pretty hotel located just steps from the Arena on a quiet side street. With forty rooms (but only twenty with showers), the hotel also offers four apartments quite suitable for families. A parking garage is available.

Expensive

HOTEL ACCADEMIA **** *Via Scala, 12. Tel. (39)(045)596-222. Fax (39)(045)800-8440. Web: www.accademiavr.it/eng/index.cfm. Breakfast.*
If you love to shop, this hotel's for you. It is located near the Via Mazzini, Verona's shopping promenade in the center of town. The common areas nicely balance Old and New World styles. Children up to two-years-old stay free of charge with families. There is also a good restaurant, although it is quite upscale.

DUE TORRI HOTEL BAGLIONI **** *Piazza Sant' Anastasia, 4. Tel. (39)(045)595-0444. Fax (39)(045)800-4130. Web: duetorrihotel.hotelsinverona.com/ ?source=googleh.*

One of the nicest hotels in Verona, situated in the city center. Antiques grace both common

areas and guestrooms, which are quite comfortable. There are 96 rooms all with bath. Breakfast. The hotel faces the front of Sant' Anastasia.

Expensive/Moderate

HOTEL TOURING *** *Via Quintino Sella, 5. Tel. (39)(045)590-944. Fax (39)(045)590-290.*
In the shadow of the Lamberti tower in Piazza Erbe is the renovated 45-room Hotel Touring. While a recent makeover has made the hotel more modern, it still retains its Liberty style. All rooms have private baths, TV, air-conditioning and fridge bar. Parking is available. Keep in mind that the rooms are small, but quiet. The marbled lobby has wonderful Persian carpets.

HOTEL MILANO *** *Via Tre Marchetti, 11. Tel. (39)(045)591-692. Fax (39)(045)801-1299. Web: www.hotelmilano-vr.it.*
Recently renovated, Hotel Milano's image is clean and sharp. Leather chairs, wood floors, Persian rugs decorate the common rooms. The fifty guestrooms are a bit small, quite modern but comfortable. The hotel's three connecting rooms best accommodate families.

GIULIETTA E ROMEO *** *Vicolo Tre Marchetti, 3. Tel. (39)(045)800-3554. Fax (39)(045)801-0862. Web: www.giuliettaeromeo. com. 30 rooms with bath. Breakfast included.*
Can you resist the name? Giulietta E Romeo is a competently run hotel situated in a quiet spot of the city, just off the main streets. The friendly staff made our stay here with children quite pleasant. It is also very quiet, as it is situated in the *Zona Pedonale* or car-free zone of Verona.

HOTEL MASTINO *** *Corso Porta Nuova, 16. Tel. (39)(045)595-388. Fax (39)(045)597-718. Web: www.hotelmastino.it. 33 rooms all with bath.*
Tucked into the historic district, Hotel Mastino also serves families well. Ask for one of the two quad rooms or a connecting room. A view of the Arena and delightful Piazza Bra can be had from some of the rooms.

HOTEL TORCOLO *** *Vicolo Listone, 3. Tel. (045)800.7512. Web: www.hoteltorcolo.it/en/index.html. 19 rooms.*
Clean and cozy, Hotel Torcolo is situated just steps from the Arena and Piazza Bra. Breakfast, which is optional except in July and August, is served on the terrace during summer months.

I'M HUNGRY!

RISTORANTE DANTE $$-$$$ *Piazza dei Singori. Tel. (39)(045)595-249. Closed Sundays.*

Homemade pasta. Need we say more? Meals at Ristorante Dante were superb. Start with the *Antipasta "Dante."* Go simple and order the *tagliolilno con pomodoro e basilico* or the more unique *risotto ai Scampi e Porri.* The *tiramisu' dello chef* is divine. This is one of several cafes where you can enjoy the lovely Piazza Dante. Originally opened as a café over 115 years ago, Dante is also locally well regarded. You can sit back, relax, or plan your itinerary here while your children safely play in the big-enough piazza. Italian mothers bring their little ones here to bicycle and play soccer. A pick-up game, perhaps?

RISTORANTE IL DESCO $$$ *Via Dietro S. Sebastiano, 7. Tel. (39)(045)595-358. Closed Sundays and sometimes in June or July, so call ahead.*

One of the best in Verona. The wine list is extensive, the menu *degustazione*, which includes antipasto, pasta, entrée, salad and dessert, is a great deal.

RISTORANTE NUOVO MARCONI $$$ *Via Fogge, 4. Tel. (39)(045)591-910. Closed Sundays.*

The manager at Giuletta E Romeo recommended this restaurant, and we're pleased we took his advice. An elegant restaurant, with private booths, even the kids were on good behavior. If you enjoy veal, this is the place for you.

TRATTORIA IMPERIO $ *Piazza dei Signori, 8. Tel. (39)(045)803-0160. Fax (39)(045)800-7328. Closed Mondays.*

Pizza, pizza, pizza. So many pizzas, so little time. The selection is vast (32 varieties), the quality excellent (and the price just right). The kids will be pleased, and so will you.

RISTORANTE CIPETTA $$ *Vicolo Teatro Filarmonico, 2. Tel. (39)(045)800843. Closed Friday night and Saturday.*

Off the beaten tourist track, in a quiet piazza off Via Roma. Cipetta specializes in local Veronese cooking.

RISTORANTE LE ARCHE $$$$ *Via Arche Scaligere. Tel. (39)(045)800-7415. Closed Sundays and Monday for dinner and most of January.*

Formal, meaning dress up the kids in clothes they do not naturally want to wear. An elegant dining experience, serving succulent fish dishes. Try a sample of the chef's favorite fish entrees. The meal is exquisite, the price expensive. Throw out the etiquette books: let your kids bring that game-boy to the dinner table, discretely, of course. Whatever it takes, within reason, to let you enjoy this meal is well worth it.

7. NAPLES & THE AMALFI COAST

Naples and the **Amalfi Coast** are a study of contrasts. From the ashes of Pompeii to the sweet song of the Sirens still mesmerizing travelers in the resort towns to the hurly-burly of chaotic Naples and its strong taste for coffee and animated conversation – this is southern Italy.

Naples delivers a punch of boisterous Italian living. It is a living stage, with citizens portraying tragedy or comedy and nothing in between. Walk through the neighborhoods, daytime only please, under flags of laundry waving in the breeze, as women shout to one another from their windows. Lots of hugging going on in these streets, and yelling and singing. Sometimes, usually, their melodic voices are drowned out by the clash of traffic – beeping cars, revving engines, screeching tires – a disquieting dissonance of human activity against the backdrop of natural beauty.

Even the beauty of the mountains, one in particular, takes on large-scale drama. **Mount Vesuvius**, when she isn't wrapped in fog and smog, gloriously rises above the Bay of Naples, a constant reminder that life is short, so why not make the best out of every minute you have. The Neapolitans, throughout the years, adopted this philosophy with open arms, welcoming strangers into their home – sometimes with drastic outcomes. Lombards, Goths, Normans, Spanish, Napoleon and French Bourbons have come and gone, leaving the Neapolitans with heads spinning over changing governments. Perhaps this is the basis for the city's chaotic state. They have rarely been left to run anything by themselves and

their "don't worry, be happy" attitude may be simply a self-defense against the merry-go-round of outside rule. Who knows? This is the city that doesn't work, and it is having fun being broken.

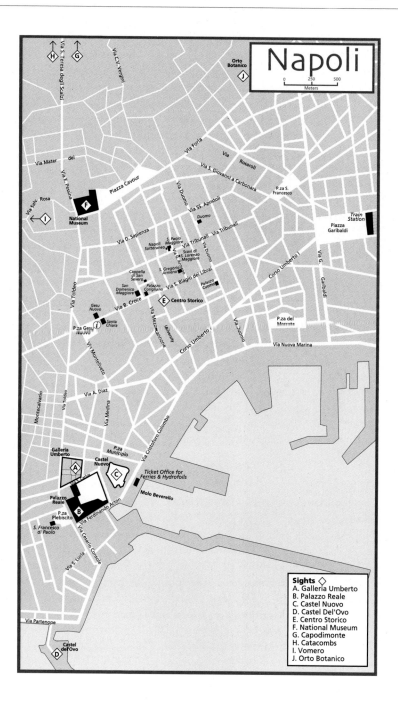

Napoli

0   250   500
Meters

Orto Botanico J

Train Station

Piazza Garibaldi

Via S. Teresa degli Salzi

Via C.V. Vergini

Via Foria

Via Rosaroli

Via S. Giovanni a Carbonara

P.za S. Francesco

Via Mater dei

Via E. Pessina

Piazza Cavour

Via Duomo

Via SS. Apostoli

Via San. Rosa

F **National Museum**

I

Duomo

Via D. Sapienza

Napoli Sotterraneo

S. Paolo Maggiore

Via Tribunali   Via Tribunali

Scavi di S. Lorenzo Maggiore

Corso Umberto I

Via G.

Garibaldi

Cappella di San Severo

S. Gregorio Armeno

Palazzo Corigliano

Via S. Biagio dei Librai

Palazzo Cuomo

San Domenico Maggiore

E **Centro Storico**

Gesu Nuovo

Via B. Croce

University

P.za del Mercato

Santa Chiara

P.za Gesu Nuovo i

Via Toledo

Via Monteliveto

Via Mezzacannone

Corso Umberto I

Via Duomo

Via Nuova Marina

Montecalvario

Via A. Diaz

Via Toledo

Via Medina

Via Cristoforo Colombo

Galleria Umberto

P.za Municipio

A

Castel Nuovo

C

Ticket Office for Ferries & Hydrofoils

Palazzo Reale

B

P.za Plebiscito

S. Francesco di Paolo

Via Ferdinando Acton

Molo Beverello

Via Cesario Console

Via S. Lucia

Via Partenope

Castel del'Ovo D

Sights ◇
A. Galleria Umberto
B. Palazzo Reale
C. Castel Nuovo
D. Castel Del'Ovo
E. Centro Storico
F. National Museum
G. Capodimonte
H. Catacombs
I. Vomero
J. Orto Botanico

H   G

234 ITALY WITH KIDS

Families have several options for feasting on all that this region, **Campania**, has to offer. If the drama of Naples invigorates you, use the city as a base to visit Pompeii, Vesuvius, the islands and the Amalfi Coast. However, if perpetual traffic jams and horns blaring and loud talk with hands flailing aren't your cup of espresso, then choose the more tranquil Sorrento. Each location has easy access to all the desired destinations: Vesuvius, Pompeii and Herculeneum, the Amalfi Coast, Capri and other islands.

GETTING AROUND TOWN

So how do you get around Naples? Walking is your best option. The bus system is unpredictable and you're still left to face the onslaught of keystone cop traffic. Naples has a metro, although it runs as smoothly as the buses and you must beware of pickpockets. The *funicolari*, inclined railway, up to Vomero is a fun mode of transportation, but it only gets you up and down the hill.

WHERE ARE WE GOING NOW?

Naples is Castles-'R-Us, so give flight to your children's imagination at these intriguing castles and palaces. And what a journey it is!

PIAZZA DEL PLEBISCITO

Naples gets a round of applause for the urban renewal undertaking that transformed Piazza del Plebiscito into the elegant square it once was. Bring a soccer ball and join the Neapolitan children at their favorite game. And, make sure to visit the nearby enchanting castles fit for young princes and princesses to explore.

PALAZZO REALE

Via Ferdinando Acton. Tel. (081)400.547. Web: www.palazzoreale napoli.it (in Italian). Open Thursday through Tuesday 9am to 7pm.

Regally walk up one of the most spectacular staircases in the world, the marble and monumental **Scalone d'Onore** to enter this grand palace. It was built in 1600 but not used as a permanent residence for anyone until Charles III of Bourbon moved into the opulent digs in the 1700s. The first doors on the right open to the **Court Theater**, created in Ferdinando Fuga for Charles III. A big hit with the kids was the **Throne Room** (Room IV). Visit Room VIII for the Titian portrait of Pier Luigi Farnese and Room XIII to see Jocahim Murat's writing room. Kids like the last room, the **Bodyguard Room**, with a door to the Throne Room.

In another wing is the **Biblioteca Nazionale Vittorio Emanuele III**, an incredible collection of rare books and manuscripts. The library is available to researchers. Enjoy the pleasant garden outside the library with a view of the next castle, Castel Nuovo.

CASTEL NUOVO

Via Ferdinando Acton. Tel. (081)795-2003. Open Monday-Saturday 9am-6pm.

Guests have been entertained in the castle with five towers for almost 800 years, although some also saw their last days here, lying waste in the prison or torture chamber. Parts of the castle are eerie and sinister. But kids and adults alike are enthralled with pretending to be king or queen for a day. The moat once used as a watery shield to protect the castle now oversees a lovely morning flower market.

Many Neapolitans continue to refer to Castel Nuovo as Maschio Angionino. It was built in 1279 by Guillermo Sagrera, commissioned by Charles of Anjou, to protect the port of Naples — which it gallantly tried to do for more than 700 years. The five towers add an imposing touch. Stretched between two of the towers is the **Arco di Tronfo** (Triumphal Arch), a resplendent Renaissance sculpture, including the figure of St. Michael looming high above. Built between 1443-1468, the arch was inspired by ancient Roman triumphal arches, yet uniquely mixes in elements of Renaissance style.

Once through the arch, the courtyard looms large. Across the way is the Palatine chapel, where Giotto and company decorated the inside in the 14th century, although only fragments of the original frescoes are visible. Next to the chapel on the left, is the infamous **Sala dei Baroni**. The city council met in this room, where villainous King Ferrante in 1486 hosted a fabulous ball for the kingdom's chief barons, only to arrest and execute them. The dungeon/torture chamber was conveniently located under the chapel! It was even rumored that there were crocodiles kept in the dungeons to indulge on a special menu of live prisoners. Today, many of the city's administrative offices are housed inside the castle walls – we wonder

if any council members hesitate when invited to a party hosted by the mayor?

MUSEO CIVICO
Tel. (081)795-2023. Monday-Saturday 9am-7pm. Admission.
Housed in the rest of the castle, with a collection of painting and sculpture. Of particular interest are the bronze doors that ferocious Ferrante commissioned William the Monk to design in 1475. The doors chronicle Ferrante's wins over John d'Anjou.

CASTEL DELL'OVO
Borgo Marinaro, near the Castel Nuovo and Palazzo Reale, off the causeway from the Via Partenope. Tel. (081)240-0055. Open weekdays 8am-2pm.
Looming over the bay on its own islet is Naples oldest castle, Castel Dell'Ovo. Its name originates from Virgil's vision of a magic egg ascending from the sea spray here. Castel dell'Ovo was begun in the 1100s and completed by the 16th century. It is impenetrable, although time has wasted many of its battlements. Today, it is used as a convention center, and sadly is open only for special events. Check to see if any activity is scheduled for the castle, and if you can, peek in to see the enormous rooms and tunnels.

GALLERIA UMBERTO I
Enter Via San Carlo, Via Toledo, Via Santa Brigida, Via Verdi.
The glass arcade built in the late 1800s is the world's precursor to the shopping mall. Light streams in from the glass ceiling, illuminating the marble inlay and, perhaps, ghosts from an era when the galleria was the center of social life. Today, it remains serenely empty, except for Christmas time when a huge Nativity crèche is set up and festivities follow.

TEATRO SAN CARLO
Via San Carlo, 98f. Tel. (081)797-2331, Fax (081)400-902. Web: www.teatrosancarlo.it. Ticket office open Tuesday-Sunday 10am-1pm and 4:30-6pm. Guided tours daily 9am-6pm.
Naples and opera go hand in hand. Theatrical Neapolitans are the perfect audience for the extravagance of opera. And the Teatro San Carlo is made for them – much more exquisite than Milan's La Scala. The auditorium is richly draped in red and gold, with awe-inspiring ceilings frescoed by Giuseppe Camarano. The theme: Apollo reciting poetry to

Athena. If that doesn't get you in the mood for opera, cast a glance at the royal box crowned with gold.

Operas staged here are breathtaking, with incredible special effects. The stage is huge enough to support horses, camels or whatever the opera's script calls for. The backdrop can be cleverly lifted to reveal the stunning **Palazzo Reale Gardens**. If you can't get a ticket, or opera isn't your favorite pastime, you can get a guided tour (Saturday and Sunday 2am-3:30pm. Admission).

SPACCANAPOLI

The pulse of Naples beats strong in this neighborhood. Talk is loud, punctuated by a whirlwind of hand gestures. Music blares from open windows while colorful laundry dances uninhibitedly from above. Welcome to Spaccanapoli, where Naples lives and breathes among squalor and riches.

Spaccanapoli, literally meaning, "split Naples," slices the city in half. In true Neapolitan style, the street's name changes from Spaccanapoli to Benedetto Corce to Via San Biagio dei Librai to numerous other names, adding confusion to an already chaotic neighborhood. Walking through the neighborhood is like descending into a virtual reality game, where the streets are arms-length wide and surprise lurks at every corner. The neighborhood is not for the faint of heart, nor the claustrophobic. But if you can muster up enough energy, your family will enjoy the warmth and special charms of this unique neighborhood.

It is advisable not to travel through the neighborhood at night and be on the lookout for pickpockets.

Churches are a specialty in Spaccanapoli. Here are a few you may want to peek into:

GESU NUOVO

Piazza del Gesu Nuovo. Tel. (39)(081)551-8613. Open Monday-Saturday 6:30am-12:45pm and 4:15pm-7:15pm. Sunday 6:30am-1:30pm.

This Jesuit church built between 1585 and 1600 is a fine example of Baroque style. Enjoy a few relaxing minutes on the benches and take in the lovely garden.

SANTA CHIARA

Piazza del Gesu Nuovo. Tel. (39)(081)552-6209. Web: www.santachiara.info. Open 7am-12:30pm and 3:30pm-6:30pm.

Across the piazza from Gesu Nuovo sits the more plainly dressed Santa

Chiara. The church dates from the 14th century. Originally, the interior competed with Gesu Nuovo's rich Baroque style, and some fine Giotto frescoes adorned the walls. But on August 4, 1943, Allied bombings and subsequent fires destroyed the interior and all traces of Giotto's work. It was rebuilt in a Gothic style. To the left of the church is a gate that leads to the Chiostro delle Clarisse, a convent for the Poor Claires (*Monday-Saturday 8:30am-12:30pm and 3:30pm-6:30pm, Sunday 9:30am-1pm*). Children enjoy visiting the cloister and entertaining all the resident cats.

CHURCH OF SAN DOMENICO MAGGIORE
Piazza San Domenico Maggiore. Open daily 8:00am-12:30pm and 4:30pm-7:00pm.

Saint Thomas Aquinas once resided in the monastery adjacent to the church. It was built in the late 13th century and contains over 40 sarcophagi of the Anjou family. The Gothic facade was added in the 1800s.

SANT'ANGELO A NILO
Piazza San Domenico Maggiore. Open daily 8am-1pm and 4pm-7:15pm.

Located across the piazza from San Domenico Maggiore, Sant'Angelo a Nilo is home to a relief of the *Assumption of the Virgin* by Donatello.

CAPELLA DI SAN SEVERO
Via F de Sanctis. Open Monday and Wednesday-Saturday 10am-5pm and Tuesday and Sunday 10am-1:30pm. Admission.

Just east of San Domenico Maggiore, is the Sansevero Chapel, tucked away down a tiny side street. The chapel was constructed in 1590 as a burial chamber for the Sangro family. Down in the creepy crypt are two human cardiovascular systems taken from bodies, hopefully after their death, by Prince Raimondo, a Sangro who dabbled in alchemy.

DUOMO
Via Duomo. Open daily 8am-12:30pm and 5pm-7pm.

Naples's Cathedral is dedicated to San Gennaro, the city's patron saint. The Cathedral was built in the late 13th century and contains the tomb of Charles of Anjou. A collection of archaeological remains can be viewed in a small museum located off the Santa Restituta chapel (*open daily 9am-12pm and 4:30pm-7pm. Sunday and holidays 9am-12pm; admission*). Inside the Duomo, on the main altar, is a bust of **San Gennaro** with his skull inside. In the tabernacle are vials of the saint's blood that legend holds liquefied three times in the past!

PIO MONTE DELLA MISERICORDIA
Via Tribunali, 253. Tel. (081)446-973. Weekdays 9:30am-1:30pm.
A beautiful church inspired by a desire to perform good deeds. The octagonal church, around the corner from the Duomo, was built by seven noblemen in 1601 for an institution for charity and now is famous for Caravaggio's passionate *Seven Acts of Mercy*. Combining the seven acts of mercy – feeding the hungry, clothing the poor, nursing the sick, sheltering pilgrims, visiting prisoners, ransoming Christine slaves and burying the indigent dead – the painting is a masterpiece of religious art.

The **Pinacoteca Museum** (*open Thursday-Saturday 9am-1pm*), located up a stairway in the church's courtyard, presents more paintings from Neapolitan artists.

NAPOLI SOTTERRANEA
Vico S. Anna di Palazzo, 52. Tel. (081)400-256. Email: laes@lanapoli sotterranea.it. Web: www.lanapolisotterranea.it.
Naples down under is a thrill for young and old alike. Here, beneath the hot hectic city are the cool catacombs, tunnels and aqueducts of ancient Naples. Be prepared to creep by candlelight in the dark, damp passageways of this underground city. Also be ready to climb up and down steps and squeeze through narrow passages. From the

> **Fun Fact**
> Troops as far back as the 6th century used this underground to sneak past enemies and gain an upper hand through a surprise attack. Sort of like a Star Trek cloaking device of yore. During World War II, the underground served as a bomb shelter and a secret passageway for anti-Nazi activity. On their way out, the Germans bombed the entrances, essentially trapping thousands of souls. But their neighbors quickly warned incoming American soldiers, who dug out the trapped Neapolitans just in the nick of time.

underground, you can walk from the Palazzo Reale to the Porta Capuana without venturing above ground. Tours are the best way to see the underground. Check your hotel or the tourist office in the Piazza del Gesu Nuovo for more information.

FILANGIERI MUSEUM
Via del Duomo. Tel. (081)203-175. Open Tuesday-Saturday 9:30am-2pm and 3:30pm-7pm, Sunday and holidays 9:30am-1:30pm. Admission.
Close to the Duomo is this small museum housed in the Palazzo Cuomo. Kids especially like to check out the armor, weapons and costumes. Also on display is a china collection and paintings by some of Naples' finest: Giordano, Preti, and Ribera. The museum once was the palace of Prince Filangieri, who donated his abode to the city in 1888.

MUSEO NAZIONALE FERROVIARIO
Corso San Giovanni a Teduccio. Tel. (081)472-003. Monday-Saturday 8:30am-1:30pm. Free.
Kids love this change of pace from art and churches. This museum houses old-fashioned cars, railroad equipment and engines. It is located slightly east of the center city.

CAPODIMONTE
Park open daily 7:30am-8pm. Off-season, 7:30am-5pm. Museum opens Tuesday-Saturday 9am-2pm, Sunday 9am 1pm. Admission.
This is Naples' picture gallery, nestled snugly inside the Parco di Capodimonte. The museum, built by Charles III in 1738 to serve as a royal palace, is where you will find some great works by Titian, Caravaggio, Lippi and Botticelli. One room is filled with delightful porcelain figures, which are still made today. For your young soldiers, there also is a display of arms and armor.
Remember, the museum is surrounded by a 297-acre park – just enough room for energetic youngsters to bounce and jump.

MUSEO ARCHEOLOGICO NAZIONALE
Piazza Museo Nazionale, 19. Tel. (081)292.823. Web: museoarcheologiconazionale.campaniabeniculturali.it/. Open daily 9am to 7:30pm. Closed Tuesdays, Christmas, New Years and May 1.
Extended hours. Great, you may say. But check your ticket. Not all the rooms may be open for the longer hours. If you want to see the entire museum, virtually impossible with kids in tow, start early.
Children especially will enjoy the lost treasures dug up in the ruins of

Herculaneum and Pompeii after Vesuvius erupted and buried the ancient cities. Do see the *Farnese Bull, Farnese Hercules and the Tyrannicides* all on the first floor. Upstairs are incredible finds from Pompeii, especially the collection of Roman mosaics. *Chicken Run* fans will get a kick out of the posing poultry in many of the paintings.

Look for Andy Warhol's *Mount Vesuvius* (1985), then compare it to the real thing just a glance away. And don't forget the room of elaborate gladiator suits and the infamous *sezione pornografica* (known as the *Gabinetto Segreto,* the Secret Room) – in case you need a translation, this is a room of erotic art that recently several years ago was reopened. Use parental discretion.

THE VILLA COMUNALE

Past the Castel Dell'Ovo is the tranquil Villa Comunale, a gorgeous park that parallels the shore. It is a refreshing place to let your little ones run and play, and it is home to the city's aquarium (see next entry below).

AQUARIO

Stazione Zoologica. Viale A. Dohrn. Tel. (081)583-3111. May-September, Tuesday-Saturday 9am-6pm and Sunday 9:30am-7:30pm. October-April, Tuesday-Saturday 9am-5pm and Sunday 9am-2pm.

Over 200 species of fish and plant life reside at the aquarium, built by German naturalist Dr. Anton Dohrn, a friend of Darwin's, in the late 19th century. The aquarium makes for a great break from the art and church circuit.

VILLA FLORIDIANA PUBLIC PARK

Via Cimarosa, 77. Tel. (081)578-8418. Monday-Saturday 9am-2pm. Admission.

Up the funicular into the southern part of Vomero, is the once elegant Villa Floridiana estate built in 1817. Inside is a museum of historical knick-knacks – fans, majolica vases, gold watches (**Museo Nazionale della Ceramica**, *open Tuesday-Sunday 9am-2pm, admission*). Surrounding the estate is the English-style garden by Degenhardt (19th century), where young children and infants enjoy a view from the pram as nannies and mamas leisurely stroll through the winding paths. Unfortunately, the park has seen better days. Graffiti is here and there; the pools are dry and the grass unattended.

VIRGIL'S TOMB, PARCO VIRGILIANO
Via Salita Grotta, 20. Tel. (39)(081)669-390.
Just beyond the western end of the Villa Comunale is the area called
Mergellina, a popular location in Naples. Mergellina rises steeply from the
sea and a funicular runs up the mountain every 15 minutes. Virgiliano
Park, named after Virgil, holds what is believed to be the poet's tomb.
Napoli was dear to Virgil. It is where he wrote the *Aeneid*. When he died
in Brindisi in 19 BC on a trip back from Greece, his body was shipped to
Naples.
To find Virgil's grave in the park, look for the Roman *columbarium* or
funerary monument. Some Virgil aficionados, however, believe his burial
spot is nearer to the Aquario.

SPORTS & RECREATION
Amusement Park
Edenlandia Viale Kennedy, *Mostra d'Oltremare. Tel. (39)(081)239-
1182.* Not that impressive.

Fitness & Swimming
Magic World Licola, *Tel. (081)804-8389.* Large outdoor fitness and
swimming center.
Piscina Scandone, *Via Giochi dei Mediterraneo. Tel. ((081)570-9154.*
Public swimming and fitness center.
Hotel Vesuvio, *Via Partenope, 45. Tel. (081)764-0044.* Fitness center.

Tennis
Tennis Club Napoli, *Viale Dohrn. Tel. (081)761-4656*
Tennis Club Vomero, *Via Rossini, 8. Tel. (081)658-912*
Virgilio Sporting Club, *Via Tito Lucrezio Caro, 6. Tel. ((081)769-
5261*

Shopping
L'Ospedale delle Bambole, *Via San Biagio dei Librai, 81. Tel.
(081)203-067.* Every little girl's dream is to take a broken doll to a warm
and loving doll hospital. Here in the midst of centro storico is just that
loving store. Shattered dolls, torn dolls, head-broken-off dolls all scattered
around, all seeking love and getting it. Ancient dolls and puppets are
hanging from nooks. You must visit this shop when in Naples.
Baracca e Burattina, *Piazza Museo, 2. Tel. (081)203-067.* A great
shop to purchase a doll – some porcelain dolls are available, but be extra •

careful if you travel with them. We've lost several and our daughter wants yet another trip to the Doll Hospital for repair.

Naples Theatrical Costumes, *Via Generro Sera, 75. Tel. (39)(081)425-711.* Cool place to take a break from traditional tourism. The costumes are magnificent and the staff welcoming.

Giuseppe Ferrigno, *Via di San Gregorio Armeno, 10. Tel. (081)552-3148.* If it's a Nativity crèche you want, Naples is the place to buy and Ferrigno is one of the most popular shops due to their commitment to Old World techniques. Most of the crèche shops congregate around the Via di San Gregorio Armeno in Spaccanapoli.

Markets

Mercato di Sant'Antonio, *Via Sant'Antonio Abate. Open daily 9am-8pm*

Mercatino della Torretta, *Viale Gramsci. Monday through Saturday 8am-1pm.* Fresh fish, vegetables to cheap clothes.

Flower Market, *Castel Nuovo.* Open daily from dawn until noon.

Antiques market, *Villa Communale.* Open daily from 8am-4pm on the last two weekends of each month.

WHICH ONE IS MY ROOM?

Lungomare & Santa Lucia *(seacoast)*

VESUVIO **** *Via Partenope, 45. Tel. (39)(081)764-0044, Fax (39)(081)764-4483. Web: www.vesuvio.it.*

Modern and elegant, with a breathtaking view of Vesuvius, the 183-room Vesuvio is a very comfortable place to stay in Naples. The 100-year-old hotel has a history. Caruso died here and the Vesuvio was a favorite haunt of Oscar Wilde. Service is excellent and you can enjoy a lovely dinner at the hotel's Caruso  restaurant, situated on the top floor with a stunning view of the bay. For anyone who refused our advice and drove into the city, Vesuvio offers underground parking.

EXCELSIOR **** *Via Partenope, 48. Tel. (39)(081)764-0111, Fax (39)(081)764-9743. Web: www.excelsior.it.*

Another top-flight hotel; one that caters to the corporate clientele.

Large rooms, with especially large beds, and incredible views of the volatile Vesuvius. Of course there is a rooftop restaurant and solarium, as well as the much coveted parking garage. With a good location, the Excelsior has been earning its reputation since 1909.

MIRAMARE **** *Via N. Sauro, 24. Tel. (39)(081)764-7589, Fax (39)(081)764-0775. Web: www.hotelmiramare.com.*

The Liberty style is the rage at Miramare, a welcoming turn-of-the-century hotel. Some rooms are small, but the hospitality comes big – Napoli-style. Enzo Rosalino, manager, is a most gracious and helpful host. Your every wish is his command. The hotel is about a 10-minute walk to the center of Naples. Intimate and cozy are the adjectives that come to mind for this hotel's 31 rooms.

Chiaia-Vomero-Posillipo *(ritzy neighborhood)*

PARKER'S GRAND HOTEL **** *Corso Vittorio Emanuele 135. Tel. (39)(081)761-2474. (39)(081)663-527. Breakfast included. Web: www.grandhotelparkers.it.*

Large comfortable rooms make your stay at Parker's a welcome relief

 from the hubbub of Naples. The elegant Parker's, which opened in 1870, sits halfway up the Vomero Hill, quite convenient to all the funicular lines. This is one of those places to see and be seen. If your room doesn't have a great view, make your way to the rooftop-garden restaurant. Check out the marvelous chandeliers in many of the rooms. Parking garage.

VILLA CAPODIMONTE **** *Via Moiarello, 66. Tel. (39)(081)459-0000, Fax (39)(081) 299-344. Web: www.villacapodimonte.it. Children under 4 stay free.*

Tranquility is yours at Villa Capodimonte. It is located above hectic Naples near Capodimonte Park, which means lots of space for kids to romp. The 64-room hotel opened in 1995 and has a beautiful garden, terrace, library and tennis courts. The rooms have wonderful views.

COSTANTINOPOLI 104 ** *Via Costantinopoli 104, Spaccanapoli. Tel. (081)557.1035. Web: www.costantinopoli104.com.*

Small, charming outdoor pool. A rarity in Naples, this hotel offers a wonderful place for kids and parents to unwind and cool off after a day of touring. Thirteen rooms and six junior suites are beautifully appointed, with a modern touch. Take breakfast outside in the garden by the pool during the summer months, or inside in a cozy breakfast room for cooler days.

I'M HUNGRY!
City Center
PIZZERIA DA BRANDI $ *Via Miano, 27/29. Tel. (39)(081)741-0455 Closed Sunday. Credit Cards not accepted here.*

This is the birthplace of our kids' favorite food, pizza Margherita, named after King Umberto's lovely queen. The pizza is out-of-this-world. Touristy, yes. Good food, big yes. And a pretty restaurant as well. Patrons who have enjoyed the 19th-century decor and wood-burning pizza ovens include Luciano Pavarotti and Chelsea Clinton.

CIRO A SANTA BRIGIDA $$ *Via Santa Brigida, 71. Tel. (390(081)552-4072. Closed Sunday and last two weeks of August.*

A Neapolitan's culinary delight, this restaurant near the Castel Nuovo packs 'em in – and for good reason. Pizza, *pasta e fagioli* (one of our favorites), the exotic *sartu* (a rice loaf), all are made to perfection since its opening in 1932.

LA FILA $$ *Via Nazionale, 6/C. Tel. (39)(081)206-717. Closed Monday. No credit cards accepted.*

This family-run restaurant takes simple Southern Italian cooking and turns it into an art form. Meatballs to die for, smoked provolone and mouth-watering pastas are featured. Pizza also is available for those more finicky eaters.

Santa Lucia & Chiaia
I RE DI NAPOLI $$$ *Via Partenope, 29/30. Tel. (39)(081)764-7775.*

Cool, real cool place to hang out. On the seafront, where Naples' hip youth linger, cigarettes dangling, eyes lost behind dark glasses, their golden bodies adorned by Versace and Prada. Well, we weren't so cool, and our kids in their younger days were more into hip-hopping around than looking hip, but the food was good and the sea breeze fine. Try the excellent stuffed pizzas named after kings.

RISTORANTE CALIFORNIA $$$ *Via Santa Lucia, 101. (39)(081)764-9752. Closed Sunday.*

The Ristorante California is the place for you, serving both American and Italian cuisine.

LA BERSAGLIERA $$ *Borgo Marinaro, 10. Tel. (39)(081)764-6016. Closed Sunday and last two weeks of August.*

A tourist restaurant, located at the foot of the medieval Castel dell'Ovo, but the food is *molto bene*. Nothing fancy, yet it lives up to its nearly 100-year history. Just the best ingredients, made with love and kissed by the sea – the restaurant is on the port at Santa Lucia. Try the grilled fish. Interesting trivia – Sophia Loren, a Napoli native, is a reputed fan of La Bersagliera.

Mergellina & Posillipo

LA SACRESTIA $$$ *Via Orazio, 116. Tel. (39)(081)664-186. Closed Sunday for dinner and lunch on Monday. Closed August.*

Fine dining that mixes traditional Neapolitan dishes with a dash of nouveau cuisine. La Sacrestia is located in the heights above Mergellina with a charming terrace. Don't know what to order? Be daring, try the *bucatini alla Principe di Napoli*, pasta noodles laced with its famous heavenly truffles. Seafood is a standout here.

GAMBRINU *Piazza Trieste e Trento. Tel. (39)(081)417-482.*

Opened in 1850, Gambrinus is not in the best location, but the coffee is sooo good.

SCATURCHIO *Piazza San Domenico Maggiore, 19. Tel. (39)(081)551-6944.*

This is one of Naples's finest pastry shops, where the action is high drama, boisterous and fun.

LA CAFFETERIA *Piazza dei Martiri, 30. (and also in Vomero). Tel. (39)(081)764-4243.*

Unlike the sound of its name, La Caffeteria caters to a chi-chi crowd.

MEGARIDE *Via Borgo Marinaro, 1. Tel. (39)(081)665-026.*

Near La Bersagliera restaurant, under the Castel dell'Ovo, sits the charming Megaride, a splendid location to enjoy a cuppa.

The Scoop on Gelato

Scimmia, Piazza della Carita, 4, in the city center. The kids voted and Scimmia came in first, with a close second to Chalet Ciro, located at Via F. Carracciolo near the Mergellina hydrofoil pier.

POMPEII

Dusty and too crow**ded describes t**he *entrance to on*e of the world's most remarkable excavations – the buried city of **Pompeii**. Miraculously the lines move faster than expected and a nearby gift shop offers welcome relief for line-weary children. Once inside the city, kids come alive at the sight of a town frozen in history.

"I had fun pretending that I was in ancient Pompeii, or on another planet," wrote our seven-year-old son in his journal. Otherworldly is a good way to describe this town still sleeping after being devastated by a blow from the volatile Vesuvius. The sun beat down on that fateful day – August 24, 79 AD – as the people of Pompeii busily went about their business. Suddenly the sky grew dark and the air more suffocating than any August day they had ever known. A loud roar rings across the land as the ground shakes and trembles. People frantically try to escape the inevitable, but they are

caught by a hail of lapilli and struck down by invisible gas from the volcano. Many are quickly asphyxiated, others die more slowly as a burning rain of ash fills up even the tiniest of cracks. Soon everything is covered, the city buried seemingly forever.

Pompeii was left buried under the soil until 1748 when Charles of Bourbon ordered the first scientific exploration of the area. In 1860, Giuseppe Fiorelli invented the system of pouring liquid plaster into the spaces left in the bed of ashes. Almost magically, the forms of people and artifacts emerged from the rubble. It took until 1911 for serious and systematic excavations to begin, and still not all of Pompeii has been freed from its ashen grave.

Pompeii is vast, impossible to cover in one day by adults let alone young children. We suggest you pick the sites you are most interested in seeing and visit only them.

Upon joining the cue for entry, we engaged in a typical Mars-Venus debate – to buy a guidebook or not. Venus won in this case, and for the better (though he'll never admit it). With a map in hand, you can more easily pinpoint the sites you want to see, avoiding a lot of wasted time. Come on guys, you can do it. If a map somehow threatens the macho image, feel free to turn it over to the wife or even the kids. Here are some Pompeii highlights:

- **The Forum**. Not well preserved but huge and with a great view of the culprit – Vesuvius.
- **The House of the Faun**. Named because of the beautiful bronze statue

of a dancing Faun decorating one of its impluvia (*see photo at left*).
- **Forum Baths**. At the crossroads of Via del Foro and Via di Nola are the baths excavated in 1823. The kids enjoyed romping through here, quite curious about why everybody came here to take a bath, pondering the unthinkable – that anyone really would choose to have a bath!
- **House of Pansa**. One of the larger homes in Pompeii.
- **House of the Large Fountain**. The mosaic of the fountain is breathtaking, and influenced by eastern art.
- **House of the Vettii**. Wealth and privilege ooze from every corner of the remains of the House of Vettii – from the stunning wall decorations to the lush and well-planned garden. One painting, as you pass the vestibule, is of Priapus weighing his oh-so-enormous, shall we say, private parts, on a scale. Why? Allegedly to frighten anyone who may be jealous of all the wealth of the Vettiis. You are warned!
- **Bakeries and Mills**. Each mill is composed of two parts made out of volcanic rock and a base to hold them up. The lower part was in a conical shape and serves as the rotation axis while the upper part was biconical and hollow. The mill was rotated either by men or mules. Kids find the mills curious.
- **Temple of Isis**. The best-preserved temple in Pompeii. Sacred objects can be seen at the National Museum of Naples.
- **Stabian Baths**. The oldest baths in Pompeii, they are beautiful with light streaming through the archways. Take note of the body encased in glass supposedly found near the baths.
- **House of the Menander**. A gorgeous home named so because of the painting of the Greek poet Menander.

- **Large Theater.** Still used today for entertainment events, the horseshoe shaped theater is located at the top of the hill. Only a few fragments of the seats remain, but one retains the number of the seat. From this, archaeologists have determined that each person was allowed a width of 40 centimeters for a seat.
- **Arcaded Court of the Gladiators.** The portico is well preserved, consisting of 74 Doric columns in tuff stucco work. The facade of the entrance hall has three Ionic columns. Excavators found, in some of the rooms, gladiator equipment, including helmets made in Greek style with the top part folded back and movable visors with the eyeholes covered by a metal network.
- **House of the Lovers.** So named because of the inscription: *"Amantes ut apes vitam mellitam exigent!"* Or, "Lovers, like bees, make life as sweet as honey!"
- **House of Venus.** The painting of Venus, lounging on a seashell mesmerized us, although the painting looks much better at a distance.
- **Amphitheatre.** Built in 80 BC, Pompeii's open air theater is distinguished as the world's oldest. The building is at the far end – east – of the city, but is well worth the trip. It remains nudged into the hillside and is quite well preserved. We entered through one of the corridors into the open arena. What fun! The kids ran around the arena, then up and down the seats and hill, until we all settled down for a snack and photo.
- **Large Palaestra.** Next to the Amphitheatre, this area was used for young people as a gymnasium.
- **Garden of the Fugitives.** They struggled for their lives and lost. After all these centuries, you can still sense their pain and despair. These 13 bodies were found in 1961. The casts of these family members – babies, children and adults – were taken and left where they fell.

Parent Tip: When visiting Pompeii, keep in mind that the streets are cobblestones. We watched as many parents struggled unsuccessfully to negotiate the streets pushing conventional strollers. We suggest placing babies in backpacks and using a jogger stroller or large-tire stroller through this area.

Fun Fact

Seventeen-year-old Pliny, nephew of Pliny the Elder, watched the volcano burst and flood Pompeii and surrounding towns with burning lava. He and his family were residing in Misenum, a few miles from Pompeii. His uncle, admiral of the imperial Roman fleet, heroically commanded a fleet of ships to save anyone who might have survived. In the process, the poisonous gas and ashes smothered him. In 104 AD, Pliny the Younger writes two letters to a friend who is writing a history of Rome. His letters are the first written observations of a volcanic eruption. Pliny is hailed as the world's first vulcanologist.

• **Villa of the Mysteries.** Located to the west of the town, the frescoes are stunning in this villa.

HERCULANEUM

Pompeii was a working city, **Herculaneum** was the wealthy resort town. Herculaneum is wedged between the sea and Ercolano, a dreary suburb of Naples. It is one-third the size of Pompeii and in some ways a more interesting site. The mosaics are more elegant and many of the buildings better preserved. If you don't think you have time to see Pompeii or the thought of dust and crowds repels you, make your way to Herculaneum.

Pompeii and Herculaneum were destroyed in different ways by the eruption of Vesuvius. While Pompeii was buried under ash, Herculaneum was hammered by waves of mud. Eventually, the mud hardened and turned to stone – much like a fossil.

Each *casa* (house) offers a unique perspective on ancient life and art. If one you want to see is locked, ask the many guards roaming the site. They may unlock a favorite for you. Also, arrange ahead of time a visit to the underground theater and evening show. Inquire at your hotel, travel agent or call (39)(081)739-0963, Ercolano's tourist information center.

Tourist Information for Pompeii & Herculaneum
   Pompeii: *Tel. (081)857.5347. Email: infopompei@tin.it, Web: www.pompeiisites.org. Open November through March, every day from 8:30am to 5pm (last admission 3:30pm) and April through October, every day from 8:30am to 7:30pm (last admission 6pm). Admission: €11.*
   Herculeneum: *Tel. (081)857.5347. Email: infopompei@tin.it, Web: www.pompeiisites.org. Open November through March, every day from 8.30am to 5pm (last admission 3.30pm) and April through October, every day from 8:30am to 7:30pm (last admission 6pm). Admission: €11.*

Getting Here

To get to **Pompeii** by train, take the Circumvesuviana railway (*Tel. (39)(081)772-2444*) from either Naples (Stazione Centrale at Piazza Garibaldi) or Sorrento and exit at Pompeii Scavi. The word "Scavi" is key, otherwise you'll end up in the center of the living city of Pompeii. By car from Naples, take the A3 *Autostrada* to Pompeii Scava.

To get to **Herculeneum/Ercolano** by train, take the Circumvesuviana railway either from Naples or Sorrento and exit at Ercolano Scavi. By car from Naples, take the A3 *Autostrada* this time to Ercolano.

SORRENTO

Even the bird's chirp is more piquant in **Sorrento**. Blissful in their surroundings, they erupt with a joyous trill and twitter not heard of elsewhere. For those who love the rawness and edge of Big Sur, Sorrento and the **Amalfi Coast** possibly could disappoint. But take a day or two away from the hustle-bustle of the piazzas, the onslaught of tourists pouring from the train station. Soon the awesome splendor of the Amalfi Coast will tease you, gently, to stay.

Sorrento is a much more family-friendly launching point than is Naples for day trips in the area. It is an easy train ride to Naples, Pompeii or Herculaneum. It is just as easy to spend time in Positano, Almalfi, Ravello and other towns on the coast by taking a bus, taxi or renting a car. Or, you can opt to take a boat to any of these locations, including the island of Capri. Hydrofoils, small boats or the train will take you to these places. Or you can choose to simply walk the small town, enjoying the many lemon and orange trees, strolling on the narrow beach and skipping stones in the sea.

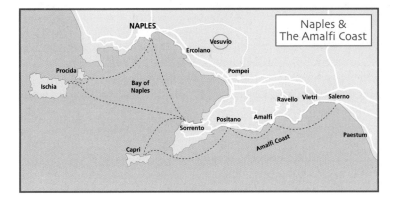

Our children enjoyed just being kids during our stay in Sorrento. Here's what they had fun doing:

- Skipping rocks into the sea and searching the waters for old decorative tiles.
- Drawing and painting from one of the many breathtaking vistas.
- Playing at the playground and pool at the Hotel Vittorio.
- Taking an evening passegiato throughout the town.
- Chasing lizards – many reside in Sorrento.

Tourist Information
   Tourist Office, *Via Luigi De Maio, 35. Tel. (081)807.4033. Fax. (081)877.3397. Web: www.sorrentotourism.com.*

WHICH ONE IS MY ROOM?
Very Expensive
   GRAND HOTEL EXCELSIOR VITTORIA **** *Piazza T. Tasso, 34. Tel. (39)(081)807-1044, Fax (39)(081)877-1206. E-mail: exvitt@exvitt.it. Web: www.exvitt.it/sorrento-hotel.html.*

A tenderly cared for five-acre park surrounds the Excelsior Vittoria, providing unending pleasures for children. Climbing and swinging in the

playground, discovering the lemon orchard, diving into the pool, and ever-so-quietly sneaking up on a lizard to get that special photo keeps kids busy. The grand is not understated in this hotel's name. Common areas are of museum-quality, the terraces splendid. Breakfast is served in an elegant room, with lots of windows and views. Rooms are spacious and well-appointed. Walk outside the gates, and you are in the middle of all the action. This is a hotel for the likes of Sophia Loren, Pavarotti and many members of royal families. Caruso spent his last days here. Yet with all the upper-crust treatment, the hotel does well by families.

   Inquire about the family apartments, which are located in a separate building on the grounds and are very spacious and private.

IMPERIAL HOTEL TRAMONTANO **** *Via V. Veneto. Tel. (39)(081)878-2588, Fax (39)(081)807-2344. Web: www.hoteltramon tano.it.*

The grand and oh-so-British Tramontano is carved out of a cliff dangling over the sea. The common areas are grand, large and many. The main building was built in 1812 and lies on the ruins of the house once owned by the son of Augustus. Most impressive are the rooms, each with a spectacular view of its own. Clearly these vistas inspire; G. B. DeCurtis wrote his famous song "Torna A Surriento" here. And the list of literary luminaries who have stayed here is daunting. Everyone from Shelley to Keats, and from Milton to Longfellow have enjoyed this hotel. Guestrooms are spacious and comfortable, many with lovely views of the sea, Vesuvius and Naples. Tramontano, like Sorrento, is a haunt for the British.

Expensive

BELLEVUE-SYRENE **** *Tel. (39)(081)878-1024, Fax (39)(081)878-3963. Web: www.bellevue.it.*

Belle Epoque murals and Venetian chandeliers make for elegant common areas at the Bellevue-Syrene. The 59 guestrooms are cozy, some with wonderful views of the bay (photo is of the Terrace Suite). Enjoy dinner at the terrace of Villa Pompeiana, the hotel's restaurant, and a walk through lush gardens. Even if you don't stay here, visit the terrace café with one of the best views in

Sorrento. In fact, Empress Eugenie of France stayed here, initially for several days and, having found the hotel and location delightful, remained for several months.

GRAND HOTEL ROYAL **** *Via Correale, 42. Tel. (39)(081)807-3434, Fax (39)(081)877-2905. Web: www.royalsorrento.com.*

Pool, beach access and all the comforts of a splendid hotel in lovely Sorrento. Ask for a sea view, not all the rooms have them. Frolic in the gardens that wrap around the hotel. The Royal has a pool and private beach. Inside, the hotel is cool and rooms are spacious.

GRAND HOTEL AMBASCIATORI **** *Via Califano, 18. Tel. (39)(081)878-2025, Fax (39)(081)807-1021. Web: www.ambasciatori sorrento.com.*
Gardens hang over the sea of this elegant hotel a bit removed from the hub of the town. The hotel is perched on a cliffside overlooking the vibrant sea. The rooms and interior match the outside and have cool, intricate mosaic tiled floors. Kids will love the pool, beach access and the resident cat.

Moderate
SETTIMO CIELO *** *Via Capo, 27. Tel. (39)(081)878-1012, Fax (39)(081)807-3290. Web: www.hotelsettimocielo.com.*
Simple, reasonable and modern, all the guestrooms here face the sea. The name of the hotel literally means "seventh heaven" and is a good reflection of the atmosphere here. Enjoy the pool and garden. A bright and cheery restaurant serves good, if not splendid, food.
HOTEL MIGNON MEUBLE *** *Via Sersale 9. Tel. (081)807.3824. Web: www.sorrentohotelmignon.com.*
Great location. Clean and neat. This is a cute hotel, with the various shades of blue décor calling to mind the deep, blue sea of Sorrento. Some rooms have balconies and the gazebo is a fun place to read books, sketch or just enjoy a few relaxing moments.

Inexpensive
LORELEY ET LONDRES ** *Via Califano, 2. Tel/Fax (39)(081)807-3187.*
Go for the sunsets – they are glorious from this hotel. Don't be disappointed in the slightly shabby decor – this is a two-star in the land of four-stars. The place is clean and the staff friendly. An elevator takes you down to a private beach, while the hotel itself takes you down an imaginary ride back into the 19th century. Ask for a room facing the sea, which is much less noisy.

I'M HUNGRY!
PANETTERIA-PIZZERIA FRANCO $ *Corso Italia, 265. Tel. (39)(081)877-2066.*
A popular local dining spot, the pizza is good and even prepared in front of your seat.

TRATTORIA DA EMILIA $$ *Via Maria Grande, 61. Tel. (39)(081)807-2720.*

Good regional cuisine at a reasonable rate. Professional and friendly staff.

LA LANTERNA $$ *Via S. Ceasareo, 23-25. Tel. (39)(081)878-1355 Closed Wednesdays.*

Situated on the site of ancient Roman baths, La Laterna features indoor and outdoor dining. We recommend the *scalloppini marsala*, a dish Michael enjoyed, or should we say, devoured?

O'PARRUCCHIANO $$$ *Corso Italia, 71. Tel. (39)(081)878-1321 Closed Wednesdays and from November to Easter.*

The name actually means "the place of the priest," although it's hard to see why as this multi-level garden and orchard of a restaurant offers sinful culinary pleasures. First opened as a restaurant in 1890, the cuisine is classic Sorrentine, with little room to go wrong.

DON ALFONSO $$$$ *Piazza Sant'Agata. Tel. (39)(081)878-0026. Closed Sunday dinners during September through May, and all day on Mondays.*

Well worth the treat, this is a special occasion waiting to happen! The food is only outdone by the presentation, something akin to sculptured art forms. The fine china and delicate crystal signal a requirement of at minimum adequate behavior from little ones. Note that it's located a good nine or ten kilometers outside of Sorrento.

APREDA $ *Via Tasso, 6. Tel. (39)(081)878-2351. Deli.*

Need to restock your provisions? The freshest of fresh in Italian lunchmeats, pickled delicacies and cheeses. The kids may enjoy shopping here, as the selection is like nowhere else in the US.

POSITANO

Sugarplum fairyland, with pastel cotton-candy homes dripping from the cliffs. **Positano** is not the sleepy fishing town it once was when so many writers and artists made a pilgrimage here seeking inspiration. But it has retained much of its charm and is beautiful to behold.

While Positano is definitely worth a day trip, it is not particularly well-suited for families as a base to explore the area. Many hotels do not accept children allegedly because of the dangers of falling from the terraces and balconies. For families, Capri is a better bet and from there you can easily take excursions by ferry to Positano, Amalfi and Naples.

Again, this is not a kid-destination, though teens may find it cool. Shopping rules in Positano. From the top of the main road down to the sandy beach, stores dominate the scenery. Positano is noted for its beach collection – some haute couture, others boardwalk-beach chic. Whatever your taste in clothes, you can find it here, although a bit more expensive than elsewhere. Also look for artisan shops and art galleries along your walks up and down shoppers' row.

For more info, go to *www.positano.com/en/positano-info*.

WHICH ONE IS MY ROOM?

When booking a reservation, make sure you mention that you are traveling with children – especially if the kids are young. Positano is the only place in Italy we found where some hotels said they did not want children under a certain age. Hotel officials at the following hotels told us they would accept children, but ask again to play it safe.

LA SIRENUSE ***** *Via Cristoforo Colombo, 30. Tel. (39)(089)875-066, Fax (39)(089)811-798. Web: www.sirenuse.it. Note: Hotel policy prefers children over eight years of age.*

Beach resort elegance, with attentive service. A former private home of local nobility, the hotel welcomed its first guests in 1951. There are 61 rooms and a hotel restaurant, La Sponda, worthy of mention. Enjoy the pool gorgeously positioned with a view of the sea and inlaid with mosaic tile work. A private ferry will shuttle you all along the coast.

EDEN ROC *** *Via G. Marconi. Tel. (39)(089)875-844 or 812-132, Fax (39)(089)875-552. Web: www.edenrocpositano.com.*

Situated with wonderful views of the sea, this hotel offers clean and comfortable rooms.

LA FENICE *** *Via G. Marconi, 4. Tel. (39)(089)875-513, Fax (39)(089)811-309. No credit cards. Web: www.lafenicepositano.com.*

Although small (only ten rooms), La Fenice offers a nice retreat from the bigger and often noisier hotels. On the quiet outskirts, there are little cottages near the sea, connected by steep walkways and ensuring privacy and romantic settings.

I'M HUNGRY!

LA CAMBUSA $$$ *Piazza Amerigo Vespucci, 4. Tel. (39)(089)875-432.*

Just up from the beach, La Cambusa has a delightful rigatoni dish with fresh *melanzane* (baby eggplant) and special green ravioli in a red or white cream sauce. Enhancing the meal is the view, looking downward onto the beach.

BUCCA DI BACCO $$$ *Via Rampa Teglia, 8. Tel. (39)(089)875-699.*

Just facing La Cambusa, this well-known eatery is one of the most popular stops after spending the day on the beach. The fish is oustanding.

CHEZ BLACK $$$ *Via Brigantino. Tel. (39)(089)875-036.* Very touristy and somewhat overpriced, Chez Black is set on beach level with a limited frontal view but the pasta dishes are as appealing as the proximity to the frothy ocean.

IL GROTTINO AZZURRO $$ *Via Chiesa Nuova. Tel. (39)(089)875-466. Closed Wednesday.*

A small but authentic family-run *tratorria* offering service as good as the food. Like most of the nearby places, try not to stray from the fish and seafood, which cannot be topped.

CAPRI

Capri is a place where descriptions fall flat. The colors reach unknown depths and the scent of perfumed flowers waft through the narrow streets. Gentle breezes woo you, and you willingly oblige. Sure tourists flood the island during the day – day-trippers come to peek at the Blue Grotto, trek to Tiberius' hilltop refuge or seek out celebrities who frequent the island. But when dusk comes and the last hydrofoil returns to Sorrento, Naples or other ports, Capri returns to its more natural state – a lush

maiden, with evening veil softly muting her rugged beauty as a blazing sunset causes her to blush sweetly with promise twinkling in her crown of stars.

Some archaeologists argue that Capri was inhabited during the Paleolithic age when the island was linked to the mainland. Prehistoric animal bones and stone weapons or tools were found when Romans began to build their enormous monuments in Capri and when, at the beginning of the 20th century, builders digging the foundation of the Quisisana Hotel uncovered similar items. Greek artifacts and inscriptions also were located on the island.

In 29 AD, Augustus, on his way home from the Eastern campaigns, stumbled upon the island and was overcome by its incredible beauty. He snatched it from the Neapolitans and gave them Ischia in return. His successor, Tiberius, also was enamored with the island and lived his "golden exile" here. Capri fell into disregard after Tiberius' death. It was used primarily as an exile for troublemakers from the mainland. When the Roman Empire collapsed, Naples and the abbots of Montecasino controlled Capri. Pirates frequently raided the island as it was passed from one ruler to another. Finally, with the emergence of the Kingdom of Italy, Capri rose as the lush island and tourist spot it is today.

Our children found the island a delight. The medieval district, with its narrow streets that zigzagged under archways, was fun to explore. The them as they spied lizards, smelled flowers and played imaginary games along the way.

Tourist Office
P.tta l. Cerio, 11. Tel. (081)837.5308. Email: capritourism@capri.it, or touristoffice@capri.it. Web: www.capritourism.com.

MARINA GRANDE

Undoubtedly, you will set foot on Capri from Marina Grande, a bustling tourist port where hotelmen seek their clients in order to help them manage their luggage to the hotel. Please note this is not Naples, and these people are only there to help, not swindle you. Once, we brushed aside their offer and struggled with our luggage through the streets. The cab driver chuckled saying many people who arrive after spending time in Naples do the same thing. Because even the taxis can only drive up to Capri's main square – and not all the way to most hotels – it's best to let your hotel transport your luggage up from Marina Grande, while your family rides up the cable car and walks the rest of the way.

Once you leave the dock, tourist shops attack all who are coming or going. The good news is you will have one last chance to grab a gift on the way out.

THE BLUE GROTTO

Take a boat either from the Marina Grande or by rowboat from Grotta Azzurra. We took a bus down the steep hill from Anacapri. Open 9am until 1 hour before sunset, closed if the water is rough.

The trip into the Blue Grotto is amazing. From stone steps that lead to the sea, you climb into a small rowboat, rocking in the waves. The rower will talk to you about the history of the grotto as you glimpse, then stare walks – up to **Augustus' Garden**, down to **Piccolo Marina** and even the exhausting trek up to **Tiberius' villa** – intrigued slack-jawed at the tiny opening your boat is expected to enter to see the grotto. How can this be? The undulating waves cause the boats to rise, and the opening turns into a mere crack in the great rock wall. Of course, you don't show your concern to the kids, but you're ready to bail out at any moment. Then, miraculously, your little boat slips through the opening into the grotto. The blue is a color unseen before, especially if you go in the morning on a sunny day. Its magic is obtained by the beams of sunlight that penetrate through the water below the cave wall. The light is diffused under the mirror of the waters that filter through an underwater opening.

The grotto was officially discovered in 1826 by poet August Koopisch and the artist Ernest Fries. Grand Tour visitors, upon hearing of the island's secret, made the grotto a special stop and were enchanted by the grotto's never-before-seen blue, shimmering between light and dark. Tourists have come in droves ever since.

After the tourist boats leave, it is possible to swim into the Grotto, although local authorities frown upon the practice. Be very careful of rising tides and stronger waves. Fatalities have occurred here and the water is quite deep, with only one resting spot toward the end of the cave, we were told by our guide.

You also can make arrangements to see the Bianca, Verde and Rossa Verde Grottos, but they will not leave quite the impression of the Blue Grotto.

FARAGLIONI

Jutting up from the depths of the sea are three stupendous rock formations called the Faraglioni. They were formed by erosion caused by the water that broke off chunks of rock, in some cases forming the grottoes or natural archways, but at the southeastern coast giving birth to these rising walls of rock. Towering at 350 feet above water, the Faraglioni symbolize Capri and have inspired artists throughout the ages, including our son who, surprisingly to us, found Capri to be his favorite place in Italy. "I like it best," he told us, "because it is so lush and the colors so deep."

ARCO NATURALE

The arch, shaped by erosion and landslides, is an awe-inspiring monument to the beauty of the island. From the center of Capri follow Via Camerelle to Via Tragara to Via Matermania. Along the way, admire the flowers, fauna, Faraglioni and picturesque coves.

GARDENS OF AUGUSTUS

Perched above the Marina Piccola is a pretty little garden originally planted by Augustus. Soaring pine trees guard this paradise, while jubilant, bright-colored flowers and palm trees hail each day. A short path winds through the garden, where you can linger to soak in the panoramic views, including the rugged Faraglioni rising from the sparkling blue sea. Or, you can gaze solemnly at the statue of Lenin, who visited Capri in the early 1900s.

VIA KRUPP

Cut into the rock is the picturesque Via Krupp, named after the German industrialist who carved the road in the early 1900s. It cuts back and forth from the Gardens of Augustus down, down to Marina Piccola. It is a long, steep but fun walk down to the Marina Piccola, with inspirational views exposed at all times. There is a bus to take you back up if necessary.

MARINA PICCOLA

A small landing is nestled at the side of the island, but the heart and soul of Marina Piccola is its cozy resort. Swimmers play in the azure waters, other sit under colorful umbrellas. The Faraglioni watch from a distance as the Scoglio della Sirene (Sirens' Rock) preoccupies travelers searching – Marina Piccola also is where you can embark on a boat ride around the island. Inquire at your hotel for details.

VILLA JOVIS

Open 9am-one hour before sunset. Admission.
From Capri, take the Via Sopramonte to Via Tiberius, which leads to Via

Moneta to the Villa Jovis. Once you are on Via Tiberius, follow the signs. The trail is long, gently sloping up. It is a beautiful hike, with gardens as borders, charming residences and lovely views. Take your time to breathe in the perfume of Capri.

Immediately before the Villa are the remains of a lighthouse. Tiberius used the lighthouse to communicate to the mainland during his reign of terror – which he enjoyed on Capri. Stories of Tiberius' cruel and demented nature continue to ring through the island. From the Villa, you will see "Tiberius' Leap," which is the spot where the Emperor would toss disloyal servants and others down to the sea.

Fun Fact

On the way up to the Villa Jovis, near the end, is a sliver of a park on your right next to the sea. Sometimes an elderly gentleman is posted there to hand out information on the Villa, protect the park from tourist trash and watch over his goats. The kids were delighted to hear the tinkling of their little bells. One frisky goat, sure to remind you of at least one of your kids, continually jumped from his terrace only to be shooed back by the old man. A lovely scene.

The Villa itself is a magnificent structure with the glorious colors of Capri as its backdrop. The ruins are a fun spot to visit, but do be careful of the cliffs.

WHICH ONE IS MY ROOM?

GRAND HOTEL QUISISANA ***** *Via Camerelle, 2. Tel. (39)(081)837-0788. (39)(081)837-6080. Closed November through March. Web: www.quisisana.com.*

All roads lead to the luxurious Hotel Quisisana. Its pale yellow facade and outdoor café beckon you inside. This is one of the island's oldest hotels, big and grand and set right in the center of all the hubbub – a place to see and be seen. The 150 rooms and 15 suites are some of the most luxurious and offer great views from the balconies. This is one of the first hotels in the area.

LA LUNA **** *Via Tragara, 57. Tel. (39)(081)370-433, Fax (39)(081)837-7790. Web: www.lunahotel.com.*

Off the beaten track, close to the Gardens of Augustus and the Via

Krupp, is pretty La Luna. From their deck, over some large cacti, is a stunning view of the Fraglioni and the sea beyond. Nothing separates La Luna from the sea but the steep, rocky cliffs. The kids especially enjoyed the long path to the streets, where lizards darted in and out and cats bounded through the grass or lazed under a noonday sun. It has a beautiful outdoor pool, although it's quite chilly off-season since they don't heat it. The rooms are comfortable with all amenities and the breakfast buffet is outstanding.

LA SCALINATELLA ***** *Via Tragara, 8. Tel. (39)(081)837-0633, Fax (39)(081)837-8291. Closed November through March. Web: www.scalinatella.com.*

The white and gold hotel is built on terraces descending, like a stairway *(salinatella)* down the hill. The 30-room Moorish building lends a mystique to the hotel. The common rooms are opulent and the guestrooms large and brightly colored. Have lunch by the pool.

VILLA BRUNELLA **** *Via Tragara, 24. Tel. (39)(081)837-0122, Fax (39)(081)837-0430. Web: www.villabrunella.it.*

A smaller family-run hotel situated on the path leading to the

Faraglioni. The rooms and views are stunning. Enjoy the swimming pool and wonderful restaurant, one of our favorites.

VILLA KRUPP ** *Viale Matteotti, 12. Tel. (39)(081)837-0362, Fax (39)(081)837-*

6489. Closed Closed November-March.

Overlooking the Gardens of Augustus and the Via Krupp is the villa once owned by the German armaments industrialist Herr Krupp. The 12 rooms are plain but large. Among the many famous guests, the Krupp has housed the great Russian author Maxim Gorky and the famous Russian revolutionary Leon Trotsky.

I'M HUNGY!

VILLA BRUNELLA $$$$ *Via Tragara, 24/a. Tel. (39)(081)837-0122, Fax (39)(081)837.0430.*

At this hotel/restaurant sunset is the best time to come – the panoramic views are startlingly beautiful. Passing time from light to dusk to night leaves you breathless. The restaurant is lit by soft candlelight, only enhancing Capri's magic. Try the *lemon risotto* – we've never had better. The kids actually loved the minestrone soup and the fish dishes are superb. Dinner ended with strawberries and ice cream and we vowed never to go home. Score one for the Sirens.

I FARAGLIONI $$$ *Via Camerelle, 75. Capri Town. Tel. (39)(081)837-0320. Closed November through March. Reservations required.*

A 100-year-old wisteria plant winds itself up I Faraglioni providing a natural umbrella to protect diners from the elements. The restaurant boasts great views, and they are right, although we've never met a view we didn't like in Capri. Dining outside is enjoyable, a place where people watching is an art  form. Although I Faraglioni is a chi-chi place, the food is good – fresh pasta, nicely done fish and tasty *crepes al formaggio*, which the kids loved. Try the *risotto alla pescatore* (rice with seafood). Not as elegant nor as child-friendly as Villa Brunella, but tolerable.

LA FONTELINA $$$ *1 Faraglioni, at the end of Via Tragara. Capri Town. Tel. (39)(081)837-0845. Lunch only. Closed from mid-October until Easter.*

Way down at the bottom of via Tragara at the foot of the Faraglioni. Given its prime beachfront location, you must sample the fish – you can bet it's fresh.

LE GROTTELLE $$$ *Via Arco Naturale, 13. Tel. (39)(081)837-5719. Closed on Thursdays in December and January. Reservations required.*

Nestled into the rocks above the Arco Naturale is this delightful *trattoria*. Seafood and pasta are featured on the menu. Try the *ravioli alla caprese* – ravioli with seafood made Caprese-style.

LA RONDINELLA $$ *Via Orlandi, 295. Anacapri. Tel. (39)(081)837-1223. Closed January 10 through February and Thursday during October-May.* There is a great view of Anacapri Street and all of that thoroughfare's interesting passers-by. There is also a nice terrace to this ristrorante-pizzeria.

LA CAPANNINA $$$ *Via delle Botteghe, 12. Tel. (39)(081)837-0732 or 0899, Fax (39)(081)837.6990. E-mail: capannina@capri.it.* Some consider La Capannina to be Capri's top restaurant – certainly many celebrities frequent this lovely upscale (and family-run) restaurant. Choice seating is on the outdoor terrace, draped with vines and lit by candlelight. The food is refined and fresh. We love the *insalata caprese*.

AMALFI

Gentle **Amalfi**, clinging to the breast of the mountainside, is a pastel-clad resort with a surprising past. At one time, the fleet docked at Amalfi's coast was feared by all in the Mediterranean. Over the years, its influence waned until the state road, built in 1800s, opened it up to tourism. In this way, Amalfi continues to flourish as that gentle resort by the sea.

For more info, go to *www.amalfitouristoffice.it.*

WHICH ONE IS MY ROOM?

GRAND HOTEL CONVENTO DI AMALFI **** *Via Annunzi atella, 46. Tel. (39)(089)871-877. Fax (39)(089)871-886. Web: www.ghconventodiamalfi.com.*

Quiet as a convent – which it once was. Originally built in the 1300s by Emperor Frederick II as a monastery, the same peaceful air still permeates the grounds. Perched on a cliff, the panoramic view is heavenly. Fifty-three guestrooms and suites are set in former cells of the friars. A Rococo chapel still shines and the reception area is located in the former cloister. Cappuccini Convento is one of the most uniquely beautiful places to stay. And babysitting is available.

LUNA CONVENTO ****
Via Comite, 33. Tel. (39)(089)871.002. Fax (39)(089)871-333. Web: www.lunahotel.it.

Also well known i1s the Luna Torre Saracena. Legend has it that St. Francis of Assisi founded the Luna Convento in the early 1200s. Now it is owned by the Barbaro family and has been since 1822. Most of the 45 rooms are large, with views of the sea. A warm and pleasant hotel, despite the fact that Mussolini was a visitor. We loved the hotel restaurant and bar set in the building's 15th-century Saracen Tower.

SANT'ANDREA * *Via Santolo Camera, 1. Tel. (39)(089)871-145.*

A pleasant two-star with lovely views of the cathedral. The rooms are simple but clean and comfortable.

I'M HUNGRY!

TARI \$\$\$\$ *Via P. Capuano. Tel. (39)(089)871-832.*

Fittingly named after a historic coin of Amalfi, Tari is expensive but well worth it. Have your pick of fresh seafood that is succulent whatever way it is prepared. There is usually a nice display of local artwork.

DA BARACCA \$\$ *Piazza dei Dogi. Tel. (39)(089)871-285. Closed Wednesday (not in summer).*

Located in a piazza just west of the cathedral, Da Baracca offers a nice variety of seafood dishes as well as its own homemade liqueur. The kids took a pass on the octopus (the *gamberini e calamari alla griglia*) but Michael gave it a thumbs up.

DA GEMMA \$\$\$\$ *Via Fra' Gerardo Sasso, 10. Tel. (39)(089)871-345. Closed Wednesday (not in summer) and November and January.*

Established in 1872, Da Gemma offers a pleasant dining experience, most notably on the terrace. We couldn't help but notice the beautiful tile floors.

RAVELLO

Ravello is Amalfi's crowned jewel, sitting on its ridge throne atop

Monte Cerreto. Terraced lemon groves and vineyards and forests of chestnut are her court. Refinement is Ravello's banner, and she lives it regally. This little hill town is about five kilometers from Amalfi and is perched atop a 350-foot cliff.

There is a music festival in Ravello called the **Festival Musicale di Ravello**, *Via Trinita, 3, Tel. (39)(089)858-149, E-mail: info@rcs.amalfi coast.it).* Contact them for a schedule for upcoming events.

Tourist Office
Via Roma, 18. Tel. (089)857.096 Email: info@ravellotime.it Web: www.ravellotime.it.

WHICH ONE IS MY ROOM?

PALUMBO ***** *Via S. Giovanni del Toro, 28. Tel. (39)(089)857-244, Fax (39)(089)857-347. Web: www.hotel-palumbo.it.*

A place for the rich and famous – from the composer Richard Wagner to President Kennedy to Placido Domingo. Today, there are two hot tubs

on the roof, a marble atrium and all-glass elevators. Glittery, yes. Comfortable, absolutely.

VILLA MARIA *** *Via Santa Chiara, 2. Tel. (39)(089)857-255. Fax (39)(089)857-071. Web: www.villamaria.it.*

Tennis is just a few steps away at this charming villa. Or, enjoy the sunny, garden terrace. The 18-room hotel is decorated with antiques and made more airy with high ceilings. There is a heated swimming pool and tennis courts as well.

VILLA AMORE ** *Tel. (39)(089)857-135. Web: www.villaamore.it.*

A family-run hotel just 10 minutes, walking, from the main square. Rooms are small and plain, but clean and pretty.

I'M HUNGY!

All the hotels have fine restaurants, but if you want to venture out, try:

CUMPA' COSIMO $$ *Via Roma, 22. Tel. (39)(089)847-876. Closed Wednesday and January-February. Reservations a must.*

Cooking with love by the Bottone family, who have owned the *cantine* for 70 of its 300 years. Photographs of all the famous people who have enjoyed the simple but succulent meals prepared here are hung on the walls. The kids enjoyed the homemade pasta with a simple sauce of garlic, oil and basil. Try the fish – fresh from the bay.

8. MILAN & THE LAKE REGION

Milan is Italy in a suit. All dressed up for business – from high fashion to finance – Milan is the country's mighty economic engine churning out a profit, but losing a bit of la dolce vita in the process. The city resembles a German or American city more than it does a Tuscan town, or even eclectic Rome. In the morning, men and women scramble to the workplace, cell phones dangling from their ears, dressed in urban-chic attire. For centuries, Milan has been a business city. Mediolanum, its name in ancient times, sat at the crossroads of a trade route extending from the Alpine passes to the Tyrrhenian and Adriatic port cities and also to the Po River. Of course, this prime commercial location had the downside of leaving Milan vulnerable to invasion.

Invaders came and went – from Rome in 222 BC to the Huns, Goths and Germans (first in the person of "Red Beard," Frederick Barbarossa, then during World War II). Civil strife also plagued Milan over nothing

short of religion. In 313, Constantine the Great issued the **Edict of Milan**, which forced religious tolerance of Christianity. The Milanese, however, were divided between a Catholic version and one that adhered to the Egyptian bishop Arius. The city's patron saint, **Ambrose**, who rose to the level of bishop (375-397), forged unity between the sects. The Ambrosian church was so strong that it remained independent of Rome until the 11th century. Today, Mass is still performed as an Ambrosian rite and some Milanese refer to themselves as Ambrosiani.

Milan, by then called Mailand, was no pushover for outside invaders. Led by the Ambrosiani and the newly formed Lombard League, Milan waged ferocious battles against Barbarossa, eventually defeating him. Throughout this time, the commune system of government was established, initially under the rule of Bishop Heribert.

Eventually, Milan came to be ruled by a series of rich and famous families – from the Torriani in the 1200s to the Sforza family in the 14th and 15th centuries. Lodovico il Moro, son of Francesco Sforza, commissioned Leonardo da Vinci to paint the *Last Supper*, restored several years ago and a sight to behold. Leonardo spent some time in Milan, on loan to Lodovico from the Medicis. "In time of peace I am an artist," wrote da Vinci, who packed his brushes and notebooks and fled Milan when the French invaded in 1499.

During the reign of the Habsburgs of Austria in the 1700s, the world-famous **La Scala opera house** and the Brera Academy were established. In 1848, after Napoleon came, saw and conquered the Habsburgs, only to see the Habsburgs return victorious to Milan in 1814, Milan finally ousted the Austrian family to join the new Kingdom of Italy. Since then, immigrants from the poor south poured into Milan, looking for jobs at a decent wage. Milan survived World War II, albeit scarred by bombing raids, and the influx of immigrants continued. Today, Milan boasts a population of about 1.5 million. It is a fashion center of the world and is home to Italy's largest stock market.

Our hotel stays in Milan always border on the absurd: We ungracefully land in the breakfast room to see heads turn, ever so slightly. Of course, the heads shine with the latest hair gloss, both sexes are perfectly manicured, dressed to the nines in the latest chic fashion with purses shouting important names of Versace, Prada or Fendi. We, of course, at our best are an ad for Gap Kids. Our chitchat is less about the latest runway show or fab diet and more about "Stop running and eat something."

GETTING AROUND TOWN
By Metro
You can catch the **Metropolitana Milanese** (metro or subway) from the train station. Look for the M in a circle. The metro is pretty safe and clean. Choose from three lines: red, green and yellow. City maps are posted at the metro stops, but when in doubt, ask a Milanese. Purchase tickets (free under 5) at newsstands at the station, the station office or machines at each stop, although we never found a machine that worked correctly.

By Walking
The city is too big to plan to walk everywhere, unlike Florence and Venice. Use the metro or a cab.

WHERE ARE WE GOING NOW?
While Milan doesn't have as many adventures for children as other Italian cities, towns and villages, there are still fun things to do in the world's fashion capital.

DUOMO

Piazza del Duomo. Open 7am-7pm. October-May 9am-4:30pm. Admission to top.

It was the last day of our trip to Italy and even Barbara was tired of visiting churches. But Michael, a big church aficionado (he toured Chartes in France three times – in two days) successfully persuaded (resorting to negotiation tactics learned from the kids) the family to accompany him on his quest to see Milan's Duomo. And we're glad he did!

The Cathedral's imposing structure is located in the center of town, with 135 spires soaring to the heavens. It is the third largest church in the world – behind St. Peter's in Rome and the Seville Cathedral. Don't ask your kids to count the saints – there are 2,244 marble statues of the holiest of the holy, with 95 gargoyles scattered about.

This is a shining, if not monstrous, example of the Gothic style. Like the song that never ends (Sherry Lewis fans are smiling), this is the church that's never done. Construction began in 1386 and it has remained under continuous restoration since then.

The Cathedral has been the biggest public works project ever undertaken in Milan. Thousands of sculptors, artists, engineers, bricklayers have been on the Cathedral's payroll for centuries. Walk inside and you feel like a small speck in the universe of marble and brick, amazing stained glass, and rows and rows of pews for the faithful. **The Baptistery of St. Ambrose** (*open daily 10am-12pm and 3pm-5pm, admission*) showcases the baptismal font

where St. Ambrose baptized St. Augustine, who the former allegedly converted.

Gian Galeazzo Visconti called for the building of a cathedral in 1386, as an offering to Mary to grant him a son. She did, although the son, Giovanni Maria, made for a lousy ruler. Major artists and engineers of the day were hired to design and build the cathedral. Too many cooks in the *cucina* meant a lot of squabbling over how the cathedral should look, and Galeazzo was draining his city's financial pot to near ruin. He resorted to increasing court fines and bullying local churches to sell indulgences. Somehow Galeazzo's cathedral was "finished" in 1399. The biggest controversy arose over the facade, which started out in the Gothic style that no one liked and ended up going through so many revisions that it appears to have its own wedding-cake look.

The kids love walking on the **cathedral roof** *(open daily 9am-5:30pm; admission; use the steps or the elevator)*. On a clear day, you can see the Matterhorn, and certainly the sight of Milan below is well worth the climb.

Parent Tip: The **Museo del Duomo** *(open Tuesday-Sunday 9:30am-12:30pm and 3pm-6pm; admission)* is home to many of the original gargoyles from the Cathedral. Lots of kids like these little, mischievous creatures. While the kids are making faces at the gargoyles, you can enjoy the tapestries, delicate stained glass windows (the originals) and other Cathedral art and artifacts.

CIVICO MUSEO DELL'ARTE CONTEMPORANEA
Palazzo Reale. Open Tuesday-Sunday 9:30am-5:30pm. Admission.

Near the Duomo is the museum of contemporary art. Inside are works by Kandinsky, Matisse, Picasso and Klee. However, the focus is on Italian art of the last century (20th century) including the futurist Boccioni and Modigliani, Morandi, de Pises and Melotti.

VITTORIO EMANUELE GALLERIA

Walk from the Piazza Duomo to the Piazza della Scala through this glass-roofed arcade (*see photo on page 268*). Construction began in 1865 and was completed in 1877. Unfortunately, the designer, Giuseppe Mengoni, never got to enjoy his work. On the day before its opening, he slipped from the scaffolding and plummeted to his death. Today many upscale bars and shops live inside the Galleria.

See Taurus the Bull, a mosaic in the center of the Galleria? Milanese folklore says it's good luck to step on his testicles. Go figure.

TEATRO LA SCALA

Via Dei Filodrammatici, 2. Tel. (39)(02)887-97473,. Web: www.teatroallascala.org. Open Monday-Saturday 9am-noon and 2pm-6pm. Sunday 9:30am-12:30pm and 2:30pm-6pm. Admission.

Opera fans flock to La Scala, the world's most famous opera house. Most of the 19th-century operas opened in this theater built in 1778. It was decimated in World War II, but quickly restored. The Museo Teatrale alla Scala is full of costumes, scores, photos of opera stars and set designs.

Parent Tip: If you're an opera buff and your kids aren't – yet – they still may enjoy the **museum** (Museo Teatrale alla Scala). The costumes and set designs often are big hits with the younger crowd.

GALLERIA NAZIONALE DI BRERA

Via Brera, 28. Tel. (02)722.631.Email: brera.artimi@arti.benicultur ali.it. Web: www.brera.beniculturali.it. Open Tuesday through Sunday from 8:30am to 7:15pm. Admission: €11.

An outstanding collection of art is on display at the Galleria Nazionale di Brera, a collection gathered by none other than Napoleon. You can't miss him. He's the guy in the bronze toga as you enter. Make sure you see Raphael's *Marriage of the Virgin,* Caravaggio's *Supper at Emmaus* and Rembrandt's *Portrait of His Sister.*

The museum, located near La Scala, opened in 1809.

CASTELLO SFORZESCO

Foro Buonaparte. Open Tuesday-Sunday 9:30am-5:30pm.

Bigger is better in Milan. The Castello Sforzesco, although scaled back from its earlier days, is Italy's largest castle. The Visconti had claimed the site as their base, only to see it razed in 1447 by the Ambrosians. Francesco Sforza rebuilt the castle. World War II bombing did enough damage to the old castle that it again was rebuilt.

Behind the castle is the wonderful (and Milan's largest) park, **Parco Sempione**, with the **Arco della Pace**, a celebration of Napoleon's victories in war. A trip to the castle is a twofer – the kids get to see and play around the castle and you

can peek into the **Civici Musei d'Arte e Pinacoteca del Castello**, an outstanding art collection filled with Lippi, Bellini, Bramantino and the unfinished and eerie *Rondanini Pieta* by an elderly Michelangelo.

GIARDINI PUBBLICI
Situated between the train station and the Duomo. Open 6am-dusk.
The gardens are a great change of pace from city life. There is a small but uninteresting zoo and lots of wooded paths to follow. Children enjoy the pedal cars and playground. On the grounds of the Giardini Pubblici is the **Museo del Cinema** (*Viale Manin, 2; Web www.cinetecamilano.it/museo; Open Tuesday through Friday 3pm-6pm; Admission*), a good place to stop if any future filmmaker is interested to discover how animation works.
The park is a great place to take kids after a long day of traveling and touring.

LEONARDO DA VINCI MUSEUM OF SCIENCE & TECHNOLOGY
Via San Vittore, 21. Tel. (02)485.551 or 480.100.16. Email: info@museoscienza.it. Web: www.museoscienza.org. Open Wednesday through Friday from 10am to 5pm, Saturday and holidays from 10am to 6:30pm. Closed Christmas and New Year's Day. Admission: €8.00, €6 for visitors under age 25 and for persons accompanying visitors under 14 years (max 2 people).
One of our favorite museums in all of Italy. Where else would a guard lift our five-year old little girl up over the velvet rope to play her favorite song – Cukoo – on an ancient piano! "Bravo, bambina," shouted our daughter's first European audience. The museum is unique for culling Leonardo da Vinci's work and experiments in diverse fields. We paid for an English-speaking guide, who obviously thought the world of children, to explain many of Leonardo's inventions, which were built for the exhibit.
Other exhibits of equal interest to curious children focus on optics, radios, computers and astronomy. The children's exhibit was closed on our visits to the museum, but it is heralded as one of Italy's finest interactive museums.
This is a must-see on any trip to Milan. The museum has a small snack bar with tables in the outside portico. The kids can run to the courtyard below and play among the sculptures.

DA VINCI'S "THE LAST SUPPER"
Piazza Santa Maria delle Grazie 2. Tel. (02)928-00360. Web: www.cenacolovinciano.it. Open Tuesday through Friday, 9am-6pm and

Saturdays 9am-2pm. Closed Christmas, New Year's, 1 May. Admission: €6.50.

While art critics opine on the virtues or flaws of this painting, to the untrained eye it is a spectacle to be seen. The restoration efforts over the years have been Herculean. Leonardo painted the *Last Supper* between 1495 and 1497. Compelled to experiment, his unique attempt to replicate what he saw in his mind's eye has not withstood the test of time. Traditional fresco techniques called for quickly applying the paint to wet plaster. Instead, da Vinci used tempera on glue and plaster in order to go back to repaint until he achieved the effect he wanted. Nature – in this case humidity – did not bow to the genius of da Vinci and has wreaked havoc on the painting over time. Particles of paint continuously peel from the painting.

Today every precaution is taken to thwart humidity's deleterious effect on it. Huge dehumidifiers whir in the darkened room as visitors must pass through several doors and vestibules before entering – with only 15 minutes of visitation rights allowed.

Parent Tip: Try your best to get tickets ahead of time to see the **Last Supper** painting. Ask your hotel and follow-up with them before you come to ensure tickets are waiting for you. We had one hotel confirm by fax that they had tickets, only to renege when we got to town. You can book online for additional charges: *www.tickitaly.com/tickets/last-supper-tickets.php*. If all else fails, go stand in line at least a half-hour before opening.

Don't give up if a museum official says they are not giving out any daily passes that day. This happened when we visited, and like many other tourists we stayed in line and happily got in about fifteen minutes later. The line forms in a small piazza where the children can run around and play or read books, color or paint while you steadfastly remain in line. The museum shop is an excellent source of gifts for the artistically inclined.

SPORTS & RECREATION
Bookstore
　　American Bookstore, Via Camperio, 16. Tel. (39)(02)878-920. That's right, books are all in English.

Festivals
　　Festa dei Navigli, First Sunday in June. Lots of music and entertainment along the Navigli (canals) in the Ticinese part of town.
　　St. Ambrose Day, December 7. Patron saint of Milan. Opera season opens around this time.

Music
Jazz Festival in Milan. April-May. *Web: www.milanojazzfestival.it.*

Shopping
Via Montenapoleone and **Via della Spiga** and everything in between these parallel streets comprise Milan's most exclusive shopping area. The Fashion collections are shown in March and October.

Markets
Fiera Sinigallia, *Porta Ticinese.* All day Saturday.
Mercato Papiniano, *Viale Papiniano near Fiera Sinigallia at the Porta Ticinese.* Tuesday morning and all day Saturday.

WHICH ONE IS MY ROOM?
FOUR SEASONS HOTEL ***** *Via Gesu, 8. Tel. (39)(02)77088, Fax (39)(02)7708-5000. 98 rooms. Web: www.fourseasons.com/milan.*

A plush, elegant and famous hotel, this 15th century former convent lives up to the Four Seasons reputation. Located in the center of Milan, the Four Seasons is a perfect setting for indulgence *alla Milanese*! There are two fine restaurants in the hotel. Most notable are the elaborate and impressive frescoes in the entrance halls.

HOTEL DE LA VILLE **** *Via Hoepli, 6. Tel. (39)(02)867-651, Fax (39)(02)866-609. Web: www.hoteldela ville.com. 109 rooms.*

Situated between the Duomo and La Scala, the location of the Hotel De La Ville is not easily surpassed. The antique furnishings of the rooms are a smart touch of Old World style. Enjoy the hotel bar and restaurant.

ARISTON *** *Largo Carrobbio, 2. Tel. (39)(02)7200-0556. Fax (39)(02)7200-0914. Web: www.aristonhotel.com. 48 rooms.*

For the environmentally aware, the Ariston is tops for all of Italia. There are low-energy lamps, specially made beds and linens and even free bicycles. The no-smoking floor is yet another unique feature for an Italian hotel. The best part is that the comfort and style of the rooms match the level of commitment to the environment.

MARCONI **** *Via F. Filzi, 3. Tel. (39)(02)6698-5561. Fax (39)(02)669-0738. Web: www.marconihotel.it. Breakfast included. 69 rooms. Closed for part of August.*
Located near Milan's central station, the rooms are simple but comfortable. The courtyard garden provides an intimate and tranquil setting for all visitors.

CAIROLI *** *Via Porlezza, 4. Tel. (39)(02)801-371. Fax (39)(02)7200-2243. 38 rooms all with bath. Double €90-150. Breakfast included.*
This smallish, 38-room hotel offers a nice degree of tranquility in an otherwise bustling city. The rooms are quiet and afford a nice break from the Milanese routine.

ANTICA LOCANDA SOLFERINO ** *Via Castelfidardo, 2. Tel. (39)(02)657-0129, Fax (39)(02)657-1361. Web: www.anticalocandasol ferino.it. Closed August.*
Offering a nice affordable alternative, this 11-room hotel has small but clean rooms. The only downside is that its reasonable rates are mainly due to the fact that the hotel is situated near a popular late-night restaurant, which serves up noise and distraction as well as good food.

ANTICA LOCANDA LEONARDO, *Corso Magenta, 78. el. (02)463-317. Web: www.anticalocandaleonardo.com.*
So very close to da Vinci's Last Supper, this gem of a hotel resides in one of the most historic  sections of Milan. The rooms face an internal garden, adding to the tranquility of the setting. This is a tenderly cared for hotel managed by the Frefel family and is a true oasis in a bustling city.

I'M HUNGRY!
BAR RISTORANTE BIFFI $$$ *Galleria Vittorio Emanuele. Tel. (39)(02)805-7961. Closed Sundays.*
Located within the Galleria, here is a wonderful spot to observe the haute couture scene. A degree below the social pomp of Savini (see below), a tasty treat is the wonderful antipasto and appetizer selection.

SAVINI $$$$ *Galleria Vittorio Emanuele. Tel. (39)(02)805-8343. Closed Sundays.*

Prepare for the poshest of posh at Milan's well-known Savini. Amid

the upscale shoppers of the Galleria, the Savini offers a unique dining experience where high prices reflect the proximity to Milan's fashion industry. While the food is good, the atmosphere is the key ingredient. The Savini exudes style from the top of the crystal chandeliers to the plush carpets. Note that proper attire is more than required — it is essential.

CHARLESTON $ *Piazza Liberty, 8. Tel. (39)(02)798-631, Fax (39)(02)7600-1154. Closed Monday and Sunday for lunch.*

When the mood for pizza hits this is the place. Not just any pizza, but real thin crust pizza fresh from a wood-burning oven. With very reasonable prices and open late, Charleston also offers a wide array of toppings. Consider trying the namesake pizza, a hearty *calzone*.

BAGUTTA $$ *Via Bagutta. Tel. (39)(02)7600-2767. Closed Sundays.*

Bagutta offers a nice range of traditional regional dishes. You'll enjoy dining amidst an impressive collection of local art.

PAPER MOON $$ *Via Bagutta 1. Tel. (39)(02)792-297. Closed Sunday.*

Offering a real local feel, Paper Moon is a family-friendly pizzeria that offers so much more. The decor is modern and clean and gives the feeling of a Milan at ease. Paper Moon is a big hit with our kids. The waiter gave them extra scoops of gelato! A fish tank provides the all-important distraction for younger children.

CAFÉ MILANO $$$ *Via San Fermo 1. Tel. (39)(02)2900-3300. Closed Monday.*

Well known for its healthy Sunday brunch, Café Milano also is famous for its social nightlife. With after-theater specials, Café Milano attracts a diverse crowd and is set against the backdrop of the traditionally middle-class Brera section of Milan.

IL VERDI $$$ *Piazza Mirabello, 5. Tel. (39)(02)651-412. Closed Saturday at lunch and Sunday.*

Il Verdi is marked by a sleek modern design and decor that is only outdone by its wide selection of salads and appealing meat entries. Note that reservations are required.

IL RISTORANTE PECK $$$$ *Via Victor Hugo, 4. Tel. (39)(02)876-774.*

The Peck name conveys a standard of stylish excellence throughout Milan, and Il Ristorante Peck does nothing to damage that. Menu choice is an understatement here and even the most finicky of children will be overcome by the flexibility and variety of this restaurant. It is located just downstairs from Bottega del Vino, with an upscale gourmet market and a Milanese version of fast food.

DA RINO VECCHIA NAPOLI $ *Via Chavez, 4. Tel. (39)(02)261-9056. Closed Sunday and Monday lunch.*

A very reasonable choice, this restaurant's *gnocchi* (wonderful small Italian, hand-made potato dumplings) and its fresh fish selection stands out. Maybe that's why reservations are so strongly recommended.

Circa Milan: The Lake Region

The **Lake region** north of Milan is one of the most spectacular natural sites in the country. The Alps tower above and the deep blue lake water spreads across the northern region, in some places lapping at Switzerland's southern border.

While all of the lakes embrace their own special magic, we've found Lake Garda's **Sirmione** to be the most child-friendly and fun.

LAKE GARDA & SIRMIONE

Sirmione is a fairytale town, complete with drawbridge and castle. Swans glide gently by in what once was a moat. In the early morning, mist swirls like lace around the pretty face of maiden Sirmione.

This is an ideal lakeside resort for families. First, there is the beauty of Lake Garda, Italy's cleanest. The lake literally surrounds the town since Sirmione is strung out along a narrow strip of land that pokes its finger into the lake's southern shore. But Sirmione also offers a delightful medieval castle that you enter by walking across a drawbridge near the main gate of the old walled town.

Out on the point of the peninsula is the **Grotte di Catullo**, the extensive ruins of an ancient Roman villa. **GardaLand**, Italy's answer to Disneyland, is nearby. Parks, beaches and water sports are plentiful. Sirmione also is a spa town and shopping mecca – in all, a relaxing way to begin or end your visit to Italy. Sirmione is a convenient stopping point along the train and car route between Venice, Verona and Milan.

French and Germans frequent Sirmione, with few tourists from England or America. Be prepared to pull out your Italian dictionary.

GETTING HERE

From Verona: About 30 kilometers by train or bus. From the bus or train station take a cab to the gates of the walled city. By car, take *Autostrada* A4 and then SS11 at Pescheria del Garda to Sirmione.

From Milan: About 90 kilometers away by train or bus. Take a cab from the bus or train station to the gates of the walled city. By car, take the *Autostrada* A4 to Desenzano, then take the SS 572 just over six kilometers to the one road that turns left to the peninsula and Sirmione.

GETTING AROUND TOWN

Sirmione is pretty much a car-free town, a delight for families with children. A fun tram takes you to the top of the hill – the Catullo ruins and back down if the walk is too much for little ones.

Tourist Office
Viale Marconi 225019. Tel. (030)916-114. Web: www.sirmione.com/english.htm.

WHERE ARE WE GOING NOW?

Sirmione offers some beautiful and fun sightseeing for families. Here is what we recommend:

DELLA SCALA FORTRESS

Open 8:30am-2:30pm. Sunday 8:30am-7pm.

The majestic della Scala Fortress greets everyone who enters Sirmione across her drawbridge (*see photo on previous page*). Her history is intertwined with the powerful della Scala family from Verona, and the fortress was built in the 11th or 12th century, although no documentation exists to give a precise date. The fortress's military function continued through the Napoleonic period, when it held barracks equipment and other war materials and through World War II, when it became the headquarters for the German occupation army. Since then, the Ministry for Arts and Culture has protected the fortress.

The fortress is open to tour, and what a delight it is. The courtyard has interesting nooks and crannies and two staircases that lead to the upper walkway. Once up top, the kids can skip along the battlements and climb the towers, while parents enjoy a panoramic view of Sirmione and Lake Garda. At night, the bright moon casts shadows and outlines the sandy-colored fortress against the ink-black sky. A splendid sight!

We lingered until closing one night and on the way out, at the guard's entrance, marched Pinky the cat. She resides in the guard's room during the day, but is let out to rule the roost of the fortress at night. Let us know if she is still there, or if another feline has moved in!

SANTA MARIA MAGGIORE
& THE PASSEGGIATA PANORAMICA

The 15th-century church overlooks a sliver of a beach where kids hang out and skip stones on the lake. At the church begins the *passeggiata panoramica* that follows the eastern shore. This is a picture-perfect walk, the breeze fresh and sweet and the blue waters shimmering in the sun. Darker blue mountains jut up in the distance and swans follow you, hoping for a snack. Further along is another public beach where you can rent bikes and paddle boats. Or, you can choose to climb the small hill and sit on the benches to enjoy the view. Our kids loved tumbling down the hill or taking secret passageway walks in the groves.

LE GROTTE DI CATULLO

Tel. (39)(030)916-517. Open 9am-6pm, from November to March open 9am-4pm. Closed Monday. Admission.

A stunning setting, the sandy remains of an old Roman villa set against the pale blue sky, with the azure lake lapping at the shores. Olive groves and rosemary bushes decorate the land and provide a shady respite for visitors. It is thought that Catullus, the Roman poet who died in 54 BC, may have resided here, although the size of the ruins suggest that whoever lived here was the Bill Gates of ancient times. Excavation began in 1939 and the entire area was completed in 1948. A small museum displays spearheads, fragments of vases and other items found at the site.

Parent Tip: The ruins spread out across five acres of land, and are set on different levels, making it a pleasure for kids to explore. In some areas, the remains are like a maze and the kids loved to lead the way, get lost, and find their way out. Let imaginations run wild here. Bring a snack and stay up awhile. During the summer season, there is a tram to take you up and down the hill to the center of the town.

GARDALAND

GardaLand is Italy's largest amusement park, strikingly similar to Disneyland. Visit the Jungle Rapids, take a ride on the spinning Moonraker or plummet on the Magic Mountain rollercoaster with 360-degree turns. The park also has marvelous attractions for younger children – ride the Peter Pan pirate ship and the Orobruco roller coaster in caterpillar cars or visit the Villaggio degli Elfi, a trip through marzipan houses and sugar flowers. Stay around for the fun nighttime parade and the *palablu*, a dolphin show.

The entrance ticket entitles you to all attractions, with a supplemental for the dolphin show. There are plenty of restaurants and snack bars throughout the park.

Getting here by cab is surely the quickest way to reach the park, but also the most expensive. Buses leave regularly from the train station – a 4 kilometer ride to GardaLand. *Web: www.gardaland.it/en/home.php.*

SPORTS & RECREATION
Windsurfing
Centro Surf Martini, *Lido Porto Galeazzi. Tel. (39)(030)916-208*
Centro Surf Sirmione, *Lido Brema. Tel. (39)(030)624-3650*

Kayaking
Centro Surf Sirmione, *Lido Brema. Tel. (39)(030)624-3650*
Lido delle Bionde, *Porto Galeazzi*

Bicycling
Bar Chocolat, *Via Colombare. Tel. (39)(030)990-5297*
Green Walk, *Via Todeschino*
Adventure Sprint, *Via Brescia, 9. Tel. (39)(030)919-000*

WHICH ONE IS MY ROOM?
Very Expensive
HOTEL SIRMIONE **** *Piazza Castello 19. Tel. (39)(030)916-331. Web: www.termedisirmione.com/tds/en/homepage/hotel/hotel-sirmione.html. Children up to age 12 in a room with two adults are free, including breakfast. From age 12-18, ask about the 30 percent discount.*

Luxury on the lake. Perhaps the best location in Sirmione, nestled against the lakeshore and off a quiet square surrounded by cafes. The hotel is modern and sleek, as are the spacious guestrooms. Candlelight illuminates evening dinner on the terrace restaurant overlooking the lake. The hotel runs a private spa, including treatments for bambini (the kids). Enjoy the swimming pool and gym.

VILLA CORTINE PALACE HOTEL ***** *Via Grotto 12. Tel. (39)(030)990-5890, Fax (39)(030)916-390. Web: www.palacehotelvilla cortine.it. 55 rooms.*

Quiet elegance built on the very foundations of an ancient Roman ruin; it is high on a hill, with wonderful views out over the lake. The neoclassical facade sits amidst a verdant garden lined with high-reaching trees. Common rooms are opulent, adorned with frescoes, antiques and sparkling chandeliers. Guestrooms are exquisitely furnished and spacious. Of course, there is a private beach, tennis courts and a luxurious swimming pool in a most romantic setting. The views are breathtaking. Lots of protected space for kids to play. Service – perfect.

Expensive

HOTEL CONTINENTAL **** *Via Punta Staffalo 7/0. Tel. (39)(030) 990-5711, Fax (39)(030)916-278. Web: www.continentalsirmione.com. 53 rooms.*

The modern rooms are clean and simple – the view, magnificent. The hotel is located outside the crowded town, toward the Roman ruins. Enjoy a private beach, water sports equipment and a swimming pool. A nice touch is a balcony for every room.

HOTEL IDEAL **** *Via Catullio 31. Tel. (39)(030)990-4245, Fax (39)(030)990-4245. Web: www.hotelidealsirmione.it.*

Guestrooms are plain and simple, many with balconies overlooking the lake. Conveniently located for families, across from the park and Catullus ruins, Hotel Ideal's grounds also give kids a lot of running room. The terrace and gardens are lovely. A great choice for families.

Moderate

HOTEL PACE *** *Piazza Porto Valentino 5. Tel. (39)(030)990-5877, Fax (39)(030)919-6097. Web: www.pacesirmione.it. Children infants to age 3 stay free, 50% reduction for children 3-12 years of age.*

We loved the beautiful vine-covered balconies overflowing with pink flowers. The rooms are comfortable and charming. Discounts for children up to age 12. The restaurant is excellent.

Inexpensive

HOTEL GRIFONE ** *Via Bocchio 5. Tel. (39)(030)916-014. Rates: Doubles €100 and up.*

Best bargain on the peninsula. Hotel Grifone is spartan, but enjoys a splendid location next to the fortress, and on the lake front. The rooms are small, so you will need two rooms to handle a family of four. The restaurant is one of the best in Sirmione – reserve a table by the window for a beautiful lake view. The only downside, the hotel manager rigidly adheres to the rules of a two-star. There are no late night arrivals. Our train from Milan was running quite late and we phoned the Grifone to let them know of our arrival time. They would not stay open to accommodate us and we were forced to find a hotel in Milan. (Late at night and early in the morning, you let yourself in and out of the hotel with a key.) Also, checkout is promptly at 10am, no later.

I'M HUNGRY!

ALBERGO RISTORANTE PACE $$$ *Piazza Porto Valentino 5. Tel. (030)990-5877.*

Located in the Hotel Pace, this is a wonderful place to enjoy a fine meal with children. There are 36 pizza selections on the menu – something to satisfy even the most finicky of eaters. Try the *torta del garda* (grilled lake trout) and the *spaghetti aglio e olio con filetti di pomodoro mollicati*, but beware of the huge chunks of garlic tossed in the pasta. Take a corner table where the kids can duck under and visit the swans and mallards bobbing in the lake.

RISTORANTE PIZZERIA VALENTINO $$ *Piazza Porto Valentino.*
Pretty buttercup-yellow tablecloths brighten this popular restaurant. Funny clown paintings dot the walls and model ships are all around – making for a wonderful diversion for the kids. Pizza dominates the menu – 20 selections.

RESTAURANTE GRIFONE $$$$ *Via Bocchio, 5. Tel. (030)916-014. Reservations.*
Elegant but friendly dining. The lake fish is finely prepared (try the Lavarello del Garda conaglio e prezzemolo/Whitefish from Garda Lake with garlic and parsley), the pasta freshly made and seasoned to perfection (a good choice is the *Crema di pomodoro al profumo di basilico*/tomato cream with basil). Another house specialty is *Crespelle gratinate con formaggi dolci*/crepes with cheese. Reservations are essential, particularly if you want a table along the windows overlooking the lake.

After dinner we walked outside, down a small flight of stone steps to the pebbled beach. Under the watchful eye of the fortress, we skipped

The Scoop on Gelato

Gelato shops line the narrow main street and the kids ogled every one of them. Consensus between the two of them could not be reached, so, we've included both:

• Caffeteria Bar da Gino, *Via Vittoria Emanuele*. Our son loved the pistachio and tiramisu.

• Break's Bar, *Via Vittoria Emanuele 3*. Our daughter adored the stracciatella.

stones with young Italians, while the swans gracefully presented themselves ever hopeful of small morsels of food.

BOUNTY CAFÉ $ *In front of the fortress.*

A great spot for a light breakfast before beginning the day's adventures. Tender croissants of multiple varieties are the favorite, drowned with a cappuccino or hot chocolate.

LAKE COMO & COMO

Como is a romantic retreat, resting at the shores of Lake Como's southwestern corner. Years ago, the silk industry emerged in Como from secrets stolen from the Chinese. The industry continues today.

But few are drawn to Como for simply silk. It is a lakeside paradise, to expunge the hectic life from your soul. Como is made for lounging, for exploring the entire lake, or for participating in a flurry of athletic activities. It's a short trip from Milan – only 40 minutes – but it seems like a nation away.

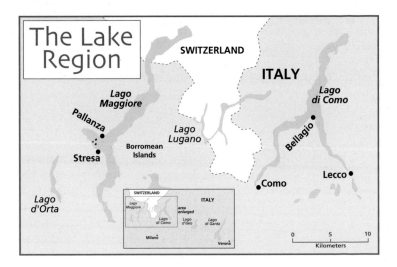

GETTING AROUND TOWN

Navigazione Lago di Como operates steamers, motor boats and hydrofoils to ferry you to many lakeside destinations. *Tel. (39)(031)304-060.*

GETTING HERE

By Car: An easy ride up *Autostrada* A9 from Milan.
By Train: Trains run frequently between Como and Milan.

Tourist Information
Piazza Cavour, 17. Tel. (39)(031)450-235. Or visit www.bellagiolakecomo.com.

SPORTS & RECREATION

Check with your hotel for tennis, rock climbing, hiking, sailing and fishing. For golf and horses, try:

Golfing
Circolo Villa d'Este, *Monteforno (four kilometers away). Tel. (39)(031)200-200*

Horseback Riding
Frazione Barella, *Tel. (39)(031)450-235*

WHICH ONE IS MY ROOM?

GRAND HOTEL VILLA D'ESTE ***** *Via Regina, 40. Tel. (39)(031)511-471, Fax (39)(031)512-027. Web: www.villadeste.com. 113 rooms, 45 suites.*

Pampered relaxation is a specialty of the Grand Hotel Villa D'Este. Dotting the 10 acres of gardens are tennis courts, swimming pool, a sauna and a private beach. Antiques and marble bathrooms await you in the guestrooms. The hotel also  offers an exceptional babysitting service, matched only by its zealous and energetic staff.

BARCHETTA EXCELSIOR **** *Piazza Cavour, 1. Tel. (39)(031)3221, Fax (39)(031)302-622. Web: www.hotelbarchetta.it.*
A lovely four-star hotel, with many rooms overlooking the glorious lake.

ALBERGO TERMINUS *** *Lungo Lario Trieste, 14. Tel. (39)(031)329-111, Fax (39)(031)302-550. Web: www.albergoterminus.com. 38 rooms.*
In the small tower is a two-floor guestroom – a delightful place to stay. Otherwise the rooms are charming and quaint. A panoramic terrace is situated on the lake. Notice the finely crafted mosaic tile work throughout the common areas of the hotel.

I'M HUNGRY!

IMBARCADERO $$ *Via Cavour, 20. Tel. (39)(031)277-341. Not open in the beginning of January.*
In the summer, the terrace is open and the family can dine on the water's edge. The food is simple but well prepared – fish, meat and fresh pasta are on the menu. For the adventurous diner, we recommend the *coniglio alle olive* (yes, rabbit), but do not tell the kids what it is!

PERLASCA $$$ *Piazza de'Gasperi, 8. Tel. (39)(031)300-263. Closed Monday.*
Wonderful views of the lake with succulent fish and traditional and homemade pasta dishes.

9. PLANNING YOUR TRIP

CLIMATE & WEATHER

Most of Italy is blessed with a Mediterranean climate – hot, dry summers and cool, rainy winters. But the weather in the north differs greatly from the south. In the north, the winters are much colder and, of course, there is snow in the Alps. The Alps, however, protect the rest of the country from cold northerly winds. Rome has a fairly moderate temperature year round, although the summers can be very hot in the city. Southern Italy and Sicily also can be boiling in the summer.

Summer is when most tourists descend on Italy. The weather varies across the country, with the north being pleasant, mid-70s in the Lake region and Milan, to high 80s and plus in Rome and the south. Fall is a gorgeous time of year to visit, with all the vibrant colors on display and the grapes ready for harvest. Winter is ski season in northern Italy, and not a bad time to see the sites elsewhere with fewer tourists. Christmas celebrations and holiday festivals brighten up the winter months, just remember to pack for bone-chilling cold days in Florence, Venice and other northern areas. Spring is rainy but the new blooms and fewer tourists make it a special time for visiting.

WHAT TO PACK

We are chuckling as we write this because packing is just another area in which our habits have changed since traveling with kids. On our bicycle trip through Tuscany before children – a three-week trip – we packed everything we needed in two saddlebags each. Suddenly we found ourselves lugging four suitcases with separate carry-on backpacks for the kids and a stroller.

What went wrong? Here's the advice we obviously have trouble following:

Pack light. Pack your bags once, then go back and remove at least one-third of what you packed. You can always do wash (carry a separate bag for dirty laundry) or buy extra clothes in Italy. Do pack warm layers if you travel in the winter months. While we expected cold winds in Venice, we were shocked at the bone-chilling cold in Florence. Be prepared.

Bring dress-up clothes. Italians tend to dress up more than Americans. Some places, like the Vatican Museum and St. Peter's, won't let you in without proper attire. For girls, this means at least one dress; for boys, bring pants and a nice top.

Pack comfortable shoes. This is key because you and your children probably will be doing more walking than you expect. Bring at least two pairs of shoes.

Come prepared for rain. Make sure you have a raincoat, preferably with a hood, and at least one umbrella. April and May can be particularly rainy, although the summers are quite dry.

Buy special snacks past security. This way, you'll be sure that you can bring them on the plane.

Have each child carry their own backpack onto the plane with books, games, coloring materials, walkmen or gameboys, Ipods, dolls and cuddlies. Pack one change of clothes, toothbrush/toothpaste in the pack just in case you miss a connection. Also, do a last-minute check of their backpacks.

Use suitcases with wheels for each of you. Each member of the family also had a separate pack or purse for carry-on items and cameras. Our kids love the independence and responsibility, and the wheels make it quite easy to move quickly through a train station.

STROLLERS & BACKPACKS

To stroll or not to stroll? The conventional small-wheeled stroller that folds up nicely as an airplane carry-on is generally useless in a country that is all cobblestones with no curb cuts. We have a novel approach. For children too big for a backpack, bring the smallest jogger stroller that collapses and folds. These strollers are tough, durable and light as a feather. We've bounced ours up the bridges of Venice, through the vineyards in Tuscany and from piazza to piazza in Rome. They go where no other stroller has gone before. When our son was too tired to walk, he climbed up on our little girl's lap and off we went. The jogger was put into use as a luggage carrier when we traveled through train stations.

For smaller children, a backpack is great for the same reason it is where you live – it's the most portable form of transportation.

PASSPORTS

Unless you plan to stay in Italy longer than 90 days and/or study or seek employment in the country, citizens from the U.S. and Canada or members of the European Economic Community do not need a visa. EU (European Union) nationals with a valid passport can stay in Italy with no time restrictions.

Children and adults do need a passport. You will be asked at each hotel to produce your passport, and most hotel clerks will keep your passport overnight as required by Italian law. Don't forget to get them back.

Parent Tip: We had the kids take turns to check if we had our passports before we left. Of course, this ultimately is the parent's responsibility, but it never hurts to have an extra person try to remember key items. Sometimes the kids remembered better than us!

CUSTOMS & ENTRANCE REQUIREMENTS

U.S. citizens may leave Italy with $800 of merchandise. Remember to keep your receipts. Pets must have a Certificate of Health from a veterinarian inspector.

Duty-free entry is allowed for personal effects that will not be sold, given away or traded while in Italy. The list is extensive, but is evolving due to the technological revolution, which every day introduces a new electronic toy for kids and adults. You cannot ship wine back to the U.S., so plan to carry back a few bottles since it is significantly less expensive than in the U.S. For up-to-date info, go to *www.cbp.gov/xp/cgov/travel.*

TRAVEL INSURANCE

You may want to purchase travel insurance, which is relatively cheap at about €30-50 for a family traveling for a two-week trip in Europe. The insurance covers a wide variety of issues – from missed connections and baggage delay to medical evacuation and medical expense. Here are several options for getting travel insurance:

• **Travelex Insurance,** *Tel. 800/228-9792, www.travelex-insurance.com*
• **Travel Insurance International,** *Tel. 800/243-3174, www.travelinsured. com*
• **Insure My Trip,** *Tel. 800/240-0369, www.insuremytrip.com*, to get a cost comparison.

ITALIAN GOVERNMENT TOURIST BOARD

Lots of information available at their website: *www.italiantourism.com.*

GETTING TO ITALY

Rules vary from airline to airline on children's fares and how to best seat babies and very young children. Check for specifics with either your travel agent or the airline.

Rome's **Leonardo da Vinci (Fiumicino)** and Milan's **Malpensa** are Italy's primary international airports. Other regional airports in Bologna, Florence, Pisa and Venice accept flights from all over Europe but not from North America or Australia.

Alitalia, *Tel. 800/223-5730. www.alitalia.it/eng/index.html,* is Italy's national airline, and most big internatinal airlines fly to Italy as well.

GETTING AROUND ITALY

Getting around Italy is easy, relaxing and a visual pleasure. There is an excellent network of highways, trains and airports. Business travelers can enjoy quick connections among major cities by flying. But for tourists with more time, take the train or car to better get to know the country.

By Car

Driving in Italy, except for Naples and maybe Rome, is not as bad as you have heard. On the *Autostrada* – a network of superhighways and toll roads – speeds are fast, but if you stay in the right lane no one bothers you. We thought the roads were better marked than in most places in America. You can typically find your way between cities and towns simply by following the signs. City driving is tougher because the streets are narrow passageways built in the Middle Ages. For the parking-challenged, getting your car into a tiny space in a tiny street on a steep hill with a line of cars waiting is a nightmare. But, once again, we saw no "road rage" incidents, just an occasional boisterous plea to the Madonna!

Then there's Naples. Forget driving. Forget parking. Naples is a caricature of Italian driving. Rome also is difficult because it is so big and the streets are not laid out on a grid. Drive around Tuscany or even the Amalfi Coast, but plan not to have a car in Rome, Florence, Venice and Naples.

Remember, driving can be dangerous with kids in the car who are miserable and distract you while you try to negotiate unknown territory. So do be careful.

Driver's License

U.S., British and Canadian driver's licenses are valid throughout Italy, but only when accompanied by a translation which can be obtainable from AAA *(www.aaa.com)*, the **Touring Club Italiano** in Italy or the **Italian Government Tourist Office** *(www.italiantourism.com)*. You also can receive an "International Drivers Permit" from the Italian Government Tourist Office. Contact **Touring Club Italilano**, *Via Marsala, 8, 00185 Roma, Tel. (39)(06)499-899.*

Having said all this, we have traveled by car in Italy without obtaining a translation or International Drivers Permit. The big rental chains – Avis, Hertz, Budget – do not ask for it. We also have rented cars from Italian agencies, which are typically cheaper, without these prerequisites. However, we have never been in any accidents or run into any other type of trouble.

Car Rental

Hertz and Avis have offices in all the major cities. If you know ahead of time when you will want a car, you can call ahead and make a reservation. The toll-free numbers are: **Hertz**, *Tel. 800/654-3001*; **Avis**, *Tel. 800/331-1084.* Or, you can wait until you get to Italy and shop around for a price.

The Touring Club Italiano (see above) provides the best road maps of Italy. You will need to call ahead. Another good source is the Michelin maps found at major bookstores or newsstands in Italy. Michelin maps have been quite dependable for us. Also, check the local tourist office for maps and ask for directions. Italians are so helpful with tourists, even when there is a language barrier, they will draw their own map.

For more information on driving in Italy, visit **Slow Travel Italy** at *www.slowtrav.com/italy/driving/maps.htm.*

By Train

Our preferred way to travel in Italy always has been by train. The government-run train system is extensive, quite efficient and relatively inexpensive. Visit Trenitalia information *(www.trenitalia.com)* for more information on rail travel throughout Italy.

Choose to travel either **first class** or **second class**. While the price difference is not huge (about 20%), first class means you have a reservation and guaranteed seating in advance. Around holidays when Italians are traveling in large numbers, a route can be completely sold out for a day or two before your travel date.

Another choice between certain destinations is the **EuroStar**. These trains are sleek and fast. A run between Florence and Rome takes no more

Train Lingo

- **Locale** means local means it stops everywhere.
- **Diretto** stops fewer times but is in no way a direct shot to your destination.
- **Expresso** is not a coffee drink. At the train station it means the train stops only at the main towns.
- **Eurocity** are trains that travel beyond Italy.
- **Intercity** trains whip between major cities.
- **EuroStar** trains are the top dog of train travel.
- **Binario** means platform. It is essential to find out which binario your train departs (**partenze**) from. A huge screen posts the binario number. Always double-check here in case the binario has been changed.
- **Biglietti** means tickets.

than two hours. Of course, the fare is higher than the regular train, but if time is of the essence, this is the way to go.

Ticket discounts also are available for certain travelers. These are only beneficial if you plan to travel many miles in Italy. Travel agents and the Italian Government Tourist Board (see above) can help you. A Green Card for Youth Travel is available for those under age 26.

To purchase tickets, visit the ticket office at the train station or stop in at one of the many travel agents in the city centers. The system is computerized and highly organized.

Keep the following tips in mind as you ride the Italian rails:

Stamp your ticket. This is a strange ritual at Italian train stations. Once you purchase your ticket, it is only good for the day of purchase. So, you must get it stamped at a yellow machine near the binario. Sometimes they actually check for the stamp on the train.

Am I on the right train? All travelers at one time or another have asked this question. The only sure way to find out is to ask: *"Scusa, ma questo treno va a Firenzie?"* (Excuse me, does this train go to Florence?) Typically, Michael loyally consults the overhead schedules while Barbara ambles off to ask – several people – if the train is going where she thinks it is. Whatever works!

There's good coffee at many train stations! Some of the best cappuccino we've had has been in train stations in small towns. Most stations have comfortable cafes – but remember they charge a *coperta* (cover charge) or higher price if you occupy a table. Feel free to purchase snacks for the train ride at the station. They are not as good nor as cheap if you had bought food items in town but the thought of going a long way with no snacks for little ones borders on insanity. Some trains provide refreshments, but they are minimal.

For current information, visit *www.europeonrail.com.*

By Bus

While long-distance traveling is best undertaken by train, the bus system does a wonderful job uniting a region's smaller towns. In most cases, the bus station is located adjacent to the train terminal. They are clean, comfortable and on longer rides have a bathroom.

By Taxi

Taxis are readily available in all major cities, but they come with a high price tag. Try not to call one from the phone because the meter clicks on when the driver begins his journey to pick you up. From the airport or train station or any other longer trip, negotiate the rate before you begin your ride. Otherwise, taxis typically run on a meter system, with extra supplements for nighttime fares, luggage, Sunday and public holidays.

The coolest cabs, according to our kids, are in Capri. They are gleaming white, long and convertible with nifty jump seats in the back.

HOTEL RATING SYSTEM

Hotel accommodations are organized by category throughout the country. All hotels are classified by the Provincial Tourist Boards, although prices have been deregulated. Here are some fast facts about hotels in Italy.

Alberghi are rated from one to five stars:

***** Five-stars are deluxe hotels, with all the fringes and conveniences plus an incredibly attentive staff. They typically have first-class restaurants, business centers and access to health clubs and other perks.

**** Four-star hotels are top-notch hotels, often only marginally less luxurious than the five-stars.

*** May have air-conditioning – but check. Slightly less professional, but still quite clean and most comfortable.

** Typically a family-run enterprise. The quality of a two-star often varies with its location. They normally do not have conveniences like in-room telephones and mini-bars. In large cities like Rome, they probably do not have air-conditioning and are smaller with no amenities. In smaller towns, a two-star could offer beautiful guestrooms with a bath, though probably not air-conditioning. Some may not have bathrooms in the room, but a shared one in the corridor.

*   One-stars offer a cheap place to go to sleep, and often nothing more.

Cribs are hard to come by, and even in the hotels that have them, they may already be in use.

We also found that Italian hotels tend to alter their rates on a rather frequent basis, which is the primary reason price ranges are shown for many hotels. Our advice: use travel books like this one and Internet sites as a base for what the rate really will be. The only way to know for sure is to check directly with the hotel or with your travel agent at the time of booking.

BUSINESS HOURS

Your best bet is to plan on stores and shops closing between 1pm and 4pm – Italy's traditional siesta time. In some of the bigger cities, especially Rome and Milan, we found that stores tend not to close for lunch. The smaller cities and towns, however, strictly observe this rule. Holidays and Sundays also are days when work stops and life begins in Italy.

BANKING

The advent of the **ATM** has made a significant difference in our traveling routine in Italy. ATMs across Italy work with the major national and regional ATM networks in the U.S. With the ATM comes freedom from constantly checking your watch and your wallet.

Banking hours in Italy tend to be Monday through Friday 8:30am-1:30pm and about 2:45pm-4:00pm. They are most definitely closed on weekends and holidays. They usually are posted on the bank's doors.

Travelers' checks can be cashed in at hotels, many shops and at the foreign exchange offices in railway stations and airports. Shop around for the best exchange rate at banks and the **Casa di Cambio**, a smaller exchange operation. Fees may be set, which is great when you want to change large amounts of money, or as a percentage of your total, more beneficial for changing smaller amounts.

CONSULATES & EMBASSIES

When in trouble, find your nearest embassy. They are your representative in a foreign city and will do their best to help you. If you lose your passport, this is the place to go. If you get in trouble anywhere in Italy, call the embassy.

Embassies and consulates in Rome include:
- **US**, *Via Veneto 119A, Tel. (39)(060)46741*
- **Canada**, *Via Zara, 30, Tel. (39)(060)445-981*
- **United Kingdom**, *Via XX Settembre, 80A, Tel. (39)(060)482-5441*

CURRENCY

The **Euro** (€)is it. Don't plan to use any left over lira from previous trips. Come to Italy with some Euros in your pocket to avoid unforeseen, but expected, chaos – like a workers' strike. There are exchange offices at most airports, but the best rates are found at the exchange bureaus and banks that are licensed by the Bank of Italy.

ELECTRICITY

Italy runs on 220v, but you will find some hotels where this is not the case! Hardware stores and chains like Staples and Office Depot sell adapter kits in the U.S. that work quite well for most appliances.

EXPRESS COURIERS

We used DHL once to ship home the too-many books we collected, along with all those extra clothes we shouldn't have packed for a trip during Italy's blazing hot summer. DHL is one of two express couriers and we strongly suggest using them rather than the Italian mail system, which does not run as efficiently as the trains.
- **DHL**, *Tel. (167)345-345 (toll-free in Italy)*
- **UPS**, *Tel. (167)822-054 (also toll-free)*

POSTAL SERVICE

The genius of Italy is not to be found in its postal system. Mail seems to get through, but not in any timely fashion – meaning you get home before the postcard. The only exception is the **Vatican Post Office** in Rome that is run by the Church – on a wing and a prayer? A town's or city's main post office typically is open from 8:30am to 6pm, Monday through Friday. On Saturday, they close at noon. Smaller post offices are open from 8:30am-2pm Monday through Friday.

SAFETY

Italian cities and towns are in general safer than most American cities, and Italians are particularly kind to families and children. Once while dining in Venice, our kids were playing very close by in the piazza. A young man walking through dressed in frayed jeans and artist's shirt handed our little girl something white. Barbara jumped up from her meal running over to our daughter, fearing the worst. The waiter, sensing her anxiety followed. The "white package" turned out to be several sticks of chalk – the gentleman was an artist. The kids ended up drawing the universe and played astronaut for the remainder of the evening, with the young man giving art tips when he returned. We felt quite foolish.

All this said, it still pays to be careful. Except for one near incident on a Naples train platform where a potential pickpocket eyed us for awhile, we never have had problems with crime.

Some street-smart tips:
• If you like, wear a money belt.
• Don't walk next to the road with a shoulder-strap purse. Some bandits drive by on scooters and try to snatch your purse.
• Make sure your backpack is zipped and have someone keep an eye to make sure no one tries to unzip it while traveling in crowded areas.
• Don't walk in isolated places of the big cities.
• Keep your children within sight.
• Be careful on overnight train rides, when someone could steal your belongings when you are asleep.

It also is important for you to stay out of trouble with the law. Unlike America's judicial system, you are considered guilty until proven innocent in Italy. Do not bring drugs into the country or try to purchase any in Italy.

TELEPHONES, FAX & E-MAIL
You can call the U.S. or Canada from almost anywhere in Italy by using the following services:
• **AT&T Direct Service**. Just dial the AT&T access number 172-1011 and charge the calls to your AT&T Calling Card, credit card or call collect.
• **Canada Direct**. Call 172-1001, toll-free from Italy, for a connection to the Canadian telephone network with access to a bilingual operator.
• **MCI**. Call 172-1022, toll-free in Italy, for MCI's World Phone and use your MCI credit card or make a collect call.
• **Sprint**. Call 172-1877, again toll-free, for access to an English-speaking Sprint operator who can charge your phone card or make your call collect.

From hotel phones get an outside line first and then dial the access number. When calling from a public phone, please use a coin or local pre-paid card to get an outside line and then dial one of the access numbers. From outside of Italy: First dial the country code, then the city code, then the number. From inside Italy: Do not dial the country code. But you must dial the city code and number.

Italy's country code is (39). Main city codes are: Florence (055). Milan (02). Naples (081). Pisa (050). Rome (06). Siena (0577). Venice (041). Verona (045). Sorrento and Capri (081). Amalfi Coast (089).

So, for example: Calling from the US to Florence, dial 011 (international for U.S.) + 39 (country) + 055 (city) + number.

PUBLIC HOLIDAYS

Life is to be enjoyed on these holidays, including for all working Italians. Expect everything to be closed on these days:

- January 1 — New Year's Day
- January 6 — Epiphany
- April 25 — Liberation Day (1945)
- Varies — Easter/Easter Monday
- May 1 — Labor Day
- August 15 — Assumption of the Blessed Virgin
- November 1 — All Saints Day
- December 8 — Feast of the Immaculate Conception
- December 25 — Christmas
- December 26 — Santo Stefano

TIME

Italy is six hours ahead of Eastern Standard Time in North America. If it's noon in New York, it's 6pm in Rome.

TIPPING

Restaurant service charges are usually added to your bill – about 15% to 18%. For taxis, add 10% of your fare; at your hotel for chambermaids, give €1-3. For sightseeing guides, €2 minimum per person for half-day tours and €2.50 for full-day tours.

TOURIST INFORMATION

Rome

- **Azienda di promozione Turistica**, *Via Parigi, 11. Tel. (39)(06)488-991. www.romaturismo.com*

- **American Express**, *Piazza di Spagna, 39,* *Tel. (39)(06)676-41*
- **Enjoy Rome**, *Via Marghera, 2,* *Tel. (39)(06)446-3379.*
  www.enjoyrome.com
- **EPT Termini**, *Train Station, Tel. (39)(06)487-1270*
- **EPT Fiumicino**, *Airport, outside customs, Tel. (39)(06)601-1255*
- **Italian Government Travel Office**, *Via M arghera, 2. Tel. (39)(06)49711,*
  www.italiantourism.com/accomod.html
- **Rome Provincial Tourist Board/EPT**, *Via Parigi, 5, Tel. (39)(06)488-3748*

Florence
The official tourism agency **APT** has the following locations:
- in central Florence: *Via Cavour, 1/r. Tel. (39)(055)290-832 or 290-833*
- elsewhere in Florence: *Borgo S. Croce 29/r; Tel. (39)(055) 234-0444 or 226-4524*
- at Amerigo Vespucci airport (*www.airport.florence.it*), in the arrivals section
- at Piazza Stazione bus station: *on the arrival side, underneath the canopy. Tel. (39)(055) 212-245*

Two good websites are: **Tuscan Tourism**, *www.turismo.toscana.it* and **Florence Tourism**, *www.firenzeturismo.it*

Venice
Piazza San Marco, Via Ascensione, 71c. Tel. (39)(041)522-6356. We found the office hard to find on our first trip. Here's what to do: At the opposite end from St. Mark's, facing the canal, look ahead in the corner.
Other tourist offices:
- Palazetto Selva, near the San Marco vaporetto stop, *Tel. (39)(041)529-8730*
- Train Station, *Tel. (39)(041)719-078*
- Bus Station, *Tel. (39)(041)522-7402*
- Marco Polo Airport, *Tel. (39)(041)541-5887*
- Lido, *Gran Viale, 6. Tel. (39)(041)526-5721*

Verona
- **APT**, *Piazza Bra. Via degli Alpini, 9. Tel. (39)(045)806-8680. Fax (39)(045)800.3638. Web: www.tourism.verona*
  Other tourist offices:
- Railway Station. *Piazza XXV Aprile. Tel/Fax (39)(045)800-0861*

• Airport. *Aeroporto V. Catullo, Villafranca. Tel/Fax (39)(045)861-9163.*

Naples
• *Piazza dei Martiri, 58. Tel. (39)(081)405-311*
• *Stazione Centrale. Tel. (39)(081)268-779*
• *Stazione Mergellina. Tel. (39)(081)761-2102*
• *AACST, Castel dell'Ovo. Tel. (39)(081)764-5688*

Milan
   A good website is *www.milanoinfotourist.com.* In Milan, contact:
• *Piazza del Duomo. Via Marconi, 1. Tel. (39)(02)809-662. Open weekdays 8:30am-8pm, Saturday 9am-1pm and 2pm-7pm and Sunday 9am-1pm and 2pm-5pm.*
• *Stazione Centrale. Tel. (39)(02)699-0432. Monday through Saturday 8am-7pm, Sunday 9am-12:30pm and 1:30pm-6pm.*

ARRIVALS & DEPARTURES
Rome
   Rome is the main entry point to Italy from the U.S. and Canada. The main airport is **Flumicino**, *Tel. (39)(06)65-951, Web: www.airwise.com/airports/europe/rome_fco/index.html*, otherwise known as Leonardo da Vinci, located about 30 kilometers outside the city. A taxi into Rome is expensive, about €50, plus €6 flat fee, in addtion to extra surcharges, including luggage. Use only the yellow or white officially licensed cabs at the taxi cues.
   An **express train** is available from the airport to Rome's train station. It runs from 7:30am to 10pm and takes about one-half hour. A one-way ticket is about €9.50 per person. A **regular-service train** that takes about 40 minutes, sometimes shorter, and runs from 6:30am to 12:15pm costs about €5.50 per person. You can purchase tickets at the airport or train station office or from automatic machines at both stations. Don't forget to stamp your train ticket at the yellow machine near the platform.
   You can book a **shuttle** online at *www.initaly.com/regions/latium/ciamshutl.htm#bookjump.* Another option is *www.airportshuttle.it.* Cost runs from €25 for one person to €70 for a group of four.
   Ciampino (*www.adr.it/static/en/portal/portal/adr/Ciampino/GB_Pastine.html*) is the city's secondary airport. You can opt for a shuttle bus or a COTRAL bus, which is rather inconvenient for getting to the historic center.
   By car: if you are coming from the north, the fastest road into town is the A1 (*Autostrada del Sole*). From there take the GRA (*Grande Raccordo*

Anulare – Anulare for short) into Rome. The Anulare is a beltway around the city. From the south, take the A2, also known as the Autostrada del Sole.

Here are some estimated drive times:
- Florence: 4 hours
- Milan: 6 hours
- Naples:3 1/2 hours
- Venice:7 hours

By train: Rome's **Termini** certainly was spruced up since our bycicle trip during the early 1990s. It is significantly cleaner and more sparkling than we've ever seen it – all because of the efforts to get the city prepared for the millennium. It is still crowded and hectic, but much improved. Hats off to the city! From the station, you can take a cab from the taxi stand or walk down to the Metro to take a subway to your destination. To catch a bus, leave the station for the bus station in Piazza Cinquencento, directly outside the train terminal.

Train travel times are listed below for key cities:
- Florence: 2 1/2 hours
- Milan: 4 hours
- Naples: 2 hours
- Venice: 5 hours

Florence & Tuscany

By bus: Provincial and regional buses link Florence with the entire Tuscan area. The most convenient bus company is **LAZZI**, located immediately next to the train station; *Tel. (055)351-061*. Points west (Pisa, Lucca, the coast) are frequently served by LAZZI. The two other main companies are **CAP**, *Via Nazionale 13; Tel. (055)214-637*; and **SITA**, *Via Santa Caterina da Siene 15; Tel. (055)294-955*.

By train: Almost all trains leave from **Stazione Santa Maria Novella**, *Tel. (055)2451*. In addition, some trains stop at the suburban stations at Rifredi, *Tel. (055)411-138,* or Campo di Marti, *Tel. (055)234-434.* Make sure you stamp your ticket before boarding. Inside Stazione Santa Maria Novella, there is a tourist information office that is a helpful place to stop, especially if you arrive without a hotel reservation (*open daily 7am-10 pm, Tel. (055)278-785*).

By car: You absolutely do not want to drive in Florence. When you are ready to visit the rest of Tuscany, however, a car is by far the most convenient way to travel between hill towns and along the coast. Remember that on the *Autostrada* or any other multi-lane road, stay in the right lane except at the moment you are passing – or expect a Ferrari or Mercedes to appear inches from your back bumper, brights flashing. Also, the road signs around Tuscany (and most of Italy) are superb; if you simply get started in the right direction, you can almost always find your way to your destination by following signs.

Renting a car in Florence is surprisingly straightforward – though more expensive than you might expect. One tip: Make a reservation with a brand-name chain before you leave home (for example, with Hertz, Avis or Budget) and then shop around when you are on the ground in Florence. We typically switched to an Italian rental agency once we compared prices – and most agencies, American and Italian, are located along a few streets between the train station and the Arno.

Remember that the already high cost of renting a car is made more so by high gasoline prices and a 19% VAT (sales tax), typically added to your final bill.

• **Avis**, *Borgo Ognissanti 128r, Tel. (055)21-36-29 or 239-8826*
• **Hertz**, *Via Maso Finiguerra 33, Tel. (055)239-8205, Fax (055) 230-2011*
• **Budget**, *Borgo Ognissanti 134r, Tel. (055)29-30-21 or 28-71-61*
• **Euro Dollar**, *Via il Prato 80r, Tel. (055)238-24-80, Fax (055) 238-24-79*
• **Maggiore**, *Via Maso Finiguerra 11r, Tel. (055)21-02-38*

Venice

By air: **Marco Polo Airport** *(www.veniceairport.it)* is located about 13 km north of the city. Water service is available to the city. A cheaper option is to take the bus to Piazzale Roma and then a *vaporetto* to your hotel.

By bus: Buses take you to and from numerous cities in the vicinity of Venice – Padua, Mira and Treviso, to name a few. The main bus service is **ACTV**, *www.actv.it*, Tel. *(041)2722-111*, with an office located in Piazzale Roma. If you arrive in Venice by bus, you will get off at Piazzale Roma, from which you will need to catch water transport to your destination. *Vaporetti* (public water buses), gondolas and water taxis can be found at the Piazzale Roma *vaporetto* stop on the canal. *Vaporetti* are by far the least expensive way to get around.

First-time visitors to Venice are thrilled, panicked or both at the prospect of getting around town by boat. Not only is it easy, it's fun and a real diversion for kids.

By car: If you can, don't come by car. Remember, Venice is free of cars – a blessing for Venice and for families with children. Traveling to Venice by car means you must wait in insufferably long lines to park your vehicle in perhaps the world's largest and most ugly parking garage at Piazzale Roma. Just what you need with siblings squabbling, babies crying or teens sulking. If you do drive, park your car and proceed to the *vaporetto* stop at the canal. Another option is to park on the parking island – yes, that's an island that solely serves as a parking garage – called **Tronchetto Parking**, *www.veniceparking.it.*

You also can rent a car in Piazzale Roma:
• **Avis**, *Tel. (39)(041)522-5825*
• **Hertz**, *Tel. (39)(041)528-4091*

By train: This is the way to travel into Venice. All trains terminate at Stazione di Santa Lucia. Walk down the steps to the canal and catch a *vaporetto*, water taxi or gondola to your final destination in the city. Sit back and enjoy the view.

Direct trains to major cities are available. For example:
• Verona: 1 hour
• Padua: 45 minutes
• Florence: 3 1/2 hours
• Rome: 5 hours

Verona

By air: **Verona/Villafranca airport** is located about 10 kilometer from Verona (www.aeroporto.it.) You can catch a shuttle bus, which run every 20 minutes, from the airport to Porta Nuova train station in Verona.

By car: From the *Autostrada* A4 there are two clearly marked exits for Verona. From the Mestre (outside Venice) you can also take the more scenic route 11.

By train: An easy train ride from or to Venice, the Lakes, Milan and actually anywhere in Italy. **Stazione Verona Porta Nuova**, Tel. (39)(147)888-08, is the train station, located about a 15-minute walk from the historic center. Is walking too difficult since your toddler, taking a cue from Italian railway workers, has decided to go on strike and is currently lying on the elegant, marble floor flailing miserably? Well, simply coax them to the front of the station to hop a bus (take number 1, 11 or 12). Better yet, get in the taxi line and hope the short ride and a promise of gelato is enough to stop the tears.

Naples

By air: The **Capodichino airport** links Naples with all major Italian cities and some foreign airports. Bus service includes hourly service from the airport to Piazza Municipio, which is near the harbor. This is the Sepsa line, a blue bus. Another bus, number 14, takes you to Stazione Centrale. The Curreri service runs four daily buses to Sorrento. Taxi service also is available but beware of extra charges. An extra supplement will be assessed for luggage and may be added for mysterious other reasons. Your best bet: agree on a fare before you leave the station.

By train: Stazione Centrale is located at Piazza Garibaldi, where you also can catch the local Circumvesuviana line that takes you to Pompeii or all the way through to Sorrento. Some trains also stop at the Napoli Mergellina and Napoli Campi Flegrei.

Three local lines serve the Bay of Naples: the Ferrovia Circumvesuviana that stops at Herculaneum, Pompeii and Sorrento (Stazione Centrale or Stazione Circumvesuviana in Corso Garibaldi), the Ferrovia Cumana that runs trains to Pozzuoli and Bai (from the station at Piazza Montesanto) and the Ferrovia Circumflegrea to Licola and Cuma from the station at Piazza Montesanto.

Parent Tip: Be careful in the train station, especially when using the Circumvesuviana. If you are uncomfortable traveling in big cities, this is not the place for you. As a family, we have used the line, and only once ran into trouble when Barbara was left with the kids and luggage alone for a few minutes. While a strong mean look scared the potential thief away, it was a highly uncomfortable few minutes. Stay together and try not to look too helpless; do not agree to let anyone help carry your luggage unless you are desperate and agree in advance on the price.

By sea: Remember, Naples is a port town so there are many sea options. Long-distance ferries leave from **Stazione Marittima**, near the Castel Nuovo. Major companies that run out of Stazione Marittima are Tirrenia (to Palermo) and Siremar (Aeolian Islands and Milazzo, Sicily).

Hydrofoils to the islands and Amalfi Coast ports leave from Stazione Marittima, but also from **Molo Beverello** (near Marittima) and Mergellina (to the west). Make sure you check the dock on your ticket.

By car: Driving in Naples is worse than driving in Rome. Use public transportation to get to, around and from Naples. If you choose to drive, you probably will come in from the north off the A2 *Autostrada*. Most likely you will want to take the P1 route from the *Autostrada* to Naples. Or you could take the *tangenziale*, which allows you to avoid the inner city.

What do you do with your car in Naples? Hide it as best you can. Hopefully your hotel will have a parking garage where you can stow it safely.

Milan

Milan is a hub city for the north and the network of planes, trains, automobiles and buses is excellent. Increasingly, Milan is the arrival point for flights from America. You can get to and from anywhere in Italy from Milan.

By air: Milan has two airports: **Linate** (8 kilometers from the center) and **Malpensa** (50 kilometers to the west). Intercontinental flights tend to go to Malpensa and European and domestic airlines fly to Linate. Always check your ticket to make sure you are going to the right airport

Bus shuttles run from Malpensa to the Stazione Centrale every 30 minutes from 6:30am and every hour after 4:30pm. It takes about one hour.

From Linate to Milan, STAM bus service runs every 20 minutes to Stazione Centrale.

Taxis are available at both airports, but cost an arm and leg from Malpensa. We usually take the bus to Milan and cab it back, because we're always running just a bit late to return home.

By car: From the east and west, the E64 *Autostrada* comes into Milan from the north. Use A1 (E35) from the south or the A7 (E62). The A9 (E35) and A8 are the major roads coming into Milan from the north.

Expect drive times to be:
• Rome: 6 hours
• Venice: 3 hours
• Florence: 3 hours

Milan is a huge city, not easy to negotiate, so we don't recommend driving unless you are traveling to another destination.

By taxi: Taxi stands are located around the city. There are stands at Piazza del Duomo, Piazza Scala, Piazza Cinque Giornate, Largo San Babila, Largo Treves, Piazzale Baraca and Piazza XIV Maggio. This is a great but expensive way to get around town.

By train: Over the years, we have spent a lot of time in Stazione Centrale and have come to admire its beauty. Most of the international and domestic train traffic comes through here.

Here are some sample times from or to Milan:
• Rome: 5 hours
• Venice: 3 hours
• Florence: 3 hours

PRACTICAL INFORMATION
Rome
Babysitting
Always check your hotel for babysitting services. Here are other options:
- **Angels:** *Vicolo del Babuino, 98, Tel. (39)(06)678-2877. Email: staffing italy@yahoo.co.uk.* English-speaking babysitters and nannies. Rates vary depending on service.
- **United Babies:** *Piazza Nicoloso da Recco, 9, Tel. (39)(06)5899-481.* A bilingual playgroup run by an American for children from age 1 to 3 that operates between 8am and 2:30pm, with additional hours up to 6pm provided for an extra cost. Closes in August.

Hospitals
- **Ospedale Pediatrico Bambino Gesu:** *Piazza Sant'Onofrio, 4, Tel. (39)(06)68-591; www.obg-irrcs.it.* (note: the website hasn't worked all the time).

Pharmacies
- **Farmacia del Vaticano,** *Porta Sant'Anna entrance. Citta del Vaticano, Tel. (39)(06)6988-3422. Open Monday through Friday 8:30am-6pm and Saturday 7:30am-1pm.* No credit cards. The best drugstore in Rome.
- **Internazionale,** *Piazza Barberini, 49, Tel. (39)(06)487-1195. Open 24 hours Monday-Friday. Times vary on Saturday and Sunday.*
- **Farmacia del Senato,** *Corso Rinascimento, 50, Tel. (39)(06)6880-3985. Open 24 hours Monday through Friday. Hours vary on Saturday and Sunday. Closed part of August.* A large red or green cross identifies other pharmacies throughout the city, most are open from 8:30am-1pm and 4pm-8pm Monday through Saturday.

Parking Garages
- **Villa Borghese,** Open 24 hours.

Parking Signs
- asso Carrabile = okay to park here
- Sosta Vietata = no parking
- Zona Rimozione = towaway zone
- Yellow stripes = disabled parking only

Florence
Babysitting
Ask your hotel concierge to arrange for babysitting. Most do, although you may need to book a day or more in advance.

Food & Flowers
- **San Lorenzo central market**, *Via dell'Ariento. Every morning except for Sunday and holidays.*
- **Sant'Ambrogio**, *Piazza Ghiberti. Every morning except for Sunday and holidays.*
- **Le Cure**, *Piazza delle Cure. Every morning except for Sunday and holidays.*
- **Santo Spirito market**, *Piazza Santo Spirito. Every morning except for Sunday and holidays. All day on the second Sunday of every month.*
- **Piazza della Republica** *(under the portico). Every Thursday morning.*

Clothing, leather, straw goods
- **Mercato Centrale**, the city's largest aggregation of learhter goods, jewelry and all things Florentine, in store fronts and in dozens of vendor carts. *Three blocks from the Duomo: Right on Via de Martelli, first left on Via dei Pucci and, at the front of the Basilica of San Lorenzo, turn right on La Nocee.*
- **Straw market**, *Piazza del Mercato Nuovo. Every day from 9am to 1:30pm, except Sunday and public holidays.*
- **San Lorenzo market**, *Via del Canto de'Nelli, Via dell'Ariento and Via Sant'Antonino. Daily from 9am to 7:30pm.*
- **Cascine market**, *Viale degli Olmi. Every Tuesday morning.*

Fashion
Haute couture resides primarily at **Via de'Tournauouni**, where you can find Gucci, and Vigna Nuova, home to Armani and Valentino. The **Piazza Santa Croce** boasts some superior leather goods.

Venice
Bookstores
- **Ca'Foscarina 2**, *Dorsoduro. Campiello degli Squellini. Tel. (39)(041)522-9602. Open 9am-7pm Monday-Friday. 9am-12:30pm Saturday.* The largest English-section bookstore.
- **Laboratorio Blu**, *Cannaregio. Ghetto Vecchio. Tel. (39)(041)715-819. Open 9:30am-12:30pm and 3:45pm-7:45pm Tuesday-Saturday and 3:45pm-7:45pm Monday.* A wonderful children's bookstore, with an

English session. The shop also offers courses for children and storytelling.

- **Libreria San Pantaion**, *Dorsoduro. Salizada S. Pantalon. Tel. (39)(041)522-4436. Open 10am-7pm Monday-Friday and 1pm-4pm Saturday.* Includes a selection of children's books.

Toys

- **Bambolandia** *(San Polo), Calle Madonnetta. Tel. (39)(041)520-7502. Beatrice@rialto.com. www.rialto.com/beatrice. Open 10am-12:30pm and 2pm-6pm Tuesday-Saturday.* No girl, big or little, can walk past this dollhouse of a store without stepping foot inside. Artist Beatrice Perini lovingly makes these one-of-a-kind dolls. Visit her web site to understand the art of dollmaking. Her exquisite dolls also come with a work-of-art price tag. We keep coming back and, just recently, purchased two lovely dolls for the newest members of our family, Zoe and Joya.
- **Agile** *(Cannaregio), Campo San Lio. Tel. (39)(041)528-3426. (39)(041)923-705, Web: www.virtualvenice.net/agile. Open 10am-7:30pm Monday-Saturday.* A wild collection of juggling instruments – from yo-yos to devil sticks.
- **Emporio Pettenello** *(Dorsoduro), Campo Santa Margherita. Tel. (39)(041)523-1167. Open 9am-1pm and 3:30pm-8pm Monday-Saturday.* We stumbled onto this delightful toy store during one of our walks. It's been in the same family for over 100 years.

Babysitting

Your best bet: ask your hotel a few days in advance. Almost all of the hotels in Venice offer babysitting services.

Changing Money

For **American Express**: *in San Marco – Salizzada San Moise. Tel. (39)(041)520-0844. Open 9am-5:30pm Monday-Friday and 9am-12:30pm Saturday.* For **Thomas Cook**: *In San Marco – Riva del Ferro. Tel. (39)(041)528-7358. Branch at Piazza San Marco, 142. Tel. (39)(041)522-4751. Open 9:30am-7pm Monday-Saturday and 9:30am-5pm Sunday.*

Hospitals

- **Osppedale al Mare**, *Lido. Lungomare D'Annunzio, 1. Tel. (39)(041)529-4111. Emergency Tel. (39)(041)529-5234.*
- **Ospedale Civile**, *Castello. Campo Santi Giovannie e Paolo. Tel.*

(39)(041)529-4111. Emergency Tel. (39)(041)529-4517. Vaporetto Ospedale. The main hospital where a doctor is more likely to speak English.
- **Ospedale Umberto I**, *Mestre. Via Circonvallazione, 50. Tel. (39)(041)260-7111. On the mainland.*

Pharmacies
- **Farmacia Al Mondo**, *San Marco. Frezzerie Tel. (39)(041)522-5813*
- **Farmacia Morelli**, *San Marco. Campo San Bartolomeo. Tel. (39)(041)522-4196*
- **Farmacia Baldisserotto**, *Castello. Via Garibaldi. Tel. (39)(041)522-4109*
- **Farmacia**, *Lido. Via Sandro Gallo, 74. Tel. (39)(041)526-1587*
- **Farmacia Solveni**, *Dorsoduro. Fondamenta Maravegie. Tel. (39)(041)522-0840*

Post Office
- **Posta Centrale**, *San Marco, 5554. Salizada del Fontego dei Tedeschi. Tel. (39)(041)271-7111. Open 8:15am-7pm Monday-Saturday.* The Post Office also will send faxes. Expect a long line for everything.

Verona
Changing Money
- **Cassa di Risparmio**, *Via Cappello,1 and Piazza Bra, 26/a.*
- **Banca Popolare di Verona**, *Corso Porta Nuova, 4 and Aeroporto Catullo. Via Mazzini, 0/b*
- **Banca Popolare di Bergamo**, *Piazza Bra, 4*
- **Exchange Office Porta Nuova Train Station**, *Open every day 7am-9pm*
- **American Express** *Cora Ponte Nuova, 11. Tel. (39)(045)800-9040*

Hospitals
- **Civile Maggiore**, *Borgo Trento. Tel. (39)(041)807-1111*
- **Policinico**, *Borgo Roma. Tel. (39)(041)807-1111*

In a medical emergency, call 582-222.

Naples
At the risk of sounding like a parent, we again caution you about driving in Naples. The traffic, while romantically wild and crazy, soon will get on your nerves if children are not as thrilled by having cars careening at you from all directions, with no attention paid to the traffic light as a lone

bicyclist weaves foolishly around the drivers who are anxious to rev up and make it the next few feet – before everything comes to a grinding halt only to have a bus ram into the side of a car in front of you causing a traffic jam to turn into a parking lot. Whew! Which is why we enjoy staying in Sorrento or Capri and take day trips by ferry to Naples.

Changing Money
• **Ufficio di Cambio**. *Stazione Centrale. Open daily 7:15am-8:30pm*
• **Cambio San Pietro**, *Corso Umberto, 292, in Piazza Garibaldi*

There are many banks to choose from in the financial district near Piazza Municipio.

Hospitals
• **Ospedale Cardarelli**, *Via Cardarellli, 0. Tel. (39)(081)757-2956*
• **Universitaria Policinco Federico II**, *Via S. Pansini. Tel. (39)(081)746-2937*
• **Ospedale dei Pellegrini**, *Via Portamedina, 41. Tel. (39)(081)563-3234*
• **Ospedale San Paolo**, *Via Terracina, 219. Tel. (39)(081)768-6284*

Emergency
Dial 113. For police, dial 112.

Pharmacy
• **Via Carducci**, *21-21. Above the Villa Communale. Tel. (39)(081)417-283*
• Call 192 for a list of the late-night pharmacies, which frequently change.

Milan
Changing Money
Milan banks are open weekdays from 8:30am-1:30pm and 3:00pm-4:00pm. *Ufficio di cambio*, exchange offices, are located throughout the city, including near the Duomo and the Via Vittorio Emanuele. **American Express** is located at *Via Brera, 3, Tel. (39)(02)85571,*

Postal Services
• **Main Post Office**, *Via Cordusio, 4. Tel. (39)(02)869-2069*

A TASTE OF ITALY
In Italy, food is an obsession. Often the food is simple but elegantly prepared with a balance of tastes and spices. Many Italian dishes we enjoy

today were discovered in the courts of the Medicis of Florence, the Sforzas of Milan, the doges of Venice and the Popes of Rome. Besides good taste, the Italians obsess about *digestivio* and what contributes positively to this health goal.

Italian cooking is a regional occupation, with different dishes and styles of cooking. Here is a sampling of some regional dishes:

Liguria

Visitors to Cinque Terre, Genova and Portofino can expect to be served Ligurian cuisine. Green is their color – pesto sauce reigns supreme. We have never tasted better pesto than in the Cinque Terre, with one restaurant's version as good as another's. Besides pesto, Ligurian cooking specialties include:

Torta Pasqualina: An Easter tart made of 33 very thin layers of pastry stuffed with chard, artichokes, ricotta and whole hard-boiled eggs.

Farinata: A chick-pea-flour crepe baked in an oven and served in wedges.

Mesciua: Chick-pea soup with wheat and beans served with pepper and olive oil.

Trenette col pesto: Thin strips of pasta with pesto containing string beans and pieces of boiled potato.

Tuccu de nuxe: Creamy paste of walnuts, bread and garlic.

Buridda: Fish stew.

Cima alla genovese: Veal breast stuffed with veal pate, sweetbreads, peas, pine nuts, parmesan and eggs wrapped in a cloth boiled, then chilled and sliced.

Coniglio in umido: Rabbit cooked with rosemary, bay leaves, white wine, pine nuts and nutmeg.

Lattughe ripiene: Braised lettuce stuffed with eggs, vegetables, fish, ground meat or chicken.

Pandolce genovese: Christmas yeast bread with candied fruit and pine nuts.

Veneto

Venice and Verona are part of the Veneto, with some of the best and unique cooking in Italy – fit for a doge. The basis of cooking in this region is rice and corn and that means *Polenta* (ground cornmeal) served with almost anything. Here are some ideas for dining in the Veneto:

Bigoli con l'anatra: Homemade pasta cooked in duck broth and topped with duck sauce.

Casunziei: Ravioli stuffed with ricotta, beets, winter squash or spinach.

Pasta e fagioli: Bean soup with homemade pasta (it's great).

Baccala mantecato: Poached salt cod, pureed with olive oil and parsley.

Bisato alla Veneziana: Eel sautéed in olive oil with bay leaves and vinegar.

Capesante alla Veneziana: Sautéed scallops.

Seppie alla Veneziana: Cuttlefish cooked with its black ink and white wine (Michael loved it).

Radicchio: Red chicory eaten raw and cooked.

Tuscany

Simple cooking is an art form in Tuscany. Start with the bread – the freshest. Add the olive oil – the richest. Wash it all down with a great Brunella or Chianti. Need you ask for more? You can. Here are just a few tantalizing tastes from a Tuscan menu.

Bruschetta: Toasted bread pasted with garlic and extra virgin olive oil, sometimes sprinkled with pepper and salt.

Prosciutto di Cinghiale: Salt- and air-cured wild boar.

Crostini: Traditional minced chicken-liver canapés.

Donzelle: Fried dough balls.

Aquacotta: Vegetable mushroom soup served over toasted bread crowned with a poached egg.

Panzanella: A summer salad of tomatoes, basil, cucumber, onion and bread, topped with olive oil.

Pici: Egg pasta that is thick and short.

Ribollita: Thick vegetable soup enhanced with bread and olive oil. (Barbara makes a meal out of this, and surprisingly, so do the kids!).

Bistecca alla Fiorentina: Charcoal-grilled T-bone steak.

Fritto misto: Mixed fried foods that can include chicken or rabbit, and many types of fresh vegetables.

Stracotto: Pot roast.

Trippa alla Fiorentina: Tripe with tomatoes and Parmesan cheese.

Fagioli al fiasco: White beans in chaos!! Actually the fiasco refers to a wine flask and the beans were at one time cooked slowly in a wine flask laid in the hearth.

Umbria

The home of St. Francis and Perugian candy brings rustic cooking to the table. Here are a few nibbles of Umbrian cuisine.

Schiacciata: Similar to pizza crust, this bread is baked with olive oil and sometimes-cooked greens and onions.

Spaghetti alla norcina: Spaghetti covered with black truffle sauce, garlic and usually anchovies.

Frittata di tartuffi: Basically, a black truffle omelet.

Lepre alle olive: Wild hare cooked with herbs white wine and olives.

Regina in porchetta: Carp from Lake Trasimeno baked in a wood-burning oven with wild fennel, garlic and other spices.

Campania

Cooking of the South sometimes is referred to as *la cucina povera*, the cooking of the poor. But the cuisine of southern Italy is anything but impoverished. It is opulent in its simplicity, with the zesty tomato always at center stage. Say Italian cooking to most people in the world, and they automatically dream of lasagna draped in a tasty red sauce or plain, old-fashioned pizza. While we know there is no such thing as generic Italian cooking, what still surprises some travelers is the cornucopia of culinary pleasures coming from Campania's kitchens. Savor the lasagna and pizza of Naples, but leave room for these succulent dishes:

Grappoli di Pomodoro con Mozzarella di Bufala: Tiny tomatoes with buffalo mozzarella (the kids' favorite).

Zupa di Soffritto di Maiale: Red wine tomato soup with spiced pork.

Brasato di Maiale con Ragu Nero: Pork braised in black sauce.

Timballo di Maccheroni: Macaroni pie.

Panzarotti: Deep-fried mozzarella-stuffed dumplings.

Cassuola di Vongole e Cozze: Casserole of clams and mussels (Amalfi Coast).

Gamberoni Grigliati in Foglile di Limone: Prawns grilled in lemon leaves (Amalfi and Capri).

INDEX

Things Change!

If you come across any new information, let us know. Contact us at:
jopenroad@aol.com or*www.openroadguides.com.*

Open Road Publishing

Open Road has launched a radical new concept in travel guides that we call our *Best Of* guides: matching the time you *really* have for your vacation with the right amount of information you need for your perfect trip! No fluff, just the best things to do and see, the best places to stay and eat. Includes one-day, weekend, one-week and two-week trip ideas – in living color! Now what could be more perfect than that?

Best Of Guides

Open Road's Best of Arizona, $12.95
Open Road's Best of The Florida Keys, $14.95
Open Road's Best of Las Vegas, $14.95
Open Road's Best of New York City, $14.95
Open Road's Best of Southern California, $14.95
Open Road's Best of Belize, $14.95
Open Road's Best of Costa Rica, $14.95
Open Road's Best of Honduras, $14.95
Open Road's Best of Panama, $14.95
Open Road's Best of Ireland, $14.95
Open Road's Best of Italy, $16.95
Open Road's Best of Paris, $12.95
Open Road's Best of Provence &
    The French Riviera, $12.95
Open Road's Best of Spain, $14.95

Family Travel Guides

Open Road's Italy with Kids, $14.95
Open Road's Paris with Kids, $16.95
Open Road's Caribbean with Kids, $14.95
Open Road's London with Kids, $14.95
Open Road's Best National Parks With Kids, $12.95
Open Road's Washington, DC with Kids, $14.95

Order now at www.openroadguides.com